CAREER EXAMINATION SERIES

THIS IS YOUR **PASSBOOK**® FOR ...

DIRECTOR OF FACILITIES I, II, III

NLC®

NATIONAL LEARNING CORPORATION®
passbooks.com

PASSBOOK® SERIES

THE *PASSBOOK® SERIES* has been created to prepare applicants and candidates for the ultimate academic battlefield – the examination room.

At some time in our lives, each and every one of us may be required to take an examination – for validation, matriculation, admission, qualification, registration, certification, or licensure.

Based on the assumption that every applicant or candidate has met the basic formal educational standards, has taken the required number of courses, and read the necessary texts, the *PASSBOOK® SERIES* furnishes the one special preparation which may assure passing with confidence, instead of failing with insecurity. Examination questions – together with answers – are furnished as the basic vehicle for study so that the mysteries of the examination and its compounding difficulties may be eliminated or diminished by a sure method.

This book is meant to help you pass your examination provided that you qualify and are serious in your objective.

The entire field is reviewed through the huge store of content information which is succinctly presented through a provocative and challenging approach – the question-and-answer method.

A climate of success is established by furnishing the correct answers at the end of each test.

You soon learn to recognize types of questions, forms of questions, and patterns of questioning. You may even begin to anticipate expected outcomes.

You perceive that many questions are repeated or adapted so that you can gain acute insights, which may enable you to score many sure points.

You learn how to confront new questions, or types of questions, and to attack them confidently and work out the correct answers.

You note objectives and emphases, and recognize pitfalls and dangers, so that you may make positive educational adjustments.

Moreover, you are kept fully informed in relation to new concepts, methods, practices, and directions in the field.

You discover that you arre actually taking the examination all the time: you are preparing for the examination by "taking" an examination, not by reading extraneous and/or supererogatory textbooks.

In short, this PASSBOOK®, used directedly, should be an important factor in helping you to pass your test.

DIRECTOR OF FACILITIES I, II, III

DUTIES:

Director of Facilities I, II and III are found throughout public school districts in New York State and are primarily responsible for the management of school facilities in the school districts. The work is performed according to established policies and procedures and in accordance with applicable state, local, and federal laws, rules, and regulations which apply to school district facility operations and maintenance.

As a Director of Facilities I in a school district or BOCES, you would ensure that buildings and grounds maintenance, repair, and cleaning related tasks and activities are properly performed. A Director of Facilities I is typically responsible for supervision of a unit and may also work alongside lower-level employees in carrying out and overseeing work details. A Director of Facilities I may perform manual labor and operate equipment related to the work. You would be responsible for direct supervision of staff, and oversee work details, to ensure the work is performed in a safe, efficient, and timely manner. The work may be performed indoors or outdoors under adverse working conditions.

As a Director of Facilities II in a school district or BOCES, you would be responsible for planning, organizing, and directing the custodial and maintenance activities of a school district's buildings and grounds department. Although certain activities are performed in the office, on occasion you could be required to perform maintenance, repair, and cleaning related tasks and activities, which may be performed indoors or outdoors under adverse working conditions. This position differs from Director of Facilities I in that a Director of Facilities II has a greater scope of responsibility, and is typically responsible for the supervision of more than one unit. Supervision is exercised over the work of custodial and maintenance staff and, where applicable, employees of the transportation department or those responsible for building safety and security. This position differs from Director of Facilities III in that this position is not primarily administrative in nature. The work is performed under general supervision of a school district administrator. Supervision is exercised over the work of subordinate staff through subordinate supervisors.

As a Director of Facilities III in a school district or BOCES, you would be responsible for the administration of a school district's buildings and grounds department. The majority of activities are performed in the office, but you will spend time at various work sites ensuring that work is being performed and completed in an efficient manner by subordinates and contractors. Due to the complexity and scope of the position of Director of Facilities III, a Director of Facilities III may have an assistant director to assist with the management of day to day activities of the department. This position differs from Director of Facilities II in that a Director of Facilities III has primarily administrative responsibilities, while the Director of Facilities II has supervisory and administrative responsibilities over custodial, maintenance staff, and where applicable, employees of the transportation department, or those responsible for building safety and security, and subordinate supervisors. The work is performed under the general supervision of a school district administrator, which may include the Superintendent. Supervision is exercised over the work of subordinate supervisors.

1. **Building and grounds maintenance** - These questions test for knowledge of the basic principles, practices, and techniques essential to proper building and grounds maintenance, including preventive maintenance and minor repair of building structures, electrical systems, mechanical systems, plumbing, and grounds. Questions may cover such areas as the maintenance and repair of roofs, windows, walls, floors, masonry, pipes, valves, sanitary systems, electrical wiring, switches, and painting; the operation and maintenance of heating, ventilating, and air conditioning systems, including boilers; lawn, tree, and shrub planting and maintenance, insect control, and snow and ice removal. Questions may also cover the proper use of tools and materials involved in maintenance activities, as well as the safety practices that should be followed when using these tools and materials.

2. **Supervision** - These questions test for knowledge of the principles and practices employed in planning, organizing, and controlling the activities of a work unit toward predetermined objectives. The concepts covered, usually in a situational question format, include such topics as assigning and reviewing work; evaluating performance; maintaining work standards; motivating and developing subordinates; implementing procedural change; increasing efficiency; and dealing with problems of absenteeism, morale, and discipline.

3. **Facilities management** - These questions test for knowledge of the methods and materials used in the construction, alteration, maintenance and repair of physical plant facilities; the principles and practices involved in managing a building maintenance and energy conservation program; knowledge of typical contract documents; establishing and maintaining accident prevention and safety programs; and the principles and practices used by administrators when participating in the budget process. Questions may cover such areas as building structural elements, electrical and mechanical systems; proper building maintenance techniques, including determining the need for and scheduling repairs; energy conservation practices, including optimal heating plant and cooling system operation; reviewing and interpreting contracts; work place safety, including safety inspections, accident investigations, safety training, hazardous materials, personal protective equipment, and the mitigation of unsafe conditions; and program and capital budgeting, including estimating costs, budget proposals and justifications, controlling expenditures, and implementing the budget.

4. **Administrative supervision** - These questions test for knowledge of the principles and practices involved in directing the activities of a large subordinate staff, including subordinate supervisors. Questions relate to the personal interactions between an upper level supervisor and his/her subordinate supervisors in the accomplishment of objectives. These questions cover such areas as assigning work to and coordinating the activities of several units, establishing and guiding staff development programs, evaluating the performance of subordinate supervisors, and maintaining relationships with other organizational sections.

5. **Administrative techniques and practices** - These questions test for a knowledge of management techniques and practices used in directing or assisting in directing a program component or an organizational segment. Questions cover such areas as interpreting policies, making decisions based on the context of the position in the organization, coordinating programs or projects, communicating with employees or the public, planning employee training, and researching and evaluating areas of concern.

HOW TO TAKE A TEST

I. YOU MUST PASS AN EXAMINATION

A. WHAT EVERY CANDIDATE SHOULD KNOW

Examination applicants often ask us for help in preparing for the written test. What can I study in advance? What kinds of questions will be asked? How will the test be given? How will the papers be graded?

As an applicant for a civil service examination, you may be wondering about some of these things. Our purpose here is to suggest effective methods of advance study and to describe civil service examinations.

Your chances for success on this examination can be increased if you know how to prepare. Those "pre-examination jitters" can be reduced if you know what to expect. You can even experience an adventure in good citizenship if you know why civil service exams are given.

B. WHY ARE CIVIL SERVICE EXAMINATIONS GIVEN?

Civil service examinations are important to you in two ways. As a citizen, you want public jobs filled by employees who know how to do their work. As a job seeker, you want a fair chance to compete for that job on an equal footing with other candidates. The best-known means of accomplishing this two-fold goal is the competitive examination.

Exams are widely publicized throughout the nation. They may be administered for jobs in federal, state, city, municipal, town or village governments or agencies.

Any citizen may apply, with some limitations, such as the age or residence of applicants. Your experience and education may be reviewed to see whether you meet the requirements for the particular examination. When these requirements exist, they are reasonable and applied consistently to all applicants. Thus, a competitive examination may cause you some uneasiness now, but it is your privilege and safeguard.

C. HOW ARE CIVIL SERVICE EXAMS DEVELOPED?

Examinations are carefully written by trained technicians who are specialists in the field known as "psychological measurement," in consultation with recognized authorities in the field of work that the test will cover. These experts recommend the subject matter areas or skills to be tested; only those knowledges or skills important to your success on the job are included. The most reliable books and source materials available are used as references. Together, the experts and technicians judge the difficulty level of the questions.

Test technicians know how to phrase questions so that the problem is clearly stated. Their ethics do not permit "trick" or "catch" questions. Questions may have been tried out on sample groups, or subjected to statistical analysis, to determine their usefulness.

Written tests are often used in combination with performance tests, ratings of training and experience, and oral interviews. All of these measures combine to form the best-known means of finding the right person for the right job.

II. HOW TO PASS THE WRITTEN TEST

A. NATURE OF THE EXAMINATION

To prepare intelligently for civil service examinations, you should know how they differ from school examinations you have taken. In school you were assigned certain definite pages to read or subjects to cover. The examination questions were quite detailed and usually emphasized memory. Civil service exams, on the other hand, try to discover your present ability to perform the duties of a position, plus your potentiality to learn these duties. In other words, a civil service exam attempts to predict how successful you will be. Questions cover such a broad area that they cannot be as minute and detailed as school exam questions.

In the public service similar kinds of work, or positions, are grouped together in one "class." This process is known as *position-classification*. All the positions in a class are paid according to the salary range for that class. One class title covers all of these positions, and they are all tested by the same examination.

B. FOUR BASIC STEPS

1) Study the announcement

How, then, can you know what subjects to study? Our best answer is: "Learn as much as possible about the class of positions for which you've applied." The exam will test the knowledge, skills and abilities needed to do the work.

Your most valuable source of information about the position you want is the official exam announcement. This announcement lists the training and experience qualifications. Check these standards and apply only if you come reasonably close to meeting them.

The brief description of the position in the examination announcement offers some clues to the subjects which will be tested. Think about the job itself. Review the duties in your mind. Can you perform them, or are there some in which you are rusty? Fill in the blank spots in your preparation.

Many jurisdictions preview the written test in the exam announcement by including a section called "Knowledge and Abilities Required," "Scope of the Examination," or some similar heading. Here you will find out specifically what fields will be tested.

2) Review your own background

Once you learn in general what the position is all about, and what you need to know to do the work, ask yourself which subjects you already know fairly well and which need improvement. You may wonder whether to concentrate on improving your strong areas or on building some background in your fields of weakness. When the announcement has specified "some knowledge" or "considerable knowledge," or has used adjectives like "beginning principles of…" or "advanced … methods," you can get a clue as to the number and difficulty of questions to be asked in any given field. More questions, and hence broader coverage, would be included for those subjects which are more important in the work. Now weigh your strengths and weaknesses against the job requirements and prepare accordingly.

3) Determine the level of the position

Another way to tell how intensively you should prepare is to understand the level of the job for which you are applying. Is it the entering level? In other words, is this the position in which beginners in a field of work are hired? Or is it an intermediate or advanced level? Sometimes this is indicated by such words as "Junior" or "Senior" in the class title. Other jurisdictions use Roman numerals to designate the level – Clerk I, Clerk II, for example. The word "Supervisor" sometimes appears in the title. If the level is not indicated by the title, check the description of duties. Will you be working under very close supervision, or will you have responsibility for independent decisions in this work?

4) Choose appropriate study materials

Now that you know the subjects to be examined and the relative amount of each subject to be covered, you can choose suitable study materials. For beginning level jobs, or even advanced ones, if you have a pronounced weakness in some aspect of your training, read a modern, standard textbook in that field. Be sure it is up to date and has general coverage. Such books are normally available at your library, and the librarian will be glad to help you locate one. For entry-level positions, questions of appropriate difficulty are chosen – neither highly advanced questions, nor those too simple. Such questions require careful thought but not advanced training.

If the position for which you are applying is technical or advanced, you will read more advanced, specialized material. If you are already familiar with the basic principles of your field, elementary textbooks would waste your time. Concentrate on advanced textbooks and technical periodicals. Think through the concepts and review difficult problems in your field.

These are all general sources. You can get more ideas on your own initiative, following these leads. For example, training manuals and publications of the government agency which employs workers in your field can be useful, particularly for technical and professional positions. A letter or visit to the government department involved may result in more specific study suggestions, and certainly will provide you with a more definite idea of the exact nature of the position you are seeking.

III. KINDS OF TESTS

Tests are used for purposes other than measuring knowledge and ability to perform specified duties. For some positions, it is equally important to test ability to make adjustments to new situations or to profit from training. In others, basic mental abilities not dependent on information are essential. Questions which test these things may not appear as pertinent to the duties of the position as those which test for knowledge and information. Yet they are often highly important parts of a fair examination. For very general questions, it is almost impossible to help you direct your study efforts. What we can do is to point out some of the more common of these general abilities needed in public service positions and describe some typical questions.

1) General information

Broad, general information has been found useful for predicting job success in some kinds of work. This is tested in a variety of ways, from vocabulary lists to questions about current events. Basic background in some field of work, such as sociology or economics, may be sampled in a group of questions. Often these are principles which have become familiar to most persons through exposure rather than through formal training. It is difficult to advise you how to study for these questions; being alert to the world around you is our best suggestion.

2) Verbal ability

An example of an ability needed in many positions is verbal or language ability. Verbal ability is, in brief, the ability to use and understand words. Vocabulary and grammar tests are typical measures of this ability. Reading comprehension or paragraph interpretation questions are common in many kinds of civil service tests. You are given a paragraph of written material and asked to find its central meaning.

3) Numerical ability

Number skills can be tested by the familiar arithmetic problem, by checking paired lists of numbers to see which are alike and which are different, or by interpreting charts and graphs. In the latter test, a graph may be printed in the test booklet which you are asked to use as the basis for answering questions.

4) Observation

A popular test for law-enforcement positions is the observation test. A picture is shown to you for several minutes, then taken away. Questions about the picture test your ability to observe both details and larger elements.

5) Following directions

In many positions in the public service, the employee must be able to carry out written instructions dependably and accurately. You may be given a chart with several columns, each column listing a variety of information. The questions require you to carry out directions involving the information given in the chart.

6) Skills and aptitudes

Performance tests effectively measure some manual skills and aptitudes. When the skill is one in which you are trained, such as typing or shorthand, you can practice. These tests are often very much like those given in business school or high school courses. For many of the other skills and aptitudes, however, no short-time preparation can be made. Skills and abilities natural to you or that you have developed throughout your lifetime are being tested.

Many of the general questions just described provide all the data needed to answer the questions and ask you to use your reasoning ability to find the answers. Your best preparation for these tests, as well as for tests of facts and ideas, is to be at your physical and mental best. You, no doubt, have your own methods of getting into an exam-taking mood and keeping "in shape." The next section lists some ideas on this subject.

IV. KINDS OF QUESTIONS

Only rarely is the "essay" question, which you answer in narrative form, used in civil service tests. Civil service tests are usually of the short-answer type. Full instructions for answering these questions will be given to you at the examination. But in case this is your first experience with short-answer questions and separate answer sheets, here is what you need to know:

1) Multiple-choice Questions

Most popular of the short-answer questions is the "multiple choice" or "best answer" question. It can be used, for example, to test for factual knowledge, ability to solve problems or judgment in meeting situations found at work.

A multiple-choice question is normally one of three types—

- It can begin with an incomplete statement followed by several possible endings. You are to find the one ending which *best* completes the statement, although some of the others may not be entirely wrong.
- It can also be a complete statement in the form of a question which is answered by choosing one of the statements listed.
- It can be in the form of a problem – again you select the best answer.

Here is an example of a multiple-choice question with a discussion which should give you some clues as to the method for choosing the right answer:

When an employee has a complaint about his assignment, the action which will *best* help him overcome his difficulty is to
- A. discuss his difficulty with his coworkers
- B. take the problem to the head of the organization
- C. take the problem to the person who gave him the assignment
- D. say nothing to anyone about his complaint

In answering this question, you should study each of the choices to find which is best. Consider choice "A" – Certainly an employee may discuss his complaint with fellow employees, but no change or improvement can result, and the complaint remains unresolved. Choice "B" is a poor choice since the head of the organization probably does not know what assignment you have been given, and taking your problem to him is known as "going over the head" of the supervisor. The supervisor, or person who made the assignment, is the person who can clarify it or correct any injustice. Choice "C" is, therefore, correct. To say nothing, as in choice "D," is unwise. Supervisors have and interest in knowing the problems employees are facing, and the employee is seeking a solution to his problem.

2) True/False Questions

The "true/false" or "right/wrong" form of question is sometimes used. Here a complete statement is given. Your job is to decide whether the statement is right or wrong.

SAMPLE: A roaming cell-phone call to a nearby city costs less than a non-roaming call to a distant city.

This statement is wrong, or false, since roaming calls are more expensive.

This is not a complete list of all possible question forms, although most of the others are variations of these common types. You will always get complete directions for answering questions. Be sure you understand *how* to mark your answers – ask questions until you do.

V. RECORDING YOUR ANSWERS

Computer terminals are used more and more today for many different kinds of exams.

For an examination with very few applicants, you may be told to record your answers in the test booklet itself. Separate answer sheets are much more common. If this separate answer sheet is to be scored by machine – and this is often the case – it is highly important that you mark your answers correctly in order to get credit.

An electronic scoring machine is often used in civil service offices because of the speed with which papers can be scored. Machine-scored answer sheets must be marked with a pencil, which will be given to you. This pencil has a high graphite content which responds to the electronic scoring machine. As a matter of fact, stray dots may register as answers, so do not let your pencil rest on the answer sheet while you are pondering the correct answer. Also, if your pencil lead breaks or is otherwise defective, ask for another.

Since the answer sheet will be dropped in a slot in the scoring machine, be careful not to bend the corners or get the paper crumpled.

The answer sheet normally has five vertical columns of numbers, with 30 numbers to a column. These numbers correspond to the question numbers in your test booklet. After each number, going across the page are four or five pairs of dotted lines. These short dotted lines have small letters or numbers above them. The first two pairs may also have a "T" or "F" above the letters. This indicates that the first two pairs only are to be used if the questions are of the true-false type. If the questions are multiple choice, disregard the "T" and "F" and pay attention only to the small letters or numbers.

Answer your questions in the manner of the sample that follows:

32. The largest city in the United States is
    A. Washington, D.C.
    B. New York City
    C. Chicago
    D. Detroit
    E. San Francisco

1) Choose the answer you think is best. (New York City is the largest, so "B" is correct.)
2) Find the row of dotted lines numbered the same as the question you are answering. (Find row number 32)
3) Find the pair of dotted lines corresponding to the answer. (Find the pair of lines under the mark "B.")
4) Make a solid black mark between the dotted lines.

VI. BEFORE THE TEST

Common sense will help you find procedures to follow to get ready for an examination. Too many of us, however, overlook these sensible measures. Indeed, nervousness and fatigue have been found to be the most serious reasons why applicants fail to do their best on civil service tests. Here is a list of reminders:

- Begin your preparation early – Don't wait until the last minute to go scurrying around for books and materials or to find out what the position is all about.
- Prepare continuously – An hour a night for a week is better than an all-night cram session. This has been definitely established. What is more, a night a week for a month will return better dividends than crowding your study into a shorter period of time.
- Locate the place of the exam – You have been sent a notice telling you when and where to report for the examination. If the location is in a different town or otherwise unfamiliar to you, it would be well to inquire the best route and learn something about the building.
- Relax the night before the test – Allow your mind to rest. Do not study at all that night. Plan some mild recreation or diversion; then go to bed early and get a good night's sleep.
- Get up early enough to make a leisurely trip to the place for the test – This way unforeseen events, traffic snarls, unfamiliar buildings, etc. will not upset you.
- Dress comfortably – A written test is not a fashion show. You will be known by number and not by name, so wear something comfortable.
- Leave excess paraphernalia at home – Shopping bags and odd bundles will get in your way. You need bring only the items mentioned in the official notice you received; usually everything you need is provided. Do not bring reference books to the exam. They will only confuse those last minutes and be taken away from you when in the test room.
- Arrive somewhat ahead of time – If because of transportation schedules you must get there very early, bring a newspaper or magazine to take your mind off yourself while waiting.
- Locate the examination room – When you have found the proper room, you will be directed to the seat or part of the room where you will sit. Sometimes you are given a sheet of instructions to read while you are waiting. Do not fill out any forms until you are told to do so; just read them and be prepared.
- Relax and prepare to listen to the instructions
- If you have any physical problem that may keep you from doing your best, be sure to tell the test administrator. If you are sick or in poor health, you really cannot do your best on the exam. You can come back and take the test some other time.

VII. AT THE TEST

The day of the test is here and you have the test booklet in your hand. The temptation to get going is very strong. Caution! There is more to success than knowing the right answers. You must know how to identify your papers and understand variations in the type of short-answer question used in this particular examination. Follow these suggestions for maximum results from your efforts:

1) Cooperate with the monitor

The test administrator has a duty to create a situation in which you can be as much at ease as possible. He will give instructions, tell you when to begin, check to see that you are marking your answer sheet correctly, and so on. He is not there to guard you, although he will see that your competitors do not take unfair advantage. He wants to help you do your best.

2) Listen to all instructions

Don't jump the gun! Wait until you understand all directions. In most civil service tests you get more time than you need to answer the questions. So don't be in a hurry. Read each word of instructions until you clearly understand the meaning. Study the examples, listen to all announcements and follow directions. Ask questions if you do not understand what to do.

3) Identify your papers

Civil service exams are usually identified by number only. You will be assigned a number; you must not put your name on your test papers. Be sure to copy your number correctly. Since more than one exam may be given, copy your exact examination title.

4) Plan your time

Unless you are told that a test is a "speed" or "rate of work" test, speed itself is usually not important. Time enough to answer all the questions will be provided, but this does not mean that you have all day. An overall time limit has been set. Divide the total time (in minutes) by the number of questions to determine the approximate time you have for each question.

5) Do not linger over difficult questions

If you come across a difficult question, mark it with a paper clip (useful to have along) and come back to it when you have been through the booklet. One caution if you do this – be sure to skip a number on your answer sheet as well. Check often to be sure that you have not lost your place and that you are marking in the row numbered the same as the question you are answering.

6) Read the questions

Be sure you know what the question asks! Many capable people are unsuccessful because they failed to *read* the questions correctly.

7) Answer all questions

Unless you have been instructed that a penalty will be deducted for incorrect answers, it is better to guess than to omit a question.

8) Speed tests

It is often better NOT to guess on speed tests. It has been found that on timed tests people are tempted to spend the last few seconds before time is called in marking answers at random – without even reading them – in the hope of picking up a few extra points. To discourage this practice, the instructions may warn you that your score will be "corrected" for guessing. That is, a penalty will be applied. The incorrect answers will be deducted from the correct ones, or some other penalty formula will be used.

9) Review your answers

If you finish before time is called, go back to the questions you guessed or omitted to give them further thought. Review other answers if you have time.

10) Return your test materials

If you are ready to leave before others have finished or time is called, take ALL your materials to the monitor and leave quietly. Never take any test material with you. The monitor can discover whose papers are not complete, and taking a test booklet may be grounds for disqualification.

VIII. EXAMINATION TECHNIQUES

1) Read the general instructions carefully. These are usually printed on the first page of the exam booklet. As a rule, these instructions refer to the timing of the examination; the fact that you should not start work until the signal and must stop work at a signal, etc. If there are any *special* instructions, such as a choice of questions to be answered, make sure that you note this instruction carefully.

2) When you are ready to start work on the examination, that is as soon as the signal has been given, read the instructions to each question booklet, underline any key words or phrases, such as *least, best, outline, describe* and the like. In this way you will tend to answer as requested rather than discover on reviewing your paper that you *listed without describing*, that you selected the *worst* choice rather than the *best* choice, etc.

3) If the examination is of the objective or multiple-choice type – that is, each question will also give a series of possible answers: A, B, C or D, and you are called upon to select the best answer and write the letter next to that answer on your answer paper – it is advisable to start answering each question in turn. There may be anywhere from 50 to 100 such questions in the three or four hours allotted and you can see how much time would be taken if you read through all the questions before beginning to answer any. Furthermore, if you come across a question or group of questions which you know would be difficult to answer, it would undoubtedly affect your handling of all the other questions.

4) If the examination is of the essay type and contains but a few questions, it is a moot point as to whether you should read all the questions before starting to answer any one. Of course, if you are given a choice – say five out of seven and the like – then it is essential to read all the questions so you can eliminate the two that are most difficult. If, however, you are asked to answer all the questions, there may be danger in trying to answer the easiest one first because you may find that you will spend too much time on it. The best technique is to answer the first question, then proceed to the second, etc.

5) Time your answers. Before the exam begins, write down the time it started, then add the time allowed for the examination and write down the time it must be completed, then divide the time available somewhat as follows:

- If 3-1/2 hours are allowed, that would be 210 minutes. If you have 80 objective-type questions, that would be an average of 2-1/2 minutes per question. Allow yourself no more than 2 minutes per question, or a total of 160 minutes, which will permit about 50 minutes to review.
- If for the time allotment of 210 minutes there are 7 essay questions to answer, that would average about 30 minutes a question. Give yourself only 25 minutes per question so that you have about 35 minutes to review.

6) The most important instruction is to *read each question* and make sure you know what is wanted. The second most important instruction is to *time yourself properly* so that you answer every question. The third most important instruction is to *answer every question*. Guess if you have to but include something for each question. Remember that you will receive no credit for a blank and will probably receive some credit if you write something in answer to an essay question. If you guess a letter – say "B" for a multiple-choice question – you may have guessed right. If you leave a blank as an answer to a multiple-choice question, the examiners may respect your feelings but it will not add a point to your score. Some exams may penalize you for wrong answers, so in such cases *only*, you may not want to guess unless you have some basis for your answer.

7) Suggestions
   a. Objective-type questions
      1. Examine the question booklet for proper sequence of pages and questions
      2. Read all instructions carefully
      3. Skip any question which seems too difficult; return to it after all other questions have been answered
      4. Apportion your time properly; do not spend too much time on any single question or group of questions
      5. Note and underline key words – *all, most, fewest, least, best, worst, same, opposite,* etc.
      6. Pay particular attention to negatives
      7. Note unusual option, e.g., unduly long, short, complex, different or similar in content to the body of the question
      8. Observe the use of "hedging" words – *probably, may, most likely,* etc.
      9. Make sure that your answer is put next to the same number as the question
      10. Do not second-guess unless you have good reason to believe the second answer is definitely more correct
      11. Cross out original answer if you decide another answer is more accurate; do not erase until you are ready to hand your paper in
      12. Answer all questions; guess unless instructed otherwise
      13. Leave time for review

   b. Essay questions
      1. Read each question carefully
      2. Determine exactly what is wanted. Underline key words or phrases.
      3. Decide on outline or paragraph answer

4. Include many different points and elements unless asked to develop any one or two points or elements
5. Show impartiality by giving pros and cons unless directed to select one side only
6. Make and write down any assumptions you find necessary to answer the questions
7. Watch your English, grammar, punctuation and choice of words
8. Time your answers; don't crowd material

8) Answering the essay question

Most essay questions can be answered by framing the specific response around several key words or ideas. Here are a few such key words or ideas:

M's: manpower, materials, methods, money, management
P's: purpose, program, policy, plan, procedure, practice, problems, pitfalls, personnel, public relations
  a. Six basic steps in handling problems:
    1. Preliminary plan and background development
    2. Collect information, data and facts
    3. Analyze and interpret information, data and facts
    4. Analyze and develop solutions as well as make recommendations
    5. Prepare report and sell recommendations
    6. Install recommendations and follow up effectiveness

  b. Pitfalls to avoid
    1. *Taking things for granted* – A statement of the situation does not necessarily imply that each of the elements is necessarily true; for example, a complaint may be invalid and biased so that all that can be taken for granted is that a complaint has been registered
    2. *Considering only one side of a situation* – Wherever possible, indicate several alternatives and then point out the reasons you selected the best one
    3. *Failing to indicate follow up* – Whenever your answer indicates action on your part, make certain that you will take proper follow-up action to see how successful your recommendations, procedures or actions turn out to be
    4. *Taking too long in answering any single question* – Remember to time your answers properly

IX. AFTER THE TEST

Scoring procedures differ in detail among civil service jurisdictions although the general principles are the same. Whether the papers are hand-scored or graded by machine we have described, they are nearly always graded by number. That is, the person who marks the paper knows only the number – never the name – of the applicant. Not until all the papers have been graded will they be matched with names. If other tests, such as training and experience or oral interview ratings have been given, scores will be combined. Different parts of the examination usually have different weights. For example, the written test might count 60 percent of the final grade, and a rating of training and experience 40 percent. In many jurisdictions, veterans will have a certain number of points added to their grades.

After the final grade has been determined, the names are placed in grade order and an eligible list is established. There are various methods for resolving ties between those who get the same final grade – probably the most common is to place first the name of the person whose application was received first. Job offers are made from the eligible list in the order the names appear on it. You will be notified of your grade and your rank as soon as all these computations have been made. This will be done as rapidly as possible.

People who are found to meet the requirements in the announcement are called "eligibles." Their names are put on a list of eligible candidates. An eligible's chances of getting a job depend on how high he stands on this list and how fast agencies are filling jobs from the list.

When a job is to be filled from a list of eligibles, the agency asks for the names of people on the list of eligibles for that job. When the civil service commission receives this request, it sends to the agency the names of the three people highest on this list. Or, if the job to be filled has specialized requirements, the office sends the agency the names of the top three persons who meet these requirements from the general list.

The appointing officer makes a choice from among the three people whose names were sent to him. If the selected person accepts the appointment, the names of the others are put back on the list to be considered for future openings.

That is the rule in hiring from all kinds of eligible lists, whether they are for typist, carpenter, chemist, or something else. For every vacancy, the appointing officer has his choice of any one of the top three eligibles on the list. This explains why the person whose name is on top of the list sometimes does not get an appointment when some of the persons lower on the list do. If the appointing officer chooses the second or third eligible, the No. 1 eligible does not get a job at once, but stays on the list until he is appointed or the list is terminated.

X. HOW TO PASS THE INTERVIEW TEST

The examination for which you applied requires an oral interview test. You have already taken the written test and you are now being called for the interview test – the final part of the formal examination.

You may think that it is not possible to prepare for an interview test and that there are no procedures to follow during an interview. Our purpose is to point out some things you can do in advance that will help you and some good rules to follow and pitfalls to avoid while you are being interviewed.

What is an interview supposed to test?
The written examination is designed to test the technical knowledge and competence of the candidate; the oral is designed to evaluate intangible qualities, not readily measured otherwise, and to establish a list showing the relative fitness of each candidate – as measured against his competitors – for the position sought. Scoring is not on the basis of "right" and "wrong," but on a sliding scale of values ranging from "not passable" to "outstanding." As a matter of fact, it is possible to achieve a relatively low score without a single "incorrect" answer because of evident weakness in the qualities being measured.

Occasionally, an examination may consist entirely of an oral test – either an individual or a group oral. In such cases, information is sought concerning the technical knowledges and abilities of the candidate, since there has been no written examination for this purpose. More commonly, however, an oral test is used to supplement a written examination.

Who conducts interviews?

The composition of oral boards varies among different jurisdictions. In nearly all, a representative of the personnel department serves as chairman. One of the members of the board may be a representative of the department in which the candidate would work. In some cases, "outside experts" are used, and, frequently, a businessman or some other representative of the general public is asked to serve. Labor and management or other special groups may be represented. The aim is to secure the services of experts in the appropriate field.

However the board is composed, it is a good idea (and not at all improper or unethical) to ascertain in advance of the interview who the members are and what groups they represent. When you are introduced to them, you will have some idea of their backgrounds and interests, and at least you will not stutter and stammer over their names.

What should be done before the interview?

While knowledge about the board members is useful and takes some of the surprise element out of the interview, there is other preparation which is more substantive. It *is* possible to prepare for an oral interview – in several ways:

1) Keep a copy of your application and review it carefully before the interview

This may be the only document before the oral board, and the starting point of the interview. Know what education and experience you have listed there, and the sequence and dates of all of it. Sometimes the board will ask you to review the highlights of your experience for them; you should not have to hem and haw doing it.

2) Study the class specification and the examination announcement

Usually, the oral board has one or both of these to guide them. The qualities, characteristics or knowledges required by the position sought are stated in these documents. They offer valuable clues as to the nature of the oral interview. For example, if the job involves supervisory responsibilities, the announcement will usually indicate that knowledge of modern supervisory methods and the qualifications of the candidate as a supervisor will be tested. If so, you can expect such questions, frequently in the form of a hypothetical situation which you are expected to solve. NEVER go into an oral without knowledge of the duties and responsibilities of the job you seek.

3) Think through each qualification required

Try to visualize the kind of questions you would ask if you were a board member. How well could you answer them? Try especially to appraise your own knowledge and background in each area, *measured against the job sought*, and identify any areas in which you are weak. Be critical and realistic – do not flatter yourself.

4) Do some general reading in areas in which you feel you may be weak

For example, if the job involves supervision and your past experience has NOT, some general reading in supervisory methods and practices, particularly in the field of human relations, might be useful. Do NOT study agency procedures or detailed manuals. The oral board will be testing your understanding and capacity, not your memory.

5) Get a good night's sleep and watch your general health and mental attitude

You will want a clear head at the interview. Take care of a cold or any other minor ailment, and of course, no hangovers.

What should be done on the day of the interview?

Now comes the day of the interview itself. Give yourself plenty of time to get there. Plan to arrive somewhat ahead of the scheduled time, particularly if your appointment is in the fore part of the day. If a previous candidate fails to appear, the board might be ready for you a bit early. By early afternoon an oral board is almost invariably behind schedule if there are many candidates, and you may have to wait. Take along a book or magazine to read, or your application to review, but leave any extraneous material in the waiting room when you go in for your interview. In any event, relax and compose yourself.

The matter of dress is important. The board is forming impressions about you – from your experience, your manners, your attitude, and your appearance. Give your personal appearance careful attention. Dress your best, but not your flashiest. Choose conservative, appropriate clothing, and be sure it is immaculate. This is a business interview, and your appearance should indicate that you regard it as such. Besides, being well groomed and properly dressed will help boost your confidence.

Sooner or later, someone will call your name and escort you into the interview room. *This is it.* From here on you are on your own. It is too late for any more preparation. But remember, you asked for this opportunity to prove your fitness, and you are here because your request was granted.

What happens when you go in?

The usual sequence of events will be as follows: The clerk (who is often the board stenographer) will introduce you to the chairman of the oral board, who will introduce you to the other members of the board. Acknowledge the introductions before you sit down. Do not be surprised if you find a microphone facing you or a stenotypist sitting by. Oral interviews are usually recorded in the event of an appeal or other review.

Usually the chairman of the board will open the interview by reviewing the highlights of your education and work experience from your application – primarily for the benefit of the other members of the board, as well as to get the material into the record. Do not interrupt or comment unless there is an error or significant misinterpretation; if that is the case, do not hesitate. But do not quibble about insignificant matters. Also, he will usually ask you some question about your education, experience or your present job – partly to get you to start talking and to establish the interviewing "rapport." He may start the actual questioning, or turn it over to one of the other members. Frequently, each member undertakes the questioning on a particular area, one in which he is perhaps most competent, so you can expect each member to participate in the examination. Because time is limited, you may also expect some rather abrupt switches in the direction the questioning takes, so do not be upset by it. Normally, a board member will not pursue a single line of questioning unless he discovers a particular strength or weakness.

After each member has participated, the chairman will usually ask whether any member has any further questions, then will ask you if you have anything you wish to add. Unless you are expecting this question, it may floor you. Worse, it may start you off on an extended, extemporaneous speech. The board is not usually seeking more information. The question is principally to offer you a last opportunity to present further qualifications or to indicate that you have nothing to add. So, if you feel that a significant qualification or characteristic has been overlooked, it is proper to point it out in a sentence or so. Do not compliment the board on the thoroughness of their examination – they have been sketchy, and you know it. If you wish, merely say, "No thank you, I have nothing further to add." This is a point where you can "talk yourself out" of a good impression or fail to present an important bit of information. Remember, *you close the interview yourself.*

The chairman will then say, "That is all, Mr. _____, thank you." Do not be startled; the interview is over, and quicker than you think. Thank him, gather your belongings and take your leave. Save your sigh of relief for the other side of the door.

How to put your best foot forward

Throughout this entire process, you may feel that the board individually and collectively is trying to pierce your defenses, seek out your hidden weaknesses and embarrass and confuse you. Actually, this is not true. They are obliged to make an appraisal of your qualifications for the job you are seeking, and they want to see you in your best light. Remember, they must interview all candidates and a non-cooperative candidate may become a failure in spite of their best efforts to bring out his qualifications. Here are 15 suggestions that will help you:

1) Be natural – Keep your attitude confident, not cocky

If you are not confident that you can do the job, do not expect the board to be. Do not apologize for your weaknesses, try to bring out your strong points. The board is interested in a positive, not negative, presentation. Cockiness will antagonize any board member and make him wonder if you are covering up a weakness by a false show of strength.

2) Get comfortable, but don't lounge or sprawl

Sit erectly but not stiffly. A careless posture may lead the board to conclude that you are careless in other things, or at least that you are not impressed by the importance of the occasion. Either conclusion is natural, even if incorrect. Do not fuss with your clothing, a pencil or an ashtray. Your hands may occasionally be useful to emphasize a point; do not let them become a point of distraction.

3) Do not wisecrack or make small talk

This is a serious situation, and your attitude should show that you consider it as such. Further, the time of the board is limited – they do not want to waste it, and neither should you.

4) Do not exaggerate your experience or abilities

In the first place, from information in the application or other interviews and sources, the board may know more about you than you think. Secondly, you probably will not get away with it. An experienced board is rather adept at spotting such a situation, so do not take the chance.

5) If you know a board member, do not make a point of it, yet do not hide it

Certainly you are not fooling him, and probably not the other members of the board. Do not try to take advantage of your acquaintanceship – it will probably do you little good.

6) Do not dominate the interview

Let the board do that. They will give you the clues – do not assume that you have to do all the talking. Realize that the board has a number of questions to ask you, and do not try to take up all the interview time by showing off your extensive knowledge of the answer to the first one.

7) Be attentive

You only have 20 minutes or so, and you should keep your attention at its sharpest throughout. When a member is addressing a problem or question to you, give him your undivided attention. Address your reply principally to him, but do not exclude the other board members.

8) Do not interrupt

A board member may be stating a problem for you to analyze. He will ask you a question when the time comes. Let him state the problem, and wait for the question.

9) Make sure you understand the question

Do not try to answer until you are sure what the question is. If it is not clear, restate it in your own words or ask the board member to clarify it for you. However, do not haggle about minor elements.

10) Reply promptly but not hastily

A common entry on oral board rating sheets is "candidate responded readily," or "candidate hesitated in replies." Respond as promptly and quickly as you can, but do not jump to a hasty, ill-considered answer.

11) Do not be peremptory in your answers

A brief answer is proper – but do not fire your answer back. That is a losing game from your point of view. The board member can probably ask questions much faster than you can answer them.

12) Do not try to create the answer you think the board member wants

He is interested in what kind of mind you have and how it works – not in playing games. Furthermore, he can usually spot this practice and will actually grade you down on it.

13) Do not switch sides in your reply merely to agree with a board member

Frequently, a member will take a contrary position merely to draw you out and to see if you are willing and able to defend your point of view. Do not start a debate, yet do not surrender a good position. If a position is worth taking, it is worth defending.

14) Do not be afraid to admit an error in judgment if you are shown to be wrong

The board knows that you are forced to reply without any opportunity for careful consideration. Your answer may be demonstrably wrong. If so, admit it and get on with the interview.

15) Do not dwell at length on your present job

The opening question may relate to your present assignment. Answer the question but do not go into an extended discussion. You are being examined for a *new* job, not your present one. As a matter of fact, try to phrase ALL your answers in terms of the job for which you are being examined.

Basis of Rating

Probably you will forget most of these "do's" and "don'ts" when you walk into the oral interview room. Even remembering them all will not ensure you a passing grade. Perhaps you did not have the qualifications in the first place. But remembering them will help you to put your best foot forward, without treading on the toes of the board members.

Rumor and popular opinion to the contrary notwithstanding, an oral board wants you to make the best appearance possible. They know you are under pressure – but they also want to see how you respond to it as a guide to what your reaction would be under the pressures of the job you seek. They will be influenced by the degree of poise you display, the personal traits you show and the manner in which you respond.

ABOUT THIS BOOK

This book contains tests divided into Examination Sections. Go through each test, answering every question in the margin. At the end of each test look at the answer key and check your answers. On the ones you got wrong, look at the right answer choice and learn. Do not fill in the answers first. Do not memorize the questions and answers, but understand the answer and principles involved. On your test, the questions will likely be different from the samples. Questions are changed and new ones added. If you understand these past questions you should have success with any changes that arise. Tests may consist of several types of questions. We have additional books on each subject should more study be advisable or necessary for you. Finally, the more you study, the better prepared you will be. This book is intended to be the last thing you study before you walk into the examination room. Prior study of relevant texts is also recommended. NLC publishes some of these in our Fundamental Series. Knowledge and good sense are important factors in passing your exam. Good luck also helps. So now study this Passbook, absorb the material contained within and take that knowledge into the examination. Then do your best to pass that exam.

EXAMINATION SECTION

EXAMINATION SECTION
TEST 1

DIRECTIONS: Each question or incomplete statement is followed by several suggested answers or completions. Select the one that BEST answers the question or completes the statement. *PRINT THE LETTER OF THE CORRECT ANSWER IN THE SPACE AT THE RIGHT.*

1. Of the following, the BEST way for you to make sure that a cleaner understands a spoken order which you have given to him is for you to   1.____

    A. ask him to repeat the order in his own words
    B. ask him whether he has understood the order
    C. watch how he begins to follow the order
    D. ask him whether he has any questions about the order

2. You have called a meeting with your cleaners to get their suggestions on ways to keep up cleaning standards in spite of budget cutbacks.   2.____
You will MOST likely be successful in encouraging them to participate in the discussion if you

    A. start the meeting by giving the cleaners all your own suggestions first
    B. keep the meeting going by talking whenever the cleaners have nothing to say
    C. get the cleaners to *think out loud* by asking them for their interpretations of the problem
    D. comment on and evaluate the suggestions made by each cleaner immediately after he makes them

3. If a custodian knows that rumors being spread by his assistants are false, he should   3.____

    A. tell the assistants that the rumors are false
    B. tell the assistants the facts which the rumors have falsified
    C. threaten to discipline any assistant who spreads the rumors
    D. find out which assistant started the rumor and have him suspended

4. One of your cleaners tells you in private that he wants to quit his job.   4.____
The FIRST thing you should do in handling this matter is to

    A. ask the cleaner why he wants to quit his job
    B. tell the cleaner to take a few days to think it over
    C. refer the cleaner to the personnel office
    D. try to convince the cleaner not to quit his job

5. The MOST important reason why a custodian should seek the suggestions of his cleaners on job-related matters is that the   5.____

    A. cleaners generally have greater knowledge of job-related matters than the custodian
    B. cleaners will tend to have a greater feeling of participation in their jobs by making suggestions
    C. custodians will be able to hold the cleaners responsible for any suggestions he follows
    D. custodians can win the respect of his cleaners by showing them the errors in their suggestions

6. Your supervisor has ordered you to announce to your cleaners a new cleaning rule with which you disagree. You should

    A. admit honestly to your cleaners that you disagree with the rule
    B. announce the rule to your cleaners without expressing your disagreement
    C. encourage your cleaners by telling them you agree with the rule
    D. tell your supervisor that you refuse to announce any rule with which you disagree

6.___

7. Of the following, the BEST practice to follow in criticizing the work performance of a cleaner is to

    A. save up several criticisms and make them all at one time
    B. soften your criticism by being humorous
    C. have another cleaner, who has more seniority, give the criticism
    D. make sure that you explain to the cleaner the reasons for your criticisms

7.___

8. Of the following, the BEST way to reduce unnecessary absences among your cleaners is to

    A. ask your cleaners the reason for their absence every time they are absent
    B. rely entirely on written warnings once every month to cleaners who have been absent too often during the month
    C. have your cleaners make a formal written report to you every time they are absent, explaining the reason for their absence
    D. threaten to fire your cleaners every time they are absent

8.___

9. A group of students complains to you about the lack of cleanliness in your building. You realize that budget cutbacks have unavoidably led to shortages in manpower and equipment for the cleaning staff.
Of the following, the BEST way for you to answer these students is to

    A. tell them frankly that the cleanliness of the building is none of their business as students
    B. apologize for the condition of the building and promise that your men will work harder
    C. tell them to take their complaints to the administration and not to you
    D. explain the reasons for the building's condition and what you are doing to improve it

9.___

10. The MOST important role of the school custodian in promoting public relations in the community should be to help

    A. increase understanding between the custodial staff and the community which it serves
    B. keep from community attention any failings on the part of the custodial staff
    C. increase the authority of the custodial staff over the community with which it deals
    D. keep the community from interfering in the operations of the custodial staff

10.___

11. A teacher conducting a class calls you to complain that the cleaners cleaning the empty classroom next to hers are being unnecessarily noisy.
Of the following, the BEST response to the teacher is to tell her that

11.___

A. she should go next door to tell the cleaners to stop the unnecessary noise
B. you will tell the cleaners about her complaint and instruct them not to make unnecessary noise
C. she should file a formal complaint against the cleaners with your superior
D. you will come to her classroom to judge for yourself whether the cleaners are being unnecessarily noisy

12. The attitude a school custodian should generally maintain toward the faculty and students is one of   12._____

A. avoidance   B. superiority
C. courtesy   D. servility

13. The flow of oil in an automatic rotary cup oil burner is regulated by a(n)   13._____

A. thermostat   B. metering valve
C. pressure relief valve   D. electric eye

14. The one of the following devices that is required on both coal-fired and oil-fired boilers is a(n)   14._____

A. safety valve
B. low water cut-off
C. feedwater regulator
D. electrostatic precipitator

15. The type of fuel which must be preheated before it can be burned efficiently is   15._____

A. natural gas   B. pea coal
C. number 2 oil   D. number 6 oil

16. A suction gauge in a fuel-oil transfer system is USUALLY located   16._____

A. before the strainer
B. after the strainer and before the pump
C. after the pump and before the pressure relief valve
D. after the pressure relief valve

17. The FIRST item that should be checked before starting the fire in a steam boiler is the   17._____

A. thermostat   B. vacuum pump
C. boiler water level   D. feedwater regulator

18. Operation of a boiler that has been *sealed* by the Department of Buildings is   18._____

A. prohibited
B. permitted when the outside temperature is below 32° F
C. permitted between the hours of 6:00 A.M. and 8:00 A.M. and 9:00 P.M. and 11:00 P.M.
D. permitted only for the purpose of heating domestic water

19. Lowering the thermostat setting by 5 degrees during the heating season will result in fuel savings of MOST NEARLY _____ percent.   19._____

A. 2   B. 5   C. 20   D. 50

3

20. An electrically-driven rotary fuel oil pump MUST be protected from internal damage by the installation in the oil line of a   20.___

    A. discharge side strainer   B. check valve
    C. suction gauge   D. pressure relief valve

21. A float-thermostatic steam trap in a condensate return line that is operating properly will allow   21.___

    A. steam and air to pass and will hold back condensate
    B. air and condensate to pass and will hold back steam
    C. steam and condensate to pass and will hold back air
    D. steam to pass and will hold back air and condensate

22. Changes in the combustion efficiency of a boiler can be determined by comparing changes in stack temperature and   22.___

    A. steam pressure in the header
    B. over the fire draft
    C. percentage of carbon dioxide
    D. equivalent of direct radiation

23. The classification of the coal that is USUALLY burned in a city school building is   23.___

    A. anthracite   B. bituminous
    C. semi-bituminous   D. lignite

24. A boiler is equipped with the following pressuretrols: 24.___
    I. Manual-reset
    II. Modulating
    III. High-limit
The CORRECT sequence in which these devices should be actuated by rising steam pressure is

    A. I, II, III   B. II, III, I
    C. III, I, II   D. III, II, I

25. The temperature of the returning condensate in a low-pressure steam heating system is 195° F.
This temperature indicates that   25.___

    A. some radiator traps are defective
    B. some boiler tubes are leaking
    C. the boiler water level is too low
    D. there is a high vacuum in the return line

26. An over-the-fire draft gauge in a natural draft furnace is USUALLY read in   26.___

    A. feet per minute   B. pounds per square inch
    C. inches of mercury   D. inches of water

27. The Air Pollution Code states that no person shall cause or permit the emission of an air contaminant of a density which appears as dark or darker than number _____ on the standard smoke chart.   27.___

    A. one   B. two   C. three   D. four

28. The equipment which is used to provide tempered fresh air to certain areas of a school   28.____
building is a(n)

    A.   exhaust fan   B.   window fan
    C.   fixed louvre   D.   heating stack

29. When a glass globe is put back over a newly replaced lightbulb in a ceiling light fixture,   29.____
the holding screws on the globe should be tightened, then loosened, one half turn.
This is done MAINLY to prevent

    A.   fires caused by electrical short circuits
    B.   cracking of the globe due to heat expansion
    C.   falling of the globe from the light fixture
    D.   building up of harmful gases inside the globe

30. Standard 120 volt type fuses are GENERALLY rated in   30.____

    A.   farads   B.   ohms   C.   watts   D.   amperes

31. A cleaner informs you that his electric vacuum cleaner is not working even though he   31.____
tried the off-on switch several times and checked to see that the plug was still in the wall
outlet.
Of the following, the FIRST course of action you should take in this situation is to

    A.   determine if the circuit breaker has tripped out
    B.   take apart the vacuum cleaner
    C.   replace the electric cord on the vacuum cleaner
    D.   replace the electrical outlet

32. The one of the following that is the MOST practical method for a school custodian to use   32.____
in making a temporary repair in a straight portion of a water pipe which has a small leak
is to

    A.   attach a clamped patch over the leak
    B.   weld or braze the pipe, depending on the material
    C.   drill and tap the pipe, then insert a plug
    D.   fill the hole with an epoxy sealer

33. The PRIMARY function of the packing which is generally found in the stuffing box of a   33.____
centrifugal pump is to

    A.   compensate for misalignment of the pump shaft
    B.   prevent leakage of the fluid
    C.   control the discharge rate of the pump
    D.   provide support for the pump shaft

34. Of the following, the MOST important reason for replacing a worn washer in a dripping   34.____
faucet as soon as possible is to prevent

    A.   overflow of the sink trap
    B.   the mixture of hot and cold water in the sink
    C.   damage to the faucet parts that can be the result of overtightening the stem
    D.   air from entering the supply line

35. In carpentry work, the MOST commonly used hand saw is the _____ saw.   35.___

    A. hack   B. rip   C. buck   D. cross-cut

36. The device which USUALLY keeps a doorknob from rotating on the spindle is a   36.___

    A. cotter pin   B. tapered key
    C. set screw   D. stop screw

37. The following tasks are frequently done when an office is cleaned: 37.___
        I.   The floor is vacuumed
        II.   The ashtrays and wastebaskets are emptied
        III.   The desks and furniture are dusted
The order in which these tasks should GENERALLY be done is

    A. I, II, III   B. II, III, I
    C. III, II, I   D. I, III, II

38. When wax is applied to a floor by the use of a twine mop with a handle, the wax should   38.___
be _____ with the mop.

    A. applied in thin coats
    B. applied in heavy coats
    C. poured on the floor, then spread
    D. dripped on the floor, then spread

39. The BEST way to clean dust from an acoustical type ceiling is with a   39.___

    A. strong soap solution   B. wet sponge
    C. vacuum cleaner   D. stream of water

40. Of the following, the MOST important reason why a wet mop should NOT be wrung out   40.___
by hand is that

    A. the strings of the mop will be damaged by hand-wringing
    B. sharp objects picked up by the mop may injure the hands
    C. the mop cannot be made dry enough by hand-wringing
    D. fine dirt will become embedded in the strings of the mop

KEY (CORRECT ANSWERS)

1.	A	11.	B	21.	B	31.	A
2.	C	12.	C	22.	C	32.	A
3.	B	13.	B	23.	A	33.	B
4.	A	14.	A	24.	B	34.	C
5.	B	15.	D	25.	A	35.	D
6.	B	16.	B	26.	D	36.	C
7.	D	17.	C	27.	D	37.	B
8.	A	18.	A	28.	B	38.	A
9.	D	19.	C	29.	B	39.	C
10.	A	20.	B	30.	D	40.	B

———

TEST 2

DIRECTIONS: Each question or incomplete statement is followed by several suggested answers or completions. Select the one that BEST answers the question or completes the statement. *PRINT THE LETTER OF THE CORRECT ANSWER IN THE SPACE AT THE RIGHT.*

1. When a painted wall is washed by hand, the wall should be washed from the _____ with a _____ sponge.   1.___

    A. top down; soaking wet   B. bottom up; soaking wet
    C. top down; damp   D. bottom up; damp

2. When a painted wall is brushed with a clean lambswool duster, the duster should be drawn _____ with _____ pressure.   2.___

    A. downward; light   B. upward; light
    C. downward; firm   D. upward; firm

3. The one of the following terms which BEST describes the size of a floor brush is   3.___

    A. 72 cubic inch   B. 32 ounce
    C. 24 inch   D. 10 square foot

4. When a slate blackboard is washed by hand, it is BEST to use   4.___

    A. a mild soap solution and allow the blackboard to air dry
    B. warm water and allow the blackboard to air dry
    C. a mild soap solution and sponge the blackboard dry
    D. warm water and sponge the blackboard dry

5. The MAIN reason why the handle of a reversible floor brush should be shifted from one side of the brush block to the opposite side is to   5.___

    A. change the angle at which the brush sweeps the floor
    B. give equal wear to both sides of the brush
    C. permit the brush to sweep hard-to-reach areas
    D. make it easier to sweep backward

6. When a long corridor is swept with a floor brush, it is good practice to   6.___

    A. push the brush with moderately long strokes and flick it after each stroke
    B. press on the brush and push it the whole length of the corridor in one sweep
    C. pull the brush inward with short brisk strokes
    D. sweep across rather than down the length of the corridor

7. Of the following office cleaning jobs performed during the year, the one which should be done MOST frequently is   7.___

    A. cleaning the fluorescent lights
    B. dusting the Venetian blinds
    C. cleaning the bookcase glass
    D. carpet-sweeping the rug

8. The BEST polishing agent to use on wood furniture is 8.____

   A. pumice   B. paste wax
   C. water emulsion wax   D. neatfoot's oil

9. Lemon oil polish is used BEST to polish 9.____

   A. exterior bronze   B. marble walls
   C. lacquered metal floors   D. leather seats

10. Cleaning with trisodium phosphate will MOST likely damage 10.____

   A. toilet bowls   B. drain pipes
   C. polished marble floors   D. rubber tile floors

11. Of the following cleaning agents, the one which should NOT be used is 11.____

   A. caustic lye   B. detergent
   C. scouring powder   D. ammonia

12. The one of the following cleaners which GENERALLY contains an abrasive is 12.____

   A. caustic lye   B. trisodium phosphate
   C. scouring powder   D. ammonia

13. The instructions on a box of cleaning powder say, *Mix one pound of cleaning powder in four gallons of water.* According to these instructions, how many ounces of cleaning powder should be mixed in one gallon of water? 13.____

   A. 4   B. 8   C. 12   D. 16

14. In accordance with recommended practice, a dust mop, when not used, should be stored 14.____

   A. hanging, handle end down
   B. hanging, handle end up
   C. standing on the floor, handle end down
   D. standing on the floor, handle end up

15. The two types of floors found in public buildings are classified as *hard* and *soft* floors. An example of a hard floor is one made of 15.____

   A. linoleum   B. cork
   C. ceramic tile   D. asphalt tile

16. The BEST way for a custodian to determine whether a cleaner is doing his work well is by 16.____

   A. observing the cleaner at work for several hours
   B. asking the cleaner questions about the work
   C. asking other cleaners to rate his work
   D. inspecting the cleanliness of the spaces assigned to the cleaner

17. A chemical frequently used to melt ice on outdoor pavements is 17.____

   A. ammonia   B. soda
   C. carbon tetrachloride   D. calcium chloride

18. A herbicide is a chemical PRIMARILY used as a(n)   18.___

    A. disinfectant   B. fertilizer
    C. insect killer   D. weed killer

19. Established plants that continue to blossom year after year without reseeding are GEN-   19.___
ERALLY known as

    A. annuals   B. parasites
    C. perennials   D. symbiotics

20. A ferrous sulfate solution is sometimes used to treat shrubs or trees that have a defi-   20.___
ciency of

    A. boron   B. copper   C. iron   D. zinc

21. A tree is described as deciduous.   21.___
This means PRIMARILY that it

    A. bears nuts instead of fruit
    B. has been pruned recently
    C. usually grows in swampy ground
    D. loses its leaves in fall

22. If you are told that a container holds a 20-7-7 fertilizer, it is MOST likely that twenty per-   22.___
cent of this fertilizer is

    A. nitrogen   B. oxygen
    C. phosphoric acid   D. potash

23. When the national flag is in such a worn condition that it is no longer a fitting emblem for   23.___
display, it should be disposed of by

    A. bagging inconspicuously with other disposables
    B. burning in an inconspicuous place
    C. laundering and then using it for cleaning purposes
    D. storing for future use as a painter's dropcloth

24. The landscape drawings for a school indicate the planting of *Acer platanoides* at a cer-   24.___
tain location on the grounds. Acer platanoides is a type of

    A. privet hedge   B. rose bush
    C. maple tree   D. tulip bed

25. Improper use of a carbon dioxide type portable fire extinguisher may cause injury to the   25.___
operator because

    A. handling the nozzle during discharge can cause frostbite to the skin
    B. carbon dioxide is highly poisonous if breathed into the lungs
    C. use of carbon dioxide on ah oil fire can cause a chemical explosion
    D. of the extremely high pressures inside the extinguisher

26. When using a portable single ladder with ten rungs, the GREATEST number of rungs   26.___
that a cleaner should climb up is

    A. 7   B. 8   C. 9   D. 10

27. Of the following types of portable fire extinguishers, the one which should be used to control a fire in or around live electrical equipment is the _____ type.

    A. foam   B. soda acid
    C. carbon dioxide   D. gas cartridge water

27.____

28. The MOST frequent cause of accidental injuries to workers on the job is

    A. unsafe working practices of employees
    B. poor design of buildings and working areas
    C. lack of warning signs in hazardous working areas
    D. lack of adequate safety guards on equipment and machinery

28.____

29. Of the following, the MOST important purpose of preparing an accident report on an injury to a cleaner is to help

    A. collect statistics on different types of accidents
    B. calm the feelings of the injured cleaner
    C. prevent similar accidents in the future
    D. prove that the cleaner was at fault

29.____

30. A cleaner is attempting to lift a heavy drum of liquid cleaner from the floor to a shelf at waist height. He will MOST likely avoid personal injury in lifting the drum if he

    A. keeps his back as straight as possible and lifts the weight
    B. arches his back and lifts the weight primarily with his back muscles
    C. keeps his back as straight as possible and lifts the weight primarily with his leg muscles
    D. arches his back and lifts the weight primarily with his leg muscles

30.____

31. Of the following, the BEST first aid treatment for a cleaner who has burned his hand with dry caustic lye crystals is to

    A. wash his hand with large quantities of warm water
    B. brush his hand lightly with a soft, clean brush and wrap it in a clean rag
    C. place his hand in a mild solution of ammonia and cool water
    D. wash his hand with large quantities of cold water

31.____

32. The purpose of the third prong in a three-prong electric plug used on a 120-volt electric vacuum cleaner is to prevent

    A. serious overheating of the vacuum cleaner
    B. electric shock to the operator of the vacuum cleaner
    C. generation of dangerous microwaves by the vacuum cleaner
    D. sparking in the electric outlet caused by a loose electrical wire

32.____

33. Of the following, the LEAST effective method for a school custodian to use to reduce window glass breakage in his school is to

    A. keep the area near the school free of sticks and stones
    B. consult with parents and civic organizations and request their assistance in reducing breakage

33.____

C. request that neighbors living near the school report afterhours incidents to the police department

D. develop a reputation as a *tough guy* with the students so that they will be afraid to break windows in the school

34. The one of the following procedures that a school custodian should use when a telephone caller makes a threat to place a bomb in the school is to

A. hang up on the caller
B. keep the caller talking as long as possible and make notes on what he says
C. tell the caller he has the wrong number
D. tell the caller his voice is being recorded and the call is being traced to its source

34.___

35. A school custodian is responsible for enforcing certain safety regulations in the school. The MOST important reason for enforcing safety regulations is because

A. every accident can be prevented
B. compliance with safety regulations will make all other safety efforts unnecessary
C. safety regulations are the law and law enforcement is an end in itself
D. safety regulations are based on reason and experience with the best methods of accident prevention

35.___

36. The safety belts that are worn by cleaners when washing outside windows should be inspected

A. before each use   B. weekly
C. monthly   D. semi-annually

36.___

37. The one of the following actions that a school custodian should take to help reduce burglary losses in the school is to

A. leave all the lights on in the school overnight
B. see that interior and exterior doors are securely locked
C. set booby traps that will severely injure anyone breaking in
D. set up an apartment in the school basement and stay at the school every night

37.___

38. The one of the following types of locks that is used on emergency exit doors is a _____ bolt.

A. panic   B. dead   C. cinch   D. toggle

38.___

39. A telephone caller tells a school custodian that a bomb has been placed in the building and immediately hangs up the phone.
The FIRST thing the school custodian should do, in the absence of the principal, is to

A. call the fire department
B. call the police department
C. let his subordinate handle it
D. ignore the call, since most threats are hoaxes

39.___

40. If an employee's bi-weekly salary is $1200.00 and 6.7% is withheld for taxes, the amount to be withheld for this purpose is MOST NEARLY

A. $62.00   B. $66.00   C. $82.00   D. $74.00

40.___

KEY (CORRECT ANSWERS).

1.	D	11.	A	21.	D	31.	D
2.	A	12.	C	22.	A	32.	B
3.	C	13.	A	23.	B	33.	D
4.	B	14.	B	24.	C	34.	B
5.	B	15.	C	25.	A	35.	D
6.	A	16.	D	26.	B	36.	A
7.	D	17.	D	27.	C	37.	B
8.	B	18.	D	28.	A	38.	A
9.	A	19.	C	29.	C	39.	B
10.	C	20.	C	30.	C	40.	C

———

EXAMINATION SECTION
TEST 1

DIRECTIONS: Each question or incomplete statement is followed by several suggested
answers or completions. Select the one that BEST answers the question or
completes the statement. *PRINT THE LETTER OF THE CORRECT ANSWER
IN THE SPACE AT THE RIGHT.*

1. Of the following, the BEST practice to follow in criticizing the work performance of a   1._____
cleaner is to

    A.   save up several criticisms and make them all at once
    B.   soften your criticisms by being humorous
    C.   have another cleaner, who has more seniority, give the criticism
    D.   make sure that you explain to the cleaner the reasons for your criticisms

2. A group of students complains to you about the lack of cleanliness in the building. You   2._____
realize that budget cutbacks have unavoidably led to shortages in manpower and equipment for the cleaning staff.
    Of the following, the BEST way for you to answer these students is to

    A.   tell them frankly that the cleanliness of the building is none of their business
    B.   apologize for the condition of the building and promise that your men will work
       harder
    C.   tell them to take their complaints to the administration and not to you
    D.   explain the reason for the building's condition and what you are doing to improve it

3. Your supervisor has ordered you to announce to your cleaners a new cleaning rule with   3._____
which you disagree. You should

    A.   admit honestly to your cleaners that you disagree with the rule
    B.   announce the rule to your cleaners without expressing your disagreement
    C.   encourage your cleaners by telling them that you agree with the rule
    D.   tell your supervisor that you refuse to announce any rule with which you disagree

4. The preparation of work schedules for custodial employees and the daily work routine of   4._____
these employees is determined and regulated by the

    A.   principal
    B.   district supervisor of custodians
    C.   chief of custodians
    D.   school custodian

5. The records and reports of school plant operations are originated by the school custo-   5._____
dian and forwarded on a monthly basis to the

    A.   borough supervisor
    B.   district superintendent
    C.   director of plant operations
    D.   chief of custodians

6. The operation, care, maintenance, and minor repair of a school building and grounds is 6.___
   the duty and responsibility of the school custodian.
   This responsibility

   A. can be delegated to the custodial staff
   B. is shared with the custodial staff
   C. cannot be delegated and is the school custodian's only
   D. is shared with the district supervisor

7. A cleaner does a very good job on the work assigned to him, but on several occasions 7.___
   you find him lounging and reading a magazine in an isolated part of the building. The
   BEST thing for you to do is

   A. tell the man to increase the time it takes to do the job so as to reduce his lax time
   B. give him a strong reprimand
   C. check the log book or personnel records and confer with the staff and principal to
      see if there are any complaints against him
   D. tell the man to report to you whenever he finishes the required work

8. If one of your employees approaches you with a suggestion on how to improve work pro- 8.___
   cedures, you should

   A. ignore it
   B. listen to the suggestion and take appropriate action
   C. refer the employee to the principal
   D. tell the employee to tell the union

9. When instructing a new employee, you should include all of the following EXCEPT 9.___

   A. the shortcomings, failures, and attitudes of fellow workers
   B. unusual situations and hazardous conditions of work assignments
   C. the normal hours of employment and special situations which require overtime
   D. the rules, regulations, customs, and policies of the assignment

10. You are newly assigned to a building in which the custodial staff has been working effec- 10.___
    tively for many years. In order to obtain the respect of the staff, you should

    A. immediately make major significant changes in procedures to establish your
       authority
    B. immediately make minor changes to show that you have new ideas, plans, and
       organizational ability
    C. criticize your predecessor to establish your identity, attitude, and authority
    D. make no changes to work schedules or assignments until you are fully aware of
       the existing practices, schedules, and assignments

11. Suppose that a cleaner has been found to be quite negligent in his work and has been 11.___
    warned repeatedly by you. If you find that your warnings have not changed the man's
    attitude or work habits, the PROPER thing to do is to

    A. discharge the employee
    B. change his assignment in the school to a less desirable job
    C. have a serious talk with the cleaner to find out why he does not do satisfactory
       work
    D. give the cleaner a final warning

12. An after-school play center is in operation in your building. On a particular afternoon, the   12._____
children in this activity are especially noisy and creating a disturbance.
The FIRST procedure to follow is to

    A. notify the day school principal of this situation
    B. notify the teacher in charge of this situation
    C. pay no attention to this situation and forget about it
    D. notify the police

13. A school custodian is required to submit several types of written reports to his supervisor   13._____
on a monthly basis. After submitting his monthly reports, a custodian discovers he has
made an error.
The CORRECT procedure for the school custodian to follow concerning this matter is
to

    A. notify the supervisor and have the supervisor correct the error
    B. notify the supervisor and request the return of the report so that the custodian can
correct the error
    C. take no action so that the error may be unnoticed
    D. take no action so that the supervisor may find the mistake

14. New cleaning materials are constantly appearing on the market.   14._____
It would be ADVISABLE for the custodian engineer to

    A. sample them to determine the cost factor
    B. trial test in an operation
    C. check materials for product safety
    D. all of the above

15. All vacuum tubes in oil burner programmers, smoke detection devices, and other elec-   15._____
tronic controls should be changed

    A. as needed   B. monthly
    C. yearly   D. every 3 years

16. In the event of flame failure, what occurs FIRST?   16._____

    A. Magnetic oil valve closes.
    B. Metering valve reduces oil flow.
    C. Magnetic gas valve closes.
    D. Primary air supply is closed.

17. A burner mounted vaporstat is a control used in conjunction with proving   17._____

    A. ignition   B. proper oil temperature
    C. flame failure   D. primary air

18. Secondary air dampers on a boiler with a rotary cup oil burner are installed PRIMARILY   18._____
to

    A. measure the flow of air into the furnace
    B. furnish air for atomization
    C. furnish air for combustion
    D. regulate boiler steam pressure

19. In a fully automatic oil burning plant, ignition of fuel oil in the firebox is accomplished by 19.____

    A. spark ignition
    B. hand torch
    C. kerosene rags
    D. spark ignition which ignites a gas pilot

20. The purpose of recirculating fuel oil is PRIMARILY to 20.____

    A. bring it up to the proper temperature
    B. heat oil in storage tanks
    C. force out air
    D. bring oil up to burner

21. The atomization of the oil in a rotary cup oil burner is PRIMARILY due to 21.____

    A. oil pressure
    B. rotary cup *only*
    C. secondary air
    D. rotary cup and primary air

22. A rotary cup oil burner is started and stopped by means of the 22.____

    A. magnetic oil valve   B. modutrol motor
    C. pressuretrol   D. vaporstat

23. The fuel oil suction strainer outside the oil storage tanks should be cleaned when 23.____

    A. burner flame fluctuates
    B. steam pressure drops
    C. flame failure occurs
    D. a differential in vacuum reading across strainer occurs

24. The LOWEST temperature at which oil gives off sufficient vapors to explode momentarily, when flame is applied, is known as _____ point. 24.____

    A. flash   B. fire
    C. pour   D. atomization

25. Air/oil ratio in a rotary cup burner is correctly arrived at with the proper setting of the following: 25.____

    A. Aquastat, vaporstat, pressurestat
    B. Metering valve, primary air, pressurestat
    C. Metering valve, primary air, secondary air
    D. Aquastat, primary air, secondary air

KEY (CORRECT ANSWERS)

1.	D		11.	A
2.	D		12.	B
3.	B		13.	B
4.	D		14.	D
5.	A		15.	C
6.	C		16.	A
7.	D		17.	D
8.	B		18.	C
9.	A		19.	D
10.	D		20.	A

21.	D
22.	C
23.	D
24.	A
25.	C

———

TEST 2

DIRECTIONS: Each question or incomplete statement is followed by several suggested answers or completions. Select the one that BEST answers the question or completes the statement. *PRINT THE LETTER OF THE CORRECT ANSWER IN THE SPACE AT THE RIGHT.*

1. The school custodian can help create goodwill and cooperation by the students, faculty, parents, visitors, and the general public through   1.___

   A. minding his own business
   B. carrying out his duties diligently
   C. reporting all infractions to the principal
   D. letting his supervisor worry about building operations

2. The school custodian has as his responsibility all of the following equipment EXCEPT   2.___

   A. that used for educational and/or culinary purposes
   B. electrical
   C. swimming pool machinery
   D. elevator and sidewalk hoist equipment

3. Upon hiring, custodial employees are required to be   3.___

   A. x-rayed or tine tested
   B. fingerprinted and police checked
   C. issued ID cards by personnel security
   D. all of the above

4. *Minor* repairs consist of   4.___

   A. mechanical adjustment and repacking
   B. clearing minor stoppages and limited glazing
   C. tightening and temporary repairs
   D. all of the above

5. Plant operation of the Board of Education is a bureau within the   5.___

   A. Division of School Buildings
   B. Office of Design and Construction
   C. Office of Business Affairs
   D. Bureau of Maintenance

6. Of the following ways of improving the success of a safety program, the one MOST likely to secure employee acceptance and interest is   6.___

   A. frequent inspection
   B. employee participation in the program
   C. posting attractive notices in work areas and employee quarters
   D. frequent meetings of employees at which safe methods are demonstrated

7. With regard to supplies, a good procedure is to utilize a daily inventory.　　　　7._____
The reason for this is that

    A. you are aware of what is on hand at all times
    B. you know if anyone is stealing
    C. it keeps you busy
    D. you can check and see if your employees are working

8. A school custodian notices a man in a corridor. This visitor identifies himself as a police　　8._____
officer and states he is observing a student in one of the classes.
The school custodian should

    A. make no further inquiries
    B. ask if the police officer has checked with the school principal
    C. ask for details—the name of the student, reason for observations, etc.—so as to
make a log book entry
    D. ask the officer to leave unless he has written permission from the principal

9. In filling out an accident report on an injured cleaner, the LEAST important item to　　9._____
include in the report is the

    A. equipment being used when the injury occurred
    B. attitude of the cleaner towards his job
    C. nature and extent of the injury
    D. work being done when the accident occurred

10. A dispute arises with a cleaner regarding his duties, where he claims the work assigned　　10._____
is *not his job*. After explaining his duties to him and showing him his work schedule, he
still refuses to perform the disputed duties. To resolve this difficulty, you would

    A. fire him for insubordination
    B. notify the school principal
    C. call in the employees union delegate
    D. call in the district supervisor of custodians

11. A number of pupil injuries have occurred while they were traveling on school stairs. Your　　11._____
inspection shows no defects or inadequacy of lighting.
The MOST desirable step to take to reduce the frequency of these accidents is to

    A. assign a cleaner to each stairway when being used
    B. put up signs warning children to be careful
    C. discuss the matter with the school principal
    D. install better stair lighting and make sure handrails are in perfect order

12. The *fuel and utility* report is a record of fuel and electricity used in a school building.　　12._____
This report should be sent to the administrative supervisor

    A. daily   B. weekly   C. monthly   D. yearly

13. One of your employees is constantly dissatisfied and is always complaining. 13._
The BEST procedure to follow regarding this man is to

    A. reprimand him and warn him that his conduct is affecting the other employees and that unless he changes his attitude he will be dismissed
    B. reassign him to a job where he will be more closely supervised
    C. discuss in detail his dissatisfaction and determine the cause
    D. supervise him less closely

14. Custodial payroll reports are submitted 14._

    A. every two weeks   B. every four weeks
    C. monthly   D. quarterly

15. An inventory of capital equipment must be filled out 15._

    A. monthly
    B. upon change of custodians
    C. semi-annually
    D. yearly

16. School custodians are required to inspect their buildings for fire prevention and fire 16._
safety

    A. daily   B. weekly   C. monthly   D. quarterly

17. A contractor working in your building is doing unsatisfactory repair work. 17._
You would notify, in writing, the

    A. borough or administrative supervisor
    B. district superintendent
    C. contract compliance division
    D. director of plant operations

18. If one of your employees frequently misplaces cleaning equipment, you would 18._

    A. notify the borough supervisor
    B. handle the problem yourself
    C. call in the chief of custodians to speak to the employee
    D. tell the principal of the school and ask for action against the employee

19. Safety education of custodial employees is the direct responsibility of the 19._

    A. school custodian
    B. principal
    C. borough supervisor
    D. director of plant operations

20. Worker's compensation insurance coverage for custodial employees is provided by all 20._
of the following EXCEPT the

    A. board of education   B. union
    C. school custodian   D. school

21. Request for plumbing repairs which cannot be performed by the custodial staff are for-   21.____
    warded to the

    A. chief of custodians
    B. director of plant operations
    C. borough supervisor
    D. plumbing shops

22. The cleaning of electrical distribution panel boxes and switchboards is the responsibility   22.____
    of the

    A. principal   B. school custodian
    C. district supervisor   D. cleaner

23. A parent complains that one of your cleaners used abusive language to him.   23.____
    As the school custodian, you should

    A. reprimand the cleaner
    B. fire the cleaner
    C. investigate the complaint to find out if there is any basis to the allegation
    D. ignore the complaint

24. Of the following, the LARGEST individual item of custodial expense in operating a school   24.____
    building is generally the cost of

    A. labor   B. fuel
    C. electricity   D. elevator services

25. A telephone caller tells a school custodian that a bomb has been placed in the building   25.____
    and immediately hangs up the phone.
    The FIRST thing the school custodian should do, in the absence of the principal, is to

    A. call the fire department
    B. call the police department
    C. let the principal's subordinate handle it
    D. ignore the call since most threats are hoaxes

———

KEY (CORRECT ANSWERS)

1.	B		11.	C
2.	A		12.	C
3.	D		13.	C
4.	D		14.	B
5.	A		15.	D
6.	B		16.	A
7.	A		17.	A
8.	B		18.	B
9.	B		19.	A
10.	A		20.	B

21.	C
22.	B
23.	C
24.	A
25.	B

EXAMINATION SECTION
TEST 1

DIRECTIONS: Each question or incomplete statement is followed by several suggested answers or completions. Select the one that BEST answers the question or completes the statement. *PRINT THE LETTER OF THE CORRECT ANSWER IN THE SPACE AT THE RIGHT.*

1. Which of the following chemicals is used to decrease the amount of oxygen in boiler water?   1._____

    A. Soda ash   B. Sodium chloride
    C. Sodium sulfite   D. Trisodium phosphate

2. The house tank in the basement of your school building has a pressure gauge 10 feet   2._____
above the bottom of the tank. If a column of water weighs .434 pounds per square inch per foot and the pressure gauge reads 47 pounds per square inch, then the pressure on the booster pump at the base of the tank is MOST NEARLY, in pounds per square inch,

    A. 47   B. 52   C. 57.50   D. 61.25

3. Assume that a shipment of ammonia and bleach have just been delivered to your school   3._____
and one of your cleaners asks to be instructed as to how the ammonia and bleach are to be stored.
You should instruct him to store them

    A. *together,* because liquids are usually stored with other liquids
    B. *separately,* because shelf life is increased when supplies are maintained in their own areas away from other supplies
    C. *together,* because it is easier to keep an accurate inventory when supplies that are delivered together are stored together
    D. *separately,* because their containers could break and mix, creating a highly toxic gas

4. Of the following, which one is the MOST effective technique for motivating your employ-   4._____
ees?

    A. Regularly remind them that they receive a good salary and other benefits
    B. Publicly commend employees when they do good work
    C. Socialize with them during breaks and after working hours
    D. Overlook minor infractions and ignore rules that you disagree with

5. Which of the following chemicals is used to melt ice and snow?   5._____

    A. Calcium chloride   B. Soda ash
    C. Trisodium soot   D. Sodium sulphite

6. Boiler *handholes* are used for   6._____

    A. climbing onto boilers   B. lighting burners
    C. cleaning soot   D. inspecting boilers

7. The true water level for a boiler in operation is determined by operating the   7._____

    A. pressure relief valve   B. blow down valve
    C. aquastat   D. tri-cocks

8. There have been a number of illegal entries into your building during school hours, and the school principal asks you to padlock certain exit doors in the building to control such entry. You and the principal are both aware that there are laws prohibiting the padlocking of exit doors, but the principal maintains that closing off the doors in question would not impede easy exit from your building.
You should

   A. have the doors locked as requested but also inform your supervisor as to your decision to do so and your reason for that decision
   B. refuse to have the doors locked and if the principal insists, refer him to your supervisor
   C. have the doors locked if, after looking into the matter, you determine that the remaining unlocked doors would be sufficient
   D. refuse to have the doors locked unless the principal overrules you and puts it in writing

8.___

9. You are in the boiler room when a steam line ruptures and the water in the gauge glass disappears.
Of the following, your FIRST action should be to

   A. secure the fire
   B. shut down the vacuum pump
   C. add water to replace the escaping water
   D. secure the steam valve

9.___

10.

The reading of the above gas meter diagram is

   A. 6929   B. 6939   C. 7929   D. 7939

10.___

11. Sight glasses are found

   A. on air compressors
   B. in classroom doors
   C. in cross-corridor doors
   D. on vision panels

11.___

12. Graphite is USUALLY used as a

   A. lubricant   B. cleaning compound
   C. sealant   D. boiler water additive

12.___

13. If you receive a yearly allowance of $52,000 for your school, what would MOST NEARLY be your bi-weekly allowance if you determined that figure based on a year of 365 days?

   A. $1,925.28   B. $1,961.30   C. $1,994.52   D. $2,000.00

13.___

14. Number 6 fuel oil is also known as   14.____

    A. crude oil   B. bunker C oil
    C. gas oil   D. kerosene

15. Of the following CO_2 readings, which one indicates the LOWEST excess in the flue gas?   15.____

    A. 10.0%   B. 12.0%   C. 14.0%   D. 15.0%

16. A large section of a ceiling in an occupied classroom is hanging loosely.   16.____
Of the following, which is the FIRST action you should take?

    A. Check for leaks in the floor above
    B. Have the ceiling replastered immediately
    C. Prepare a requisition for repair
    D. Have the room evacuated

17. If you sometimes enforce rules with strong disciplinary action and at other times you   17.____
enforce the same rules with mild disciplinary action, your practice is a

    A. *good* one, because it enables you to apply strict discipline to cleaners who accept it and to avoid confrontations with your more resistant workers
    B. *bad* one, because generally speaking strong disciplinary actions should be taken for infractions
    C. *good* one, because employees who are *kept guessing* about what supervisors are thinking are less likely to try to take advantage
    D. *bad* one, because discipline should be applied with consistency

18. If one of your employee's gross salary is $38,000 a year and you must deduct 5.85% of   18.____
that sum, you should deduct

    A. $2223.00   B. $2226.00   C. $2235.00   D. $2342.00

19. The remote control switch of an oil burning heating plant should be located   19.____

    A. at the boiler room exit door
    B. in the custodian's office
    C. between 2 and 5 feet from the boiler
    D. on the boiler at eye level

20. Fire Department personnel, while making a routine inspection, issue violations for conditions existing in your building.   20.____
Of the following, it is MOST appropriate for you to

    A. explain that because schools are city property, violations cannot be issued
    B. accept the violations as written and take follow-up action
    C. inform them that they must go through proper channels before issuing the violations
    D. volunteer information about other conditions possibly in violation

21. Assume that your school building has three-phase wiring. Assume also that when you throw the start-up switch on a motor in your boiler room, the motor hums but does not-turn.
Of the following, the MOST likely cause for this is

    A. low voltage   B. motor grounding
    C. low amperage   D. a blown fuse

21.___

22. Two of your cleaners are entitled to retroactive pay of 18 cents per hour. One of the cleaners is to be paid retroactive money for 800 hours at straight time and 50 hours at time and a half. The other cleaner is entitled to 750 hours at straight time and 100 hours at time and a half.
What is the TOTAL amount of retroactive money to be paid to the two employees?

    A. $238.50   B. $265.90   C. $319.50   D. $346.50

22.___

23. Of the following, the MOST likely cause of coal gas fumes is a(n)

    A. improperly banked fire
    B. high steam pressure
    C. improper water level
    D. heavy BTU content in coal being used

23.___

24. Boiler draft is measured in

    A. pounds per square inch   B. degrees Fahrenheit
    C. inches of water   D. cubic feet per minute

24.___

25. Of the following, which method should be used to check a CO_2 fire extinguisher?

    A. Discharge it   B. Weigh it
    C. Read the gauge   D. Shake it

25.___

26. A(n) _____ pump is used on a boiler system using number 6 oil.

    A. transfer   B. vacuum   C. ejector   D. sump

26.___

27. Your boiler water has a pH of 8. This means that the water is

    A. acidic   B. neutral   C. alkaline   D. dirty

27.___

28. Assume that the high temperature on March 14 was 72° F and the low temperature was 52° F. The standard temperature for calculation of degree days is 65° F.
The number of degree days for March 14 is

    A. 3   B. 7   C. 13   D. 20

28.___

29. Pig tails are commonly found on

    A. steam gauges   B. water meters
    C. temperature recorders   D. draft gauges

29.___

30. Your school principal complains to you that a workman making repairs to the windows in your building is making noise that is disrupting classroom instruction.
Of the following, the FIRST action you should take is to

    A. ignore the principal in the hope that the noise subsides
    B. tell the principal that there has to be a certain amount of noise when repair work is being done
    C. meet with the workman to discuss rescheduling the work in order to minimize disruption
    D. inform the workman's supervisor that you have received complaints and warn him that you will take further action if he fails to cooperate

30._____

31. *Checkerboard* floors are found in

    A. restrooms
    C. classrooms
    B. boiler rooms
    D. lunchrooms

31._____

32. One of your cleaners has a gross bi-weekly salary of $736.94.
If the federal tax deduction for that period is $127.92, the state tax deduction is $42.85, and the FICA is $61.02, the city decusion is $7.36 and the state disability is $.60, what is the cleaner's net pay?

    A. $239.75   B. $362.49   C. $497.19   D. $521.03

32._____

33. The operating automatic pressuretrol shuts down the burner when the

    A. oil pressure fluctuates due to high oil temperatures
    B. steam pressure fluctuates due to highly acidic feedwater
    C. oil pressure indicator arrow enters *red* or danger zone
    D. predetermined steam pressure setting is reached

33._____

34. The PROPER method for securing lighting globes is to tighten the thumbscrews

    A. hand tight
    B. snug and loosen 1/2 turn
    C. with pliers
    D. till they just support the globe

34._____

35. Persons running an adult program after school hours ask to use the school kitchen to set up a large coffee maker and utensils. Board of Education policy, however, prohibits such use of the kitchen by anyone other than school kitchen workers.
Of the following, it would be MOST appropriate for you to

    A. explain that you are prohibited from doing so and offer an alternative
    B. allow them to use the kitchen if you know them to be responsible and they agree to clean up afterwards
    C. politely inform them that their request does not come under your jurisdiction
    D. allow them to use the kitchen and afterwards have your staff clean up

35._____

36. A damaged or loose spinner cup will cause

    A. high oil pressure
    C. low oil pressure
    B. loss of lubricant
    D. poor atomization of oil

36._____

37. If, during a pay period, one of your employees works 80 hours at the straight time rate of $8.40 per hour and works 16 hours at time and a half, the employee's gross pay for the period is   37.___

    A. $739.20   B. $806.40   C. $873.60   D. $1,008.00

38. The low water cut-off stops the   38.___

    A. boiler on low water
    B. sump pump on low water
    C. sump pump in emergencies
    D. water on low pressure

39. Which of the following chemicals is used to increase alkalinity in feedwater?   39.___

    A. Calcium chloride   B. Sodium chloride
    C. Sodium hydroxide   D. Hydrogen peroxide

40. Which of the following should be used to remove mildew from marble surfaces?   40.___

    A. Bleach   B. Ammonia
    C. Scouring powder   D. Trisodium

KEY (CORRECT ANSWERS)

1. C	11. A	21. D	31. B
2. B	12. A	22. C	32. C
3. D	13. D	23. A	33. D
4. B	14. B	24. C	34. B
5. A	15. D	25. B	35. A
6. D	16. D	26. A	36. D
7. D	17. D	27. C	37. C
8. B	18. A	28. A	38. A
9. A	19. A	29. A	39. C
10. A	20. B	30. C	40. A

TEST 2

DIRECTIONS: Each question or incomplete statement is followed by several suggested answers or completions. Select the one that BEST answers the question or completes the statement. *PRINT THE LETTER OF THE CORRECT ANSWER IN THE SPACE AT THE RIGHT.*

1. You have been informed that your building allowance is going to be decreased as part of a city-wide economy drive.
   Of the following, which is the FIRST action you should take in this situation?

   A. Lay-off the worker with the least seniority.
   B. Reduce the amount and complexity of your work in order to absorb the decrease.
   C. Start using less expensive supplies and materials.
   D. Study your custodial operation to determine how best to minimize the effects of the cuts.

   1.____

2. The purpose of the vent line on an oil tank is to allow

   A. water in the oil to evaporate
   B. oil to drain if tank is overfilled
   C. for expansion of the oil as the oil temperature rises
   D. gases to escape into the atmosphere

   2.____

3. A reading of 45° C is indicated on your temperature recorder. This temperature, expressed in degrees Fahrenheit, is

   A. 77   B. 81   C. 113   D. 145

   3.____

4. A dark orange flame in a boiler indicates

   A. low draft
   B. that the refractory is damaged
   C. too much secondary air
   D. too much primary air

   4.____

5. *Metering* faucets

   A. are washerless   B. have aerators
   C. shut off automatically D. vent air

   5.____

6. You are allowed $72,000 for the operation of your building. Of this amount, your salary is $32,000, your fireman's salary is $25,000, your cleaner earns $10,500, and compensation insurance will cost $750.00.
   After these monies are paid, how much will remain?

   A. $3,150   B. $3,750   C. $4,550   D. $4,570

   6.____

7. It has come to your attention that the police department has one of your cleaners under surveillance.
   Of the following, your action should be to

   A. tell the cleaner that he is under surveillance
   B. tell all your cleaners about the situation and warn them to avoid trouble

   7.____

31

C. terminate the cleaner under surveillance
D. say nothing about the situation to the cleaner

8. After you prepared a monthly payroll report and sent it to headquarters, you find that you made errors in the report. Of the following, it would be MOST important to 8.___

A. do nothing since a payroll report would be thoroughly checked at headquarters
B. make all the required changes on the copy you kept
C. immediately resubmit the report to include the corrected information
D. adjust the next month's figures to compensate for the error

9. Stay bolts are found in a boiler's 9.___

A. brick setting   B. breeching
C. fire doors   D. shell

10. A *plumber's friend* is used to 10.___

A. change washers   B. stop leaks
C. open corroded fittings   D. clear stoppages

11. Ballasts are found in 11.___

A. fluorescent fixtures   B. plumbing fixtures
C. boiler equalizers   D. vacuum pumps

12. You hire a person as a cleaner on the recommendation of a friend of yours who is a custodian at another school. When dealing with the newly hired cleaner, it would be MOST appropriate for you to assign 12.___

A. him to the same types of work as you would give to another cleaner with similar abilities
B. less desirable work to him than you assign to other cleaners in order to avoid giving the impression that he will be receiving special treatment
C. him work with no regard to his abilities since all workers should be treated the same
D. him the most desirable work in order to maintain friendship with the custodian who recommended him and to encourage the newly hired cleaner to do good work

13. The size of a boiler tube is based on its 13.___

A. inside diameter   B. circumference
C. outside diameter   D. cross-sectional area

14. Of the following, the LEAST important consideration when preparing a work schedule is the 14.___

A. number of employees on your staff
B. type of work to be done
C. age of the employees on your staff
D. monies budgeted

15. A solenoid valve is also known as a _____ valve. 15.___

A. magnetic oil   B. thermo-electric
C. hydraulic   D. pressure

16. One of your employees earns $8.50 an hour and another employee earns $10.50 an hour. Last week, the employee making $8.50 an hour worked forty hours, and the employee earning $10.50 an hour worked forty-four hours. Assuming that all time in excess of forty hours a week is computed at time and a half, their combined gross pay for the week is

16.____

    A. $823.00   B. $840.00   C. $853.00   D. $876.00

17. Flame failure in a rotary cup oil burner is detected by the

17.____

    A. vaporstat   B. aquastat
    C. low draft switch   D. scanner

18. If the water coming from the faucets in your building is 95°C, it is

18.____

    A. warm   B. too hot
    C. tepid   D. too cold

19. You are writing a memorandum to your supervisor concerning problems you have been having with certain boiler room equipment.
Of the following, it would be MOST important for your memorandum to

19.____

    A. be long and include proper terminology to let your supervisor know you are technically competent and knowledgeable about proper boiler plant operation
    B. explain the problem clearly and to provide possible solutions
    C. explain the problem in such a way as to avoid giving the impression that the problems are your fault or that you did not do enough to minimize the effects
    D. be respectful in tone and grammatically correct

20. One of the classrooms in your building is often littered with paper, other trash, and in otherwise unacceptable condition at the end of the day.
Of the following, it would be MOST appropriate for you to

20.____

    A. tell the children that they are to leave the room as clean at the end of the day as they find it in the morning
    B. speak to the principal about the room's condition in order to obtain her assistance to resolve the situation
    C. advise the teacher that you will instruct your cleaners not to clean the room unless he cooperates in keeping it clean
    D. regularly check the room to determine which of the children are responsible for its condition

21. One of your employees has a gross bi-weekly salary of $600 and a FICA deduction of 5%.
His FICA deduction for a period of 4 weeks is

21.____

    A. $3   B. $6   C. $30   D. $60

22. A(n) _____ has a gauge glass.

22.____

    A. pressure gauge   B. inspection window
    C. condensate tank   D. transom

23. One standard square of roofing shingle will cover _____ square feet.

23.____

    A. 1   B. 10   C. 100   D. 144

24. _____ NOT a part of low pressure boilers.   24.____

    A. Crown sheets   B. Impellers
    C. Weep holes   D. Stay rods

25. If one person is normally assigned to a facility for every 33,000 square feet and you have   25.____
82,000 square feet, your manpower requirement is

    A. 1   B. 1 1/2   C. 2   D. 2 1/2

26. Your cleaning crew's morale is very low because the school is often vandalized, making   26.____
it very difficult for your workers to maintain the building properly.
Of the following, it would be MOST appropriate for you to tell your crew

    A. that you are aware of the effort they put in even though the building does not reflect
        the work they do
    B. not to work so hard because their work is not appreciated and it is a losing battle
    C. that they get paid for their work and, therefore, there is no justification for their low
        morale
    D. not to concern themselves about vandalism since it is a social problem, not a cus-
        todial matter

27. Nematodes are   27.____

    A. weeds   B. elevator fuses
    C. electrical circuits   D. lawn pests

28. A *supervisory* circuit is found in   28.____

    A. boiler controls   B. the principal's intercom
    C. hot water tanks   D. fire alarms

29. Braided packing is found in   29.____

    A. electrical insulation   B. stuffing boxes
    C. wall insulation   D. junction boxes

30. The gas meter in your building reads 1234 on the 1st of the month and 1356 at the end   30.____
of the month.
If the meter has a multiplier of 60, how much gas was consumed for the month?

    A. 813.60   B. 4260   C. 7320   D. 81360

31. Which of the following is NOT used to control boiler water level?   31.____
A

    A. condensate return pump   B. vacuum pump
    C. blow down valve   D. feedwater regulator

32. A water-charged fire extinguisher should NOT be used on a(n) _____ fire.   32.____

    A. paper   B. oil   C. wood   D. trash

33. A *pope's head* is used to clean   33.____

    A. floors   B. boiler tubes
    C. windows   D. sidewalks

34. The drain in your school yard is stopped up after each rainfall.   34.____
Which one of the following is the MOST appropriate action to take to correct this situation?

    A.   Remove the strainer basket
    B.   Schedule regular drain cleaning
    C.   Blank off grating
    D.   Have the drain *snaked* on an annual basis

35. Of the following, which is the LARGEST size of coal?   35.____

    A.   Rice   B. Buckwheat   C. Pea   D. Walnut

36. To perform a low water cut-off test, you should   36.____

    A.   shut off the water at the tempering valve
    B.   open the bypass valve on the feedwater regulator
    C.   shut down the water supply until the boiler shuts off
    D.   open the pressure relief valve

37. A recently hired cleaner does not complete tasks within the time periods that you believe   37.____
to be proper for his work.
Of the following, the FIRST action you should take is to

    A.   warn him that his job may be in jeopardy if he does not improve
    B.   avoid mentioning anything about his work for the first few weeks of his employment in order to give him time to learn what is expected from him
    C.   ask other employees to encourage him to work harder and faster
    D.   observe him while he works to determine the reasons he takes so long to complete this work

38. This year, the fuel consumption at your school has significantly increased over last year's   38.____
consumption even though the weather for both years has been quite similar. You are checking your heating system to determine the reason for the increase.
Which of the following is LEAST likely to be the reason for the higher consumption?

    A.   Dirty fire tubes
    B.   Leaking steam traps
    C.   High flue gas temperature
    D.   High steam temperature

39. A teacher tells you that one of your cleaners broke her classroom movie projector. She   39.____
states that when she left the room at the end of the preceding school day, the cleaner was working in her room and the projector was operating fine. The next morning it wasn't working.
For this situation, you should FIRST

    A.   accuse the cleaner of breaking it to test his reaction
    B.   order the cleaner to talk to the teacher to get the matter resolved
    C.   question the cleaner to find out what, if anything, he knows about this situation
    D.   watch the cleaner for several days to see if he does anything to indicate guilt

40. Of the following, which is the MOST likely indication of soot build-up in boiler tubes? 40._____

    A. A high CO_2 reading
    B. A high furnace draft reading
    C. High boiler pressure
    D. High stack temperature

KEY (CORRECT ANSWERS)

1.	D	11.	A	21.	D	31.	B
2.	D	12.	A	22.	C	32.	B
3.	C	13.	C	23.	C	33.	C
4.	A	14.	C	24.	B	34.	B
5.	C	15.	A	25.	D	35.	C
6.	B	16.	A	26.	A	36.	C
7.	D	17.	D	27.	D	37.	D
8.	C	18.	B	28.	D	38.	D
9.	D	19.	B	29.	B	39.	C
10.	D	20.	B	30.	C	40.	D

EXAMINATION SECTION
TEST 1

DIRECTIONS: Each question or incomplete statement is followed by several suggested answers or completions. Select the one that BEST answers the question or completes the statement. *PRINT THE LETTER OF THE CORRECT ANSWER IN THE SPACE AT THE RIGHT.*

1. Two cleaners swept four corridors in 24 minutes. Each corridor measured 12 feet x 176 feet.
   The space swept per man per minute was MOST NEARLY _____ square feet.

   A. 50   B. 90   C. 180   D. 350

   1.____

2. The BEST time of the day to dust classroom furniture and woodwork is

   A. in the morning before the students arrive
   B. during the morning recess
   C. during the students' lunch time
   D. immediately after the students are dismissed for the day

   2.____

3. A custodian-engineer wishes to order sponges in the most economical manner.
   Keeping in mind that large sponges can be cut up into many smaller sizes, the one of the following that has the LEAST cost per cubic inch of sponge is

   A. 2" x 4" x 6" sponges @ $0.24
   B. 4" x 8" x 12" sponges @ $1.44
   C. 4" x 6" x 36" sponges @ $4.80
   D. 6" x 8" x 32" sponges @ $9.60

   3.____

4. Many new products are used in new schools for floors, walls, and other surfaces.
   A custodian-engineer should determine the BEST procedure to be used to clean such new surfaces by

   A. referring to the board of education's manual of procedures
   B. obtaining information on the cleaning procedure from the manufacturer
   C. asking the advice of the mechanics who installed the new material
   D. asking the district supervisor how to clean the surfaces

   4.____

5. The one of the following chemicals that a custodian-engineer should tell a cleaner to use to remove mildew from terrazzo is

   A. ammonia   B. oxalic acid
   C. sodium hypochlorite   D. sodium silicate

   5.____

6. The type of soft floor that is basically a mixture of oxidized linseed oil, resin, and ground cork pressed upon a burlap backing is known as

   A. asphalt tile   B. cork tile
   C. linoleum   D. vinyl tile

   6.____

7. The difficulty of cleaning soil from surfaces is LEAST affected by the

   A. length of time between cleanings
   B. chemical nature of the soil

   7.____

C. smoothness of the surface being cleaned
D. standard time allotted to the job

8. The one of the following cleaning agents that is GENERALLY classified as an alkaline cleaner is

8.____

A. sodium carbonate
B. ground silica
C. kerosene
D. lemon oil

9. The one of the following cleaning agents that should be used ONLY when adequate ventilation and protective measures have been taken is

9.____

A. methylene chloride
B. sodium chloride
C. sodium carbonate
D. calcium carbonate

10. Of the following, the MOST important consideration in the selection of a cleaning agent is the

10.____

A. cost per pound or gallon
B. amount of labor involved in its use
C. wording of the manufacturer's warranty
D. length of time the manufacturer has been producing cleaning agents

11. The fan motor in a central vacuum cleaner system is found to be operating at 110% of its rated capacity.
The one of the following actions which is MOST likely to decrease the load on the motor is

11.____

A. tying-back several outlets in the open position on each floor
B. moving the butterfly damper slightly toward the closed position
C. removing ten percent of the filter bags
D. operating the bag shaker continuously

12. A groundskeeper asks how to remove an accumulation of grease from the concrete near the loading dock.
Of the following, the cleaning agent that a custodian-engineer should tell him to use to degrease the area is a(n)

12.____

A. acid cleaner
B. alkaline cleaner
C. liquid soap
D. solvent cleaner

13. The instructions for mixing a powdered cleaner in water state, *Mix three ounces of powder in a 14-quart pail three-quarters full of water.*
A cleaner asks you how much powdered cleaner he should use in a mop truck containing 28 gallons of water to obtain the same strength solution. Your answer should be _____ ounces of powder.

13.____

A. 6
B. 8
C. 24
D. 32

14. A resin-base floor finish USUALLY

14.____

A. gives the highest lustre of all floor finishes
B. should be applied in one heavy coat
C. provides a slip-resistant surface
D. should not be used on asphalt tile

15. The one of the following cleaning operations on soft floors that generally requires MOST NEARLY the same amount of time per 1,000 square feet as damp mopping is   15.____

    A. applying a thin coat of wax
    B. sweeping
    C. dust mopping
    D. wet mopping

16. Of the following cleaning jobs, the one that should be allowed the MOST time to complete a 1,000 square foot area is   16.____

    A. vacuuming carpets
    B. washing painted walls
    C. stripping and waxing soft floors
    D. machine-scrubbing hard floors

17. When instructing your staff in the use of sodium silicate, you should tell them that it is MOST commonly used to   17.____

    A. seal concrete floors   B. condition leather
    C. treat boiler water   D. neutralize acid wastes

18. Cleaners should be instructed that dust mopping is LEAST appropriate for removing light soil from _____ floors.   18.____

    A. terrazzo   B. unsealed concrete
    C. resin-finished soft   D. sealed wood

19. Of the following, the substance that should be recommended for polishing hardwood furniture is   19.____

    A. lemon oil polish   B. neat's-foot oil
    C. paste wax   D. water-emulsion wax

20. The use of concentrated acid to remove stains from ceramic tile bathroom floors USUALLY results in making the surface   20.____

    A. pitted and porous   B. clean and shiny
    C. harder and glossier   D. waterproof

21. Asphalt tile floors should be protected by coating them with   21.____

    A. hard-milled soap   B. water-emulsion wax
    C. sodium metaphosphate   D. varnish

22. Of the following, the BEST way to economize on cleaning tools and materials is to   22.____

    A. train the cleaners to use them properly
    B. order at least a three-year supply of every item in order to avpid annual price increases
    C. attach a price sticker to every item so that the people using them will realize their high cost
    D. delay ordering material for three months at the beginning of each year to be sure that the old material is used to the fullest extent

23. The MINIMUM amount of free chlorine that swimming pool water should contain for proper disinfection is _____ parts per million.   23.____

    A. 1.0   B. 10   C. 50   D. 500

24. The point at which swimming pool filters should be back-washed is when the difference between the inlet and outlet pressures EXCEEDS _____ psi.   24.____

    A. 5   B. 10   C. 15   D. 20

25. An orthotolidine test is used to test a water sample to see what quantity it contains of   25.____

    A. alum   B. ammonia   C. chlorine   D. soda ash

26. The ideal flue gas temperature in a rotary-cup oil-fired boiler should be equal to the steam temperature PLUS   26.____

    A. 50° F   B. 125° F   C. 275° F   D. 550° F

27. The carbon dioxide reading in a boiler flue when the boiler is operating efficiently should be MOST NEARLY   27.____

    A. 0.5 inches of water   B. 8 ounces per mol
    C. 10 psi   D. 12 percent

28. The one of the following that PRIMARILY indicates a low water level in a steam boiler is the   28.____

    A. pressure gauge   B. gauge glass
    C. safety valve   D. hydrometer

29. The one of the following steps that should be taken FIRST if a safety valve on a coal-fired steam boiler pops off is to   29.____

    A. add water to the boiler
    B. reduce the draft
    C. tap the side of the safety valve with a mallet
    D. open the bottom blow-off valve

30. A device that operates to vary the resistance of an electrical circuit is USUALLY part of a _____ pressurtrol.   30.____

    A. high-limit   B. low-limit
    C. manual-reset   D. modulating

KEY (CORRECT ANSWERS)

1.	C	16.	C
2.	A	17.	A
3.	B	18.	B
4.	B	19.	C
5.	C	20.	A
6.	C	21.	B
7.	D	22.	A
8.	A	23.	A
9.	A	24.	B
10.	B	25.	C
11.	B	26.	B
12.	D	27.	D
13.	D	28.	B
14.	C	29.	B
15.	A	30.	D

―――――

TEST 2

DIRECTIONS: Each question or incomplete statement is followed by several suggested answers or completions. Select the one that BEST answers the question or completes the statement. *PRINT THE LETTER OF THE CORRECT ANSWER IN THE SPACE AT THE RIGHT.*

1. A solenoid valve is actuated by   1.__

    A. air pressure   B. electric current
    C. temperature change   D. light rays

2. A sequential draft control on a rotary-cup oil-fired boiler should operate to   2.__

    A. *open* the automatic damper at the end of the post-purge perio'd
    B. *open* the automatic damper when the draft has increased during normal burner operation
    C. *close* the automatic damper just before the burner motor starts up
    D. *close* the automatic damper after the burner goes off and the burner cycle is completed

3. The one of the following components of flue gas that indicates, when present, that more   3.__
   excess air is being supplied than is being used is

    A. carbon dioxide   B. carbon monoxide
    C. nitrogen   D. oxygen

4. An advantage that a float-thermostatic steam trap has over a float-type steam trap of   4.__
   comparable rating is that a float-thermostatic trap

    A. requires less maintenance
    B. is easier to install
    C. allows non-condensable gases to escape
    D. releases the condensate at a higher temperature

5. A pump delivers 165 pounds of water per minute against a total head of 100 feet.   5.__
   The water horsepower of this pump is _____ HP.

    A. 1/2   B. 2   C. 5   D. 20

6. Of the following, the BEST instrument to use to measure over-the-fire draft is the   6.__

    A. Bourdon tube gauge   B. inclined manometer
    C. mercury manometer   D. potentiometer

7. The temperature of the water in a steam-heated domestic hot water tank is controlled by   7.__
   a(n)

    A. aquastat   B. thermostatic regulating valve
    C. vacuum breaker   D. thermostatic trap

8. The one of the following conditions that will MOST likely cause fuel oil pressure to fluctu-   8.__
   ate is

    A. a faulty pressure gauge
    B. a clean oil-strainer
    C. cold oil in the suction line
    D. an over-tight pump drive belt

9. The cooler in a Freon 12 refrigeration system that is equipped with automatic protective devices is MOST likely to be accidentally damaged by water freeze-up when the system('s)

    A. is operating at reduced load
    B. is operating at rated load
    C. condenser water-flow is interrupted
    D. is being pumped down

9.____

10. The capacity of a water-cooled condenser is LEAST affected by the

    A. water temperature
    B. refrigerant temperature
    C. surrounding air temperature
    D. quantity of condenser water being circulated

10.____

11. Of the following chemicals used in boiler feedwater treatment, the one that should be used to RETARD corrosion in the boiler circuit due to dissolved oxygen is sodium

    A. aluminate   B. carbonate   C. phosphate   D. sulfite

11.____

12. The heating system in a certain school is equipped with vacuum return condensate pumps.
The MOST likely place for an air-vent valve to be installed in this plant is on

    A. each radiator
    B. the outlet of the domestic hot water steam heating coil
    C. the pressure side of the vacuum pump
    D. the shell of the domestic hot water tank

12.____

13. *Priming* of a steam boiler is NOT caused by

    A. load swings
    B. uneven fire distribution
    C. too high a water level
    D. high alkalinity of the boiler water

13.____

14. A Hartford loop is used in school heating systems PRIMARILY to

    A. provide for thermal expansion of the steam distribution piping
    B. equalize the water level in two or more boilers
    C. prevent siphoning of water out of the boiler
    D. by-pass the electric fuel-oil heaters when the steam heaters are operating

14.____

15. Of the following, the MOST likely use for temperature-indicating crayons by a custodian-engineer is in

    A. checking the operation of the radiator traps
    B. replacing room thermometers that have been vandalized
    C. indicating possible sources of spontaneous combustion
    D. checking the effectiveness of an insulating panel

15.____

16. A stop-and-waste cock is GENERALLY used on   16.____

    A. refrigerant lines between the compressor and the condenser
    B. soil lines
    C. gas supply lines
    D. water lines subjected to low temperatures

17. A pressure-regulating valve in a compressed air line should be preceded by a(n)   17.____

    A. check valve   B. intercooler
    C. needle valve   D. water-and-oil separator

18. A house trap is a fitting placed in the house drain immediately inside the foundation wall   18.____
of a building.
The MAIN purpose of a house trap is to

    A. prevent the entrance of sewer gas into the building drainage system
    B. provide access to the drain lines in the basement for cleaning
    C. drain the basement in case of flooding
    D. maintain balanced air pressure in the fixture traps

19. The one of the following that is BEST to use to smooth a commutator is   19.____

    A. Number 1/0 emery cloth   B. Number 00 sandpaper
    C. Number 2 steel wool   D. a safe edge file

20. The electric service that is provided to MOST schools in the city is NOMINALLY   20.____

    A. 208 volt-3 phase -4 wire - 120 volts to ground
    B. 208 volt-3 phase -3 wire - 208 volts to ground
    C. 220 volt-2 phase -3 wire - 110 volts to ground
    D. 440 volt-3 phase -4 wire - 240 volts to ground

21. All the fuses in an electrical panel are good but the clips on the fuse in circuit No. 1 are   21.____
much hotter than the clips of the other fuses.
Of the following, the MOST likely cause of this condition is that

    A. circuit No. 1 is greatly overloaded
    B. circuit No. 1 is carrying much less than rated load
    C. the room temperature is abnormally high
    D. the fuse in circuit No. 1 is very loose in its clips

22. Of the following, the BEST tool to use to drive a lag screw is a(n)   22.____

    A. open-end wrench   B. Stillson wrench
    C. screwdriver   D. alien wrench

23. Of the following, the one that is MOST likely to be used in landscaping work as ground   23.____
cover is

    A. Barberry   B. Forsythia
    C. Pachysandra   D. Viburnum

24. The velocity of air in a ventilation duct is USUALLY measured with a(n)   24.____

    A. hydrometer   B. psychrometer
    C. pyrometer   D. pitot tube

25. The motor driving a centrifugal pump through a direct-connected flexible coupling burned out.
   When a new motor is ordered, it is important to specify the same NEMA frame size so that the

   A. horsepower will be the same
   B. speed will be the same
   C. conduit box will be in the same location
   D. mounting dimensions will be the same

   25.____

26. A custodian-engineer should inspect the school building for safety

   A. at least once each day
   B. at least every other day
   C. at least once a week
   D. at the end of each vacation period

   26.____

27. Of the following, the MOST important practice to follow in order to prevent fires in a school is to train the staff to

   A. fight fires of every kind
   B. detect and eliminate every possible fire hazard
   C. keep halls, corridors, and exits clear
   D. place flammables in fire-proof containers

   27.____

28. The one of the following types of portable fire extinguishers that is MOST effective in fighting an oil fire is the _____ type.

   A. soda-acid   B. loaded-stream
   C. foam   D. carbon dioxide

   28.____

29. A custodian-engineer opens the door to the boiler room and discovers that fuel oil has leaked onto the floor and caught fire.
   Of the following, the FIRST action he should take is to

   A. notify the Principal
   B. notify the fire department
   C. turn off the remote control switch
   D. fight the fire using a Class B extinguisher

   29.____

30. The MINIMUM noise level beyond which hearing may be impaired is _____ decibels.

   A. 10   B. 50   C. 90   D. 130

   30.____

KEY (CORRECT ANSWERS)

1.	B	16.	D
2.	D	17.	D
3.	D	18.	A
4.	C	19.	B
5.	A	20.	A
6.	B	21.	D
7.	B	22.	A
8.	C	23.	C
9.	D	24.	D
10.	C	25.	D
11.	D	26.	A
12.	B	27.	B
13.	D	28.	C
14.	C	29.	C
15.	A	30.	C

EXAMINATION SECTION
TEST 1

DIRECTIONS: Each question or incomplete statement is followed by several suggested answers or completions. Select the one that BEST answers the question or completes the statement. *PRINT THE LETTER OF THE CORRECT ANSWER IN THE SPACE AT THE RIGHT.*

1. An electrical device whose function is to keep boiler steam pressure from exceeding the predetermined pressure is the   1.____

    A. relief valve   B. vaporstat
    C. pressure gage   D. pressuretrol

2. Sodium sulphite is used to   2.____

    A. treat boiler water   B. detect leaks in a gas system
    C. remove ink stains   D. seal wood

3. Boiler water should have a pH value between   3.____

    A. 5 and 7   B. 9 and 11   C. 13 and 14   D. 15 and 17

4. The percentage of dryness of steam is called steam   4.____

    A. purity   B. ratio   C. priming   D. quality

5. A bottom blowdown on a boiler is used to   5.____

    A. decrease the amount of fuel consumed
    B. increase the boiler steam pressure
    C. decrease the water intake
    D. eliminate impurities from the mud drum

6. The flow of oil to a rotary cup oil burner is generally controlled by a(n)   6.____

    A. aquastat   B. steam coil
    C. solenoid valve   D. venturi

7. The unit of a rotary cup oil burner that senses primary air failure is the   7.____

    A. remote switch   B. modutrol
    C. vaporstat   D. stackmeter

8. The quantity of water delivered by a centrifugal pump varies _____ pump speed.   8.____

    A. directly as the cube of the   B. directly as the square of the
    C. directly as the   D. inversely as the

9. The volute casing of a centrifugal pump serves the MAIN purpose of   9.____

    A. a priming chamber
    B. venting the pump head
    C. converting velocity head into pressure head
    D. making the pump run quieter

10. The amount of water vapor mixed with dry air in the atmosphere is known as 10._

   A. saturation ratio   B. humidity
   C. vapor density   D. dew point

11. When water freezes at 32° F, the amount of heat lost, per lb. of water is _____ BTU. 11._

   A. 212   B. 180   C. 144   D. 100

12. The one of the following factors which does NOT affect human comfort in air conditioning 12._
   is air

   A. temperature   B. purity
   C. motion   D. absorption

13. The element of a mechanical compression refrigerating system in which the refrigerant 13._
   absorbs heat is the

   A. evaporator   B. receiver
   C. condenser   D. carnot

14. When the water level in a boiler falls below a specified level, the oil burner is shut off by 14._
   the action of a

   A. magnetic gas valve   B. purge control
   C. low water cut-out   D. bellows feed

15. A small by-pass line would be installed around a large gate valve in a water line in order 15._
   to

   A. measure the flow accurately
   B. show the direction of the flow
   C. alter the liquid flow in case of valve failure
   D. make it easier to open the gate valve

16. Flanged butterfly valves are operated by bringing them from closed to full-open position 16._
   in _____ turn(s).

   A. 3 full   B. 2 full
   C. one-half   D. one-quarter

17. A monometer measures 17._

   A. electrical energy   B. revolutions per minute
   C. difference in pressure   D. fluid volume

18. The difference between a compound gage and a standard gage is that the compound 18._
   gage measures

   A. only pressures less than atmospheric
   B. pressures above and below atmospheric
   C. only pressures greater than atmospheric
   D. only pressures greater than absolute

19. The absolute pressure indicated by a gage reading of 14 psi is *approximately* _____ psi.

19.____

    A. 18.0   B. 24.0   C. 28.0   D. 32.0

20. A boiler steam gage should be graduated so that, when indicating the normal operating pressure, its pointer is nearly

20.____

    A. horizontal
    B. vertical
    C. 45 off the vertical position
    D. 60 off the vertical position

21. The packing generally used in the expansion points of a firebrick wall is

21.____

    A. sand   B. tar
    C. asbestos   D. high-temperature cement

22. The carbon dioxide (CO_2) content of the flue gases of an efficiently fired boiler should measure about

22.____

    A. 4%   B. 6%   C. 8%   D. 12%

23. Pre-heaters are generally installed when burning fuel oil number

23.____

    A. 6   B. 4   C. 2   D. 1

24. A typical boiler heat balance would show that the GREATEST amount of heat loss in boiler operation is

24.____

    A. in the slag   B. in the flue gases
    C. by radiation   D. by moisture in the air

25. When a boiler setting leaks air, there is an increase in the

25.____

    A. amount of heat lost
    B. boiler output
    C. quantity of flue gas impurities
    D. blow down

26. The 2 in a concrete mix of 1:2:4 refers to the quantity of

26.____

    A. cement   B. sand   C. water   D. filler

27. When roofing material is specified as *5 ply 70 lbs.*, it means that, as laid, the total of 5 plies weighs 70 lbs. per 100

27.____

    A. square feet   B. yards length
    C. square inches   D. feet length

28. The choice that shows which type of equipment is designed to prevent an elevator car from starting before the hatchway door is closed and locked is the

28.____

    A. hoistway access switch   B. interlocks
    C. spring buffer   D. counterweight

29. The piping through which water from private wells is delivered to swimming pools must be painted   29.__

    A.   red   B.   purple   C.   orange   D.   black

30. A chemical commonly used to disinfect swimming pools is   30.__

    A.   ammonium nitrate   B.   chloraseptic
    C.   ammonium bicarbonate   D.   calcium hypochorite

31. Shades and Venetian blinds are cleaned BEST with a   31.__

    A.   dry cloth   B.   scouring powder
    C.   vacuum cleaner   D.   paradry.

32. The surfaces of water coolers and door kick plates are cleaned BEST by using a cleaning solution and a   32.__

    A.   brush   B.   wet cloth
    C.   cellulose sponge   D.   wad of paper

33. The BEST technique to use when washing the outside surface of the upper sash of double hung windows that are not equipped with safety belt anchors is to work from a   33.__

    A.   standing position on the outside of the sill
    B.   sitting position on the sill with the feet inside the room
    C.   standing position on the inside of the sill
    D.   standing position on the top of a stepladder

34. The one of the following that should be used to clean an acoustical ceiling is a   34.__

    A.   dry mop   B.   water wet cloth
    C.   waxed cloth   D.   vacuum cleaner

35. The BEST procedure to follow to determine the actual cleaning ability of a specific material is to   35.__

    A.   test its performance
    B.   read the specifications
    C.   ask the manufacturer
    D.   examine trade literature

36. The one of the following statements that is CORRECT concerning the application of wax by the use of a twine mop with handle is that   36.__

    A.   infrequent heavy coats are preferred
    B.   the mop used for waxing must be hard
    C.   the wax should be poured from a pail onto the floor
    D.   the wax should be applied in thin coats

37. One coat of floor sealer applied to a hardwood floor usually lasts   37.__

    A.   at least 2 years   B.   a maximum of 1 year
    C.   no more than 6 months   D.   no more than 3 months

38. The material recommended for removing blood or fruit stains from concrete is 　　38.____

    A. soft soap　　　　　　　　　　B. neatsfoot oil
    C. oxalic acid　　　　　　　　　　D. ammonia

39. To order wet mop filler replacements, you should specify the 　　39.____

    A. number of strands　　　　　　B. girth
    C. weight　　　　　　　　　　　　D. wet test strength

40. You should use chlordane in a building to control 　　40.____

    A. water seepage　　　　　　　　B. kitchen odors
    C. mildew　　　　　　　　　　　　D. roaches

――――――

KEY (CORRECT ANSWERS)

1. D	11. C	21. C	31. C
2. A	12. D	22. D	32. C
3. B	13. A	23. A	33. B
4. C	14. C	24. B	34. D
5. D	15. D	25. A	35. A
6. C	16. D	26. B	36. D
7. C	17. C	27. A	37. B
8. C	18. B	28. B	38. D
9. C	19. C	29. A	39. C
10. B	20. B	30. D	40. D

――――――

TEST 2

DIRECTIONS: Each question or incomplete statement is followed by several suggested answers or completions. Select the one that BEST answers the question or completes the statement. *PRINT THE LETTER OF THE CORRECT ANSWER IN THE SPACE AT THE RIGHT.*

1. Safety belts worn by window cleaners must meet the approval of the   1.___

    A. National Safety Council
    B. American Safety Council
    C. American National Standards Institute
    D. State Department of Labor

2. After a snowfall has stopped, all snow must be removed from sidewalks (the time   2.___
between 9 P.M. and 7 A.M. excluded) within _____ hour(s).

    A. 4   B. 3   C. 2   D. 1

3. Little white insects that look like small shrimps and feed on the roots of grass are called   3.___

    A. grubs   B. ricks
    C. praying mantes   D. crabs

4. A term used to indicate a lawn chemical weed killer is   4.___

    A. germicide   B. emulsified
    C. herbicide   D. vitrified

5. A device installed in a drainage system to prevent gases from flowing into a building is   5.___
called a

    A. trap   B. stall   C. cleanout   D. bidet

6. The plumbing fixture that contains a ball cock is the   6.___

    A. trap   B. water closet
    C. sprinkler   D. dishwasher

7. In a plumbing installation, an escutcheon is a   7.___

    A. metal collar   B. reducing tee
    C. valve   D. single sweep

8. A leaking faucet stem can be repaired by replacing the   8.___

    A. flange or the seat   B. nipple
    C. o-ring or the packing   D. cock

9. The abbreviation *O.S. and Y.,* as used in plumbing, applies to a(n)   9.___

    A. hot well   B. radiator
    C. injector   D. gate valve

10. Gas range piping should have a minimum diameter of _____ inch.   10.___

    A. 3/4   B. 1/2   C. 1/4   D. 1/8

11. The pipe fitting that would be used to connect a 2" pipe at a 45-degree angle to another   11.____
    2" pipe is called a(n)

    A. tee   B. orifice flange
    C. reducer   D. elbow

12. An instrument that measures relative humidity is called a(n)   12.____

    A. manometer   B. interferometer
    C. hygrometer   D. petrometer

13. The one of the following flat drive belts that gives the BEST service in dry places is a(n) 13.____
    _____ belt.

    A. rawhide   B. oak-tanned
    C. chrome-tanned   D. semirawhide

14. The letter representing the standard V-belt section which has the LOWEST horsepower-   14.____
    per-belt rating is

    A. E   B. C   C. B   D. A

15. A 6 x 19 wire rope has   15.____

    A. 6 strands
    B. 6 wires in each strand
    C. 19 strands
    D. 25 strands arranged in a 6 x 19 pattern

16. A water tank that is 5 feet in diameter and 30 feet high has a volume of *most nearly*   16.____
    _____ cu.ft.

    A. 150   B. 250   C. 600   D. 1200

17. The circumference of a circle with a radius of 5 inches is *most nearly* _____ in.   17.____

    A. 31.3   B. 30.0   C. 20.1   D. 13.4

18. A flexible coupling should be used to connect two shafts that   18.____

    A. have centerlines at right angles to each other
    B. may be slightly out of line
    C. start and stop too fast
    D. have different speeds

19. Of the following materials used to make pipe, the one that is MOST brittle is   19.____

    A. lead   B. aluminum
    C. copper   D. cast iron

20. Mechanical equipment is generally tested and inspected on regular schedule in order to   20.____

    A. avoid breakdowns
    B. train new personnel
    C. maintain inventory
    D. give employees something to do

21. The *united inches* for a pane of glass that measures 14 inches by 20 inches is   21._

    A. 14   B. 34   C. 40   D. 54

22. The one of the following that should NOT be lubricated is a(n)   22._

    A. spur gear train   B. motor commutator
    C. roller chain drive   D. automobile axle

23. The one of the following oils that has the LOWEST viscosity is S.A.E.   23._

    A. 70   B. 50   C. 20   D. 10W

24. A neoprene gasket would normally be used in a pipeline carrying   24._

    A. steam   B. compressed air
    C. carbon dioxide   D. light oil

25. The one of the following that would NOT be used in cleaning toilet bowls is   25._

    A. a cleaning cloth   B. oxalic acid
    C. muriatic acid   D. a detergent

26. An electric motor-driven air compressor is automatically started and stopped by a   26._

    A. thermostat   B. line air valve
    C. pressure switch   D. float trap

27. The term *kilowatt hours* describes the consumption of   27._

    A. energy   B. radiation
    C. cooling capacity   D. conductance

28. AC voltage may be converted to DC voltage by means of a   28._

    A. magneto   B. rectifier
    C. voltage regulator   D. transducer

29. When replacing a blown fuse, it is BEST to   29._

    A. install another one of slightly larger size
    B. seek the cause of the fuse failure before replacing it
    C. install another one of size smaller
    D. read the electric meters as a check on the condition of the circuit

30. A 208 volt, 3 phase, 4 wire circuit power supply has a line to grounded neutral voltage of   30._
approximately _____ volts.

    A. 120   B. 208   C. 220   D. 240

31. An interlock is generally installed on electronic equipment to   31._

    A. prevent loss of power
    B. maintain vhf frequencies
    C. keep the vacuum tubes lit
    D. prevent electric shock during maintenance operations

32. A flame should NOT be used to inspect the electrolyte level in a lead acid battery because the battery cells give off highly flammable 32.____

    A. hydrogen   B. lead oxide
    C. lithium   D. xenon

33. The purpose of the third prong in a three-prong male electric plug used in a 120-volt circuit is to 33.____

    A. make a firm connection   B. strengthen the plug
    C. prevent electric shock   D. get more electricity

34. You are informed that an employee under your supervision has just been injured in the building. The FIRST course of action you should take is to 34.____

    A. inform your superior
    B. aid the injured employee
    C. call a meeting of all the men
    D. order an investigation

35. In the prevention of accidental injuries, the MOST effective procedure is to 35.____

    A. install safety guards
    B. alert the workers to the hazard
    C. install lighting for easy sight
    D. eliminate the accident hazard

36. The one of the following practices that will INCREASE the possibility of fires occurring is the 36.____

    A. using of understairs areas for storage of all kinds
    B. wiping of machinery shafts with lubricating oil
    C. ventilating of all storage spaces
    D. cleaning of lockers at frequent intervals

37. When evaluating a building for fire hazards, the MOST important considerations are the 37.____

    A. number of stories and the height of each story
    B. location in the neighborhood and the accessibility
    C. interior lighting and the furniture
    D. number of residents and the use of the building

38. The one of the following that is a basic safety requirement for operating a power mower is: 38.____

    A. Fill gasoline-driven mowers indoors
    B. Do not operate power mowers on wet grass
    C. Keep the motor running when you leave the mower unattended for only a short while
    D. Fill the tank while the engine is running

39. You observe a red truck making a fuel delivery. The fuel being delivered is probably 39.____

    A. gasoline   B. #2 fuel oil
    C. #4 fuel oil   D. #5 fuel oil

40. The one of the following steps that is NOT taken when operating a carbon dioxide fire   40._
extinguisher is to

    A. carry the extinguisher to the fire and set it on the ground
    B. unhook the hose
    C. pull the pin in the valve wheel
    D. turn the valve and direct the gas to the top of the fire

_____

KEY (CORRECT ANSWERS)

1.	D	11.	D	21.	B	31.	D
2.	B	12.	C	22.	B	32.	A
3.	A	13.	B	23.	D	33.	C
4.	C	14.	D	24.	D	34.	B
5.	A	15.	A	25.	C	35.	D
6.	B	16.	C	26.	C	36.	A
7.	A	17.	A	27.	A	37.	D
8.	C	18.	B	28.	B	38.	B
9.	D	19.	D	29.	B	39.	A
10.	A	20.	A	30.	A	40.	D

_____

EXAMINATION SECTION
TEST 1

DIRECTIONS: Each question or incomplete statement is followed by several suggested answers or completions. Select the one that BEST answers the question or completes the statement. *PRINT THE LETTER OF THE CORRECT ANSWER IN THE SPACE AT THE RIGHT.*

1. Of the following, the *PREFERRED* sequence of tasks to be followed in office cleaning is   1._____

   A. dust desks, empty ash trays and waste baskets, mop floor
   B. mop floor, dust desks, empty ash trays and waste baskets
   C. empty ash trays and waste baskets, dust desks, mop floor
   D. mop floor, empty ash trays and waste baskets, dust desks

2. When vacuum cleaning rugs, the suction tool should be pushed   2._____

   A. diagonally across the lay of the nap
   B. with the lay of the nap
   C. across the lay of the nap
   D. against the lay of the nap

3. The brownish discoloration that sometimes occurs in hot water circulating systems is *USUALLY* due to   3._____

   A. molds   B. algae   C. bacteria   D. rust

4. The type of valve that does *NOT* have a stuffing or packing gland is a _____ valve.   4._____

   A. globe   B. radiator   C. check   D. gate

5. Assuming that the hot and cold water demand of a fixture will be the same, then the normal size of the hot water pipe with respect to that of the cold water pipe should be   5._____

   A. the same   B. twice as great
   C. one and one-half times as great   D. one half as great

6. If the pitch of a horizontal steam line is 1/2 inch in 10 feet, one end of a 45-foot steam line is lower than the other end by, *MOST NEARLY,* _____ inches.   6._____

   A. 2   B. 2 1/4   C. 3   D. 3 1/2

7. A pump that removes 30 gallons of water per minute is pumping water from a cellar 30 feet x 50 feet covered with eight inches of water. One cubic foot of water equals 7.5 gallons of water.
   The number of minutes it will take to remove the eight inches of water from the cellar is, *MOST NEARLY,*   7._____

   A. 200   B. 225   C. 250   D. 275

8. Oil preheaters are used to   8._____

   A. economize on fuel oil   B. reduce friction in the oil blower
   C. improve the flow of oil   D. reduce oil volatility

9. The *FIRST* item which should be checked when a sump pit overflows because the automatic electric sump pump is not operating properly is the

    A. feedwater pressure   B. ficat switch mechanism
    C. stat switch   D. discharge line check valve

9.___

10. Chloride of lime should be used for the removal of

    A. alkali stains on wood
    B. grass stains on wood or marble
    C. indelible pencil and marking ink stains on concrete or terrazzo
    D. ink stains on wood

10.___

11. Of the following, the lack of a vapor barrier on the inside surface of a well-insulated wall may eventually cause, during the winter,

    A. plugging of weep holes
    B. peeling of exterior paint
    C. lower heat losses through the wall
    D. improvement in insulation performance by plugging air spaces with the insulation

11.___

12. When cold water pipes in a room *sweat,* it is *USUALLY* due to the

    A. surface of the pipes being below the dew point temperature of the room air
    B. specific humidity exceeding the relative humidity
    C. air in the room exceeding 100% relative humidity
    D. surface of the pipe being below the wet bulb temperature of the room air

12.___

13. The *MAIN* reason for applying floor finish to a floor surface is to

    A. protect against germs   B. protect the floor surface
    C. increase traction   D. waterproof the floor

13.___

14. The *MAIN* reason for preventing sewer gas from entering buildings through the plumbing system is because the gas

    A. is highly inflammable and explosive in nature and could result in a fire hazard
    B. has an eroding effect on plumbing fixtures and pipe lines
    C. is highly infectious and contagious in nature
    D. has a nuisance effect on occupants

14.___

15. The one of the following that is a concrete floor sealer is

    A. sodium silicate   B. neatsfoot oil
    C. sodium hydroxide   D. linseed oil

15.___

16. To help plants survive the shock of transplanting, in most cases, it is BEST to

    A. spray them with insecticide every day for a week
    B. cover the foliage with burlap for a day or two
    C. shade them from the sun for a week or two
    D. prune them every day for a week or two

16.___

17. When cutting a branch off a tree, it is desirable to undercut because it will 17.____

    A. prevent the weight of the branch from tearing off bark and wood below the cut
    B. make the tree grow stronger and straighter
    C. let the saw work smoother and easier
    D. make it easier to cut up the limb

18. The *MAIN* reason for applying lime to soil is to control its 18.____

    A. aridity   B. fertilization
    C. acidity   D. porosity

19. The *GREATEST* danger to a tree from a large unprotected wound is that 19.____

    A. birds may build a nest in it
    B. the tree may bleed to death
    C. the wound may become infected
    D. it is open to the elements

20. The fertilizer that is used for the care of trees should have a high content of 20.____

    A. DDT   B. nitrogen   C. sulphur   D. carbon

21. The area of the plot plan shown below is _____ square feet. 21.____

    A. 25,300
    B. 26,700
    C. 28,100
    D. 30,500

22. The *BEST* of the following combinations of instruments to use in checking the combustion efficiency of a heating boiler is 22.____

    A. anemometer, stack thermometer, and orsat apparatus
    B. draft gage, psychrometer, and barometer
    C. draft gage, stack thermometer, and orsat apparatus
    D. draft gage, stack thermometer, and barometer

23. The one of the following that does NOT indicate low water in a steam boiler is the 23.____

    A. fusible plug   B. safety valve
    C. tri cocks   D. gauge glass

24. The increase in the stack temperature toward the end of the heating system above what it was at the beginning of the season is an indication that the 24.____

    A. radiators and convectors are air bound
    B. tubes and heating surfaces of the boiler are becoming insulated with soot
    C. furnace fire brick is failing
    D. heat content of the fuel is improving

25. Of the following, the one which is *NOT* a general class of oil burners is the _____ atom-   25.___
izing.

    A.   water   B.   rotary cup   C.   mechanical   D.   air

26. Of the following, the one which should be between a boiler and its safety valve is   26.___

    A.   a swing check valve of a size larger than that of the safety valve
    B.   a butterfly valve located in the boiler-nozzle
    C.   a gate valve of the same nominal size as that of the safety valve
    D.   no valve of any type

27. The term *spinner cup* refers to   27.___

    A.   screw-type stokers   B.   gun-type oil burners
    C.   rotary-type oil burners   D.   chain grate stokers

28. A *gun-type* burner is often used on a   28.___

    A.   pot-type oil burner
    B.   low pressure gas boiler
    C.   coal underfeed stoker boiler
    D.   high pressure oil-fired boiler

29. Of the following, the action that should be taken as the *FIRST* step if a properly adjusted   29.___
safety valve on a steam boiler *pops off* when in operation is

    A.   open the-draft   B.   add more water to the boiler
    C.   wire the valve shut   D.   reduce the draft

30. When the water gets below the safe level in an operating boiler, it is *BEST* to   30.___

    A.   add new water up to the safe level and open up the fire so that the water will heat
        quickly
    B.   check the fire and let the boiler cool down before new water is added
    C.   add new water to the boiler immediately
    D.   check the fire and empty the boiler

31. Vents on fuel oil storage tanks are used to   31.___

    A.   fill the fuel tanks
    B.   allow air to escape during filling
    C.   check oil flash points
    D.   make tank fuel soundings

32. Of the following, the *MOST* desirable way to remove carbon deposits from the atomizing   32.___
cup of an oil burner is to

    A.   apply a hot flame to the carbonized surfaces to burn off the carbon deposits
    B.   use kerosene to loosen the deposits and wipe with a soft cloth
    C.   wash the cup with a mild trisodium phosphate solution and dry with a cloth
    D.   use a scraper, followed by light rubbing with emery cloth

33. Of the following, the *MOST* important precaution that should be taken when *cutting in* a boiler in a battery is to see that the

    A. water column is at least 1 inch below top row of tubes
    B. non-return valve is closed when the boiler pressure is rising
    C. safety valves function properly
    D. boiler pressure is about equal to header pressure

33.____

34. A condensate feedwater tank in a low pressure steam plant

    A. is hermetically sealed to prevent contamination of feed water
    B. contains a surface blow down line
    C. is vented to the atmosphere
    D. has a vacuum breaker exposed to the atmosphere

34.____

35. Of the following, the *FIRST* action to take in the event a low pressure steam boiler gauge glass breaks is to

    A. bank the fires
    B. close the water gauge glass cocks
    C. open the safety valve
    D. blow down the boiler

35.____

36. A *barometric damper* would be used in a boiler installation fired under draft conditions that are called

    A. induced   B. natural   C. regenerate   D. forced

36.____

37. The flue gas temperature, when firing oil, should be just high enough to evaporate any contained moisture in order to

    A. prevent an acid from forming and eroding the breeching
    B. decrease the amount of excess air needed
    C. prevent an air pollution condition
    D. lower the combustion efficiency of the boiler

37.____

38. A compound gauge in a boiler room

    A. measures pressures above and below atmospheric pressure
    B. indicates the degree of compounding in a steam engine
    C. shows the quantity of boiler treatment compound on hand
    D. measures steam and water pressure

38.____

39. In the combustion of the common fuels, the *PRINCIPAL* boiler heat loss is that due to the heat

    A. carried away by the moisture in the fuel
    B. lost by radiation
    C. carried away by the flue gases
    D. lost by incomplete combustion

39.____

40. Of the following, the *CORRECT* sequence of steps to use when removing a boiler from service in order to perform extensive repairs on it is 40.___

    A. discontinue firing, drain boiler, turn off valves, cool boiler
    B. discontinue firing, drain boiler, turn off valves
    C. turn off valves, drain boiler, discontinue firing, cool boiler
    D. discontinue firing, turn off valves, cool boiler, drain boiler

---

KEY (CORRECT ANSWERS)

1.	C	11.	B	21.	C	31.	B
2.	B	12.	A	22.	C	32.	B
3.	D	13.	B	23.	B	33.	D
4.	C	14.	D	24.	B	34.	C
5.	A	15.	A	25.	A	35.	B
6.	B	16.	C	26.	D	36.	B
7.	C	17.	A	27.	C	37.	A
8.	C	18.	C	28.	D	38.	A
9.	B	19.	C	29.	D	39.	C
10.	C	20.	B	30.	B	40.	D

TEST 2

DIRECTIONS: Each question or incomplete statement is followed by several suggested answers or completions. Select the one that BEST answers the question or completes the statement. *PRINT THE LETTER OF THE CORRECT ANSWER IN THE SPACE AT THE RIGHT.*

1. With the same outdoor winter temperatures, the load on a heating boiler starting up is greater than the normal morning load *MAINLY* because of   1.____

   A. loss of heat escaping through the stack
   B. steam required to heat boiler water and piping to radiators
   C. viscosity of the fuel oil
   D. low outdoor temperatures

2. The *FIRST* operation when starting a boiler after it has been on bank overnight should be to   2.____

   A. blow down the boiler
   B. clean the furnace
   C. check the gate valves
   D. look at the water gauge and try the gauge cocks

3. *Cascading* of raw city water when filling a cleaned boiler should be avoided because it   3.____

   A. is harmful to the mud drum
   B. adds additional free oxygen in the boiler
   C. adds considerable time to the filling procedure
   D. will stress tube and sheet joints

4. The average temperature on a day in January was 24° F. The number of degree-days for that day was   4.____

   A. 12   B. 24   C. 41   D. 48

5. Under normal conditions during the growing season, lawns should receive a good saturation of water with a spray   5.____

   A. once a day   B. once a week
   C. once a month   D. twice a month

6. One of the important benefits to floors that wax does *NOT* provide is   6.____

   A. easier soil removal   B. improved stain resistance
   C. reduction in wear   D. resistance to fire

7. In the Ringelmann chart of smoke density, number 4 indicates   7.____

   A. the darkest smoke condition
   B. the lightest smoke condition
   C. smoke density of 80 per cent
   D. no smoke condition

8. Of the following, the estinguishing agent that should be used on fires in flammable liquids is   8.___

   A. steam   B. water   C. foam   D. soda and acid

9. A soda-acid fire extinguisher is recommended for use on fires consisting of   9.___

   A. wood or paper
   B. fuel oil or gasoline
   C. electrical causes or fuel oil
   D. paint or turpentine

10. The *CHIEF* reason wooden ladders should *NOT* be painted is that the paint may   10.___

   A. hide defects   B. mark up the walls
   C. make the ladder slippery D. damage the rungs

11. In accordance with the uniform method of identifying piping in public buildings, pipes car-   11.___
    rying materials classified as being dangerous are colored

   A. blue   B. red
   C. orange and yellow   D. green and white

12. The *MOST* effective way to eliminate fire hazards in public buildings is to   12.___

   A. hold frequent fire drills
   B. have the fire department inspect the building annually
   C. promote constant self-inspection
   D. supply each building with ample fire fighting equipment

13. When a room is air conditioned in the summer, the windows should be   13.___

   A. opened at the top and bottom to improve circulation
   B. screened to keep out the dirt
   C. kept closed
   D. opened at the top only to let hot air escape

14. In order to clean an office with 20,000 sq. ft. of space in four hours, using a standard of   14.___
    900 sq. ft. per hour, the number of cleaners you should assign to do the job is *MOST
    NEARLY*

   A. 4   B. 6   C. 8   D. 10

15. The area of a floor 35' wide and 45' long is, in square yards, *MOST NEARLY*   15.___

   A. 175   B. 262   C. 525   D. 1575

16. A pyrometer is an instrument used for measuring   16.___

   A. condensation and humidity
   B. high temperatures
   C. noise pollution
   D. water flow

17. It is usually desirable to assign the cleaning of an office to one employee only because 17._____

    A. the amount of time wasted through talking is decreased
    B. an employee working alone, by himself, is more efficient
    C. there is no question who is responsible for the work done
    D. working alone reduces the rate and severity of accidents

18. Of each dollar spent on the cleaning of public buildings, the amount spent on cleaning 18._____
supplies is usually not more than _____ cents.

    A. 5   B. 35   C. 55   D. 75

19. Of the following solutions, the one MOST often used in washing exterior glass is _____ 19._____
water and a small quantity of _____.

    A. cold; turpentine   B. cold; ammonia
    C. cold; glass wax   D. warm; soft soap

20. Rust stains in wash basins can BEST be prevented by 20._____

    A. applying wax film to the rusty surface
    B. replacing leaking faucet washers
    C. adding rust inhibitor to the domestic cold water storage tank
    D. sand papering the rusty surfaces

21. Of the following, the one which is likely to be MOST harmful to asphalt tile is 21._____

    A. coffee   B. ketchup   C. salad oil   D. vinegar

22. Of the following, when sweeping a corridor with a floor brush, the cleaner should 22._____

    A. lean on the brush and walk the length of the corridor
    B. give the brush a slight jerk after each stroke to free it of loose dirt
    C. make certain there is no overlap on sweeping strokes
    D. use moderately long pull strokes

23. Time standards for cleaning are of value ONLY if 23._____

    A. a bonus is promised if the time standards are beaten
    B. the cleaners determine the methods and procedures to be used
    C. accompanied by a completely detailed description of the methods to be used
    D. a schematic diagram of the area is made available to the cleaners

24. Of the following, the one which is the LEAST important factor in deciding that additional 24._____
training is necessary for the men you supervise is that

    A. the quality of work is below standard
    B. supplies are being wasted
    C. too much time is required to do specific jobs
    D. the absentee rate has declined

25. To promote proper safety practices in the operation of power tools and equipment, you 25._____
should emphasize in meetings with the staff that

    A. every accident can be prevented through proper safety regulations
    B. proper safety practices will probably make future safety meetings unnecessary

C. when safety rules are followed, tools and equipment will work better
D. safety rules are based on past experience with the best methods of preventing accidents

26. A good practical method to use in determining whether an employee is doing his job properly is to

    A. assume that if he asks no questions, he knows the work
    B. question him directly on details of the job
    C. inspect and follow up the work which is assigned to him
    D. ask other employees how this employee is making out

26.___

27. If an employee continually asks how he should do his work, you should

    A. dismiss him immediately
    B. pretend you do not hear him unless he persists
    C. explain the work carefully but encourage him to use his own judgment
    D. tell him not to ask so many questions

27.___

28. You have instructed an employee to wet-mop a certain area. To be sure that the employee understands the instructions you have given him, you should

    A. ask him to repeat the instructions to you
    B. check with him after he has done the job
    C. watch him while he is doing the job
    D. repeat the instructions to the employee

28.___

29. One of your men disagrees with your evaluation of his work.
Of the following, the *BEST* way to handle this situation would be to

    A. explain that you are in a better position to evaluate his work than he is
    B. tell him that since other men are satisfied with your evaluation, he should accept their opinions
    C. explain the basis of your evaluation and discuss it with him
    D. refuse to discuss his complaint in order to maintain discipline

29.___

30. Of the following, the one which is *NOT* a quality of leadership desirable in a supervisor is

    A. intelligence   B. integrity
    C. forcefulness   D. partiality

30.___

31. Of the following, the one which *LEAST* characterizes the *grapevine* is that it

    A. consists of a tremendous amount of rumor, conjecture, information, advice, prediction, and even orders
    B. seems to rise spontaneously, is largely anonymous, spreads rapidly, and changes in unpredictable directions
    C. can be eliminated without any great effort
    D. commonly fills the gaps left by the regular organizational channels of communication

31.___

32. Of the following, the one which is *NOT* a purpose of a cleaning job breakdown is to

    A. eliminate unnecessary steps
    B. determine the type of floor wax to use

32.___

C. rearrange the sequence of operations to save time
D. combine steps or actions where practicable

33. Of the following, the *PRINCIPAL* function of a supervisor is to   33._____

    A. train and instruct his subordinates in the proper methods of doing their work
    B. eliminate all accidents
    C. prepare reports on his activities to his supervisor
    D. prepare a thorough job methods analysis

34. The *BEST* method of making cleaning assignments in a large building is by means of   34._____

    A. daily rotation   B. specific assignment
    C. individual choice   D. chronological order

35. When one of your new cleaning employees is making little progress after the usual train-   35._____
ing period with one of your experienced men, you should

    A. recommend to your superior that he should be discharged
    B. tell your superior he is not interested in the job
    C. determine the reason for the poor results
    D. discontinue all training

36. For a supervisor to have his cleaning employees willing to follow standardized cleaning   36._____
procedures, he must be prepared to

    A. associate with his employees
    B. show that the procedures are reasonable
    C. give extra time off
    D. set up a penalty system

37. One of the employees you supervise has broken the rule against keeping liquor in his   37._____
locker.
You should

    A. make believe it never happened and forget the incident
    B. explain the rule to him and that a repetition may result in disciplinary action
    C. suspend him immediately
    D. fire him immediately

38. The *BEST* action for you to take on receiving complaints of poor illumination in one of the   38._____
offices is to

    A. wait until you have several complaints of this kind
    B. tell the complainant nothing can be done
    C. request that additional ceiling lights be installed
    D. check the office for the cause of poor illumination

39. The *MAIN* purpose of periodic inspections and tests of mechanical equipment is to   39._____

    A. keep the men busy during otherwise slack periods
    B. discover minor faults before they develop into major faults
    C. make the men familiar with the equipment
    D. encourage the men to take better care of the equipment

40. Assume that one of your employees has been slightly injured while doing a cleaning job. After the employee has been cared for, you should *NEXT*   40.___

    A. investigate the cause of the accident
    B. notify the union
    C. charge the employee with recklessness
    D. transfer the employee

KEY (CORRECT ANSWERS)

1.	B	11.	C	21.	C	31.	C
2.	D	12.	C	22.	B	32.	B
3.	B	13.	C	23.	C	33.	A
4.	C	14.	B	24.	D	34.	B
5.	B	15.	A	25.	D	35.	C
6.	D	16.	B	26.	C	36.	B
7.	C	17.	C	27.	C	37.	B
8.	C	18.	A	28.	A	38.	D
9.	A	19.	B	29.	C	39.	B
10.	A	20.	B	30.	D	40.	A

EXAMINATION SECTION
TEST 1

DIRECTIONS: Each question or incomplete statement is followed by several suggested answers or completions. Select the one that BEST answers the question or completes the statement. *PRINT THE LETTER OF THE CORRECT ANSWER IN THE SPACE AT THE RIGHT.*

1. The specification states: *The value of each change order shall be computed separately by cost of labor and materials, plus equipment allowance, plus overhead and profit.* The MOST probable value of overhead and profit is _____% of the cost of labor and materials plus equipment allowance.

   A. 5 B. 15 C. 34 D. 55

1.____

2. In the specifications is an item: *Equipment Allowance: Shall include rental of necessary equipment plus 9% of this rental.*
   According to the above specification, if a piece of equipment rents for $35 per day, Equipment Allowance for this equipment rented for 11 days is MOST NEARLY

   A. $484.00 B. $378.42 C. $385.00 D. $419.65

2.____

3. A supplier quotes a list price of $172.00 less 15 and 10 percent for twelve tools. The ACTUAL cost for these twelve tools is MOST NEARLY

   A. $146 B. $132 C. $129 D. $112

3.____

4. Which one of the following is the PRIMARY object in drawing up a set of specifications for materials to be purchased?

   A. Control of quality
   B. Outline of intended use
   C. Establishment of standard sizes
   D. Location and method of inspection

4.____

5. In order to avoid disputes over payments for extra work in a contract for construction, the BEST procedure to follow would be to

   A. have contractor submit work progress reports daily
   B. insert a special clause in the contract specifications
   C. have a representative on the job at all times to verify conditions
   D. allocate a certain percentage of the cost of the job to cover such expenses

5.____

6. You wish to order sponges in the most economical manner. Keeping in mind that large sponges can be cut up into many smaller sizes, the one of the following that has the LEAST cost per cubic inch of sponge is _____ sponges @ _____.

   A. 2" x 4" x 6"; $.24
   C. 4" x 6" x 36"; $4.80
   B. 4" x 8" x 12"; $1.44
   D. 6" x 8" x 32"; $9.60

6.____

7. The cost of a certain job is broken down as follows: 7._

    Materials $375

    Rental of equipment   120

    Labor   315

The percentage of the total cost of the job that can be charged to materials is MOST NEARLY _____ %.

    A. 40   B. 42   C. 44   D. 46

8. Partial payments to outside contractors are USUALLY based on the   8._

    A. breakdown estimate submitted after the contract was signed
    B. actual cost of labor and material plus overhead and profit
    C. estimate of work completed which is generally submitted periodically
    D. estimate of material delivered to the job

9. Building contracts usually require that estimates for changes made in the field be submit-   9._
ted for approval before the work can start.
The MAIN reason for this requirement is to

    A. make sure that the contractor understands the change
    B. discourage such changes
    C. keep the contractor honest
    D. enable the department to control its expenses

10. If the cost of a broom went up from $4.00 to $6.00, the percent INCREASE in the original   10._
cost is

    A. 20   B. 25   C. 33 1/3   D. 50

11. The AVERAGE of the numbers 3, 5, 7, 8, 12 is   11._

    A. 5   B. 6   C. 7   D. 8

12. The cost of 100 bags of cotton cleaning cloths, 89 pounds per bag, at 7 cents per pound   12._
is

    A. $549.35   B. $623.00   C. $700.00   D. $890.00

13. If 5 1/2 bags of sweeping compound cost $55,00, then 6 1/2 bags would cost   13._

    A. $60.00   B. $62.50   C. $65.00   D. $67.00

14. The cost of cleaning supplies in a project averaged $330.00 a month during the first 8   14._
months of the year.
How much can be spent each month for the last four months if the total amount that
can be spent for cleaning supplies for the year is $3,880?

    A. $124   B. $220   C. $310   D. $330

15. The cost of rawl plugs is $2.75 per gross. The cost of 2,448 rawl plugs is   15._

    A. $46.75   B. $47.25   C. $47.75   D. $48.25

16. A caretaker received $70.00 for having worked from Monday through Friday, 9 A.M. to 5 P.M. with one hour a day for lunch.
The number of hours the caretaker would have to work to earn $12.00 is   16.____

    A. 10   B. 6
    C. 70 divided by 12   D. 70 minus 12

17. Assume that an employee is paid at the rate of $5.43 per hour with time and a half for overtime past 40 hours in a week.
If he works 43 hours in a week, his gross weekly pay is   17.____

    A. $217.20   B. $219.20   C. $229.59   D. $241.64

18. Kerosene costs 36 cents a quart.
At that rate, two gallons would cost   18.____

    A. $1.44   B. $2.16   C. $2.88   D. $3.60

Questions 19-21.

DIRECTIONS: Questions 19 through 21 are to be answered on the basis of the following table.

	Man Days Borough 1		Man Days Borough 2		Man Days Borough 3		Man Days Borough 4	
	Oct.	Nov.	Oct.	Nov.	Oct.	Nov.	Oct.	Nov.
Carpenter	70	100	35	180	145	205	120	85
Plumber	95	135	195	100	70	130	135	80
House Painter	90	90	120	80	85	85	95	195
Electrician	120	110	135	155	120	95	70	205
Blacksmith	125	145	60	180	205	145	80	125

19. In accordance with the above table, if the average daily pay of the five trades listed above is $47.50, the approximate labor cost of work done by the five trades during the month of October for Borough 1 is MOST NEARLY   19.____

    A. $22,800   B. $23,450   C. $23,750   D. $26,125

20. In accordance with the above table, the Borough which MOST NEARLY made up 22.4% of the total plumbing work force for the month of November is Borough   20.____

    A. 1   B. 2   C. 3   D. 4

21. In accordance with the above table, the average man days per month per Borough spent on electrical work for all Boroughs combined is MOST NEARLY   21.____

    A. 120   B. 126   C. 130   D. 136

22. When preparing an estimate for a certain repair job, you determine that $125 worth of materials and 220 man-hours are required to complete the job.
If your man-hour cost is $5.25 per hour, the TOTAL cost of this repair job is   22.____

    A. $1,030   B. $1,155   C. $1,280   D. $1,405

23. Assume that in determining the total cost of a repair job, a 15% shop cost is to be added to the costs of material and labor.
    For a repair job which cost $200 in materials and $600 in labor, the shop cost is

    A. $30　　　　B. $60　　　　C. $90　　　　D. $120

24. Assume that in quantity purchases, the city receives a discount of 33 1/3%.
    If a one gallon can of paint retails at $5.33 per gallon, the cost of 375 gallons of this paint is MOST NEARLY

    A. $1,332.50　　B. $1,332.75　　C. $1,333.00　　D. $1,333.25

25. Assume that eight barrels of cement together weigh a total of 3004 lbs. and 12 oz.
    If there are four bags of cement per barrel, then the weight of one bag of cement is HOST NEARLY _____ lbs.

    A. 93.1　　　　B. 93.5　　　　C. 93.9　　　　D. 94.3

26. Lumber is usually sold by the board foot, and a board foot is defined as a board one foot square and one inch thick.
    If the price of one board foot of lumber is 18 cents and you need 20 feet of lumber 6 inches wide and 1 inch thick, the cost of the 20 feet of lumber is

    A. $1.80　　　　B. $2.40　　　　C. $3.60　　　　D. $4.80

27. Assume that a trench is 42" wide, 5' deep, and 100' long. If the unit price of excavating the trench is $35 per cubic yard, the cost of excavating the trench is MOST NEARLY

    A. $2,275　　　B. $5,110　　　C. $7,000　　　D. $21,000

28. No single activity has a very large effect on the final price of the complete housing structure and, therefore, the total cost is not affected appreciably by the price policy of any component.
    From the above statement, you may conclude that

    A. we cannot hope for substantial reductions in housing costs
    B. the builder must assume responsibility for the high cost of construction
    C. a 10% reduction in the cost of materials would result in much less than a 10% reduction in the cost of housing
    D. federal government financing would reduce the city's cost of public housing

29. Four board feet of lumber, listed at $350 per M, will cost

    A. $3.50　　　　B. $1.40　　　　C. $1.80　　　　D. $4.00

30. The cost of material is approximately 3/8ths of the total cost of a certain job.
    If the total cost of the job is $127.56, then the cost of material is MOST NEARLY

    A. $47.83　　　B. $48.24　　　C. $48.65　　　D. $49.06

31. It takes four men six days to do a certain job. Working at the same speed, the number of days it will take three men to do this job is

    A. 7　　　　　B. 8　　　　　C. 9　　　　　D. 10

32. A contractor on a large construction project USUALLY receives partial payments based on   32.____

    A. estimates of completed work
    B. actual cost of materials delivered and work completed
    C. estimates of material delivered and not paid for by the contractor
    D. the breakdown estimate submitted after the contract was signed and prorated over the estimated duration of the contract

33. In estimating the cost of a reinforced concrete structure, the contractor would be LEAST   33.____
concerned with

    A. volume of concrete
    B. surface area of forms
    C. pounds of reinforcing steel
    D. type of coarse aggregate

34. Assume that an employee is paid at the rate of $6.25 per hour with time and a half for   34.____
overtime past 40 hours in a week.
If she works 45 hours in a week, her gross weekly pay is

    A. $285.49   B. $296.88   C. $301.44   D. $325.49

35. Cleaning fluid costs $1.19 a quart.   35.____
If there is a 10% discount for purchases over 5 gallons, how much will 8 gallons cost?

    A. $34.28   B. $38.08   C. $42.28   D. $43.43

KEY (CORRECT ANSWERS)

1.	B	11.	C	26.	A
2.	D	12.	B	27.	A
3.	B	13.	C	28.	C
4.	A	14.	C	29.	B
5.	C	15.	A	30.	A
6.	B	16.	B	31.	B
7.	D	17.	D	32.	A
8.	C	18.	C	33.	D
9.	D	19.	C	34.	B
10.	D	20.	B	35.	A
		21.	B		
		22.	C		
		23.	D		
		24.	A		
		25.	C		

TEST 2

DIRECTIONS: Each question or incomplete statement is followed by several suggested answers or completions. Select the one that BEST answers the question or completes the statement. *PRINT THE LETTER OF THE CORRECT ANSWER IN THE SPACE AT THE RIGHT.*

1. When windows are mounted side by side, the vertical piece between them is called the   1.__

    A. muntin   B. casement   C. sash   D. mullion

2. Approximately how many pounds of 16d nails would be required for 1,000 square feet of floor framing area?   2.__

    A. 4-5   B. 7-8   C. 8-10   D. 10-12

3. What is represented by the electrical symbol shown at the right?   3.__

    A. Transformer   B. Buzzer
    C. Telephone   D. Bell

4. Which of the following structures would typically require a relatively higher grade of lumber?   4.__

    A. Vertical stud   B. Joist
    C. Column   D. Mud sill

5. A dump truck with a capacity of 10-12 cubic yards must load, drive, dump, and reposition itself over a 1-mile haul distance.
What average amount of time should be estimated for this sequence?   5.__

    A. 15 minutes   B. 30 minutes
    C. 1 hour   D. 2 hours

6. The stripping of forms that are to be reused should be charged as   6.__

    A. common labor   B. masonry labor
    C. carpentry labor   D. material credit

7. What type of brick masonry unit is represented by the drawing shown at the right?   7.__
    A. Modular
    B. Norwegian
    C. 3 core
    D. Economy

8. Which of the following would be a typical thickness of a crushed-rock base course for an area of asphalt paving?   8.__

    A. 2"   B. 5"   C. 7"   D. 10"

9. Which of the following wood floor materials would be MOST expensive to install?   9.____

    A. Unfinished plank   B. Walnut parquet
    C. Maple strip   D. Oak parquet

10. When calculating the air-conditioning needs for a building, a loss factor of _____ should   10.____
be used for the exposure of walls to common heated surfaces.

    A. 2.0   B. 3.5   C. 6.0   D. 7.5

11. Approximately how many linear feet of moldings, door and window trim, handrails, or   11.____
similar parts can a carpenter install in a typical work day?

    A. 100   B. 250   C. 400   D. 500

12. Which of the following constructions is NOT typically found in bathroom lavatories?   12.____

    A. Enameled pressed steel   B. Cast iron
    C. Cast ceramic   D. Stainless steel

13. What size reinforcing bar is typically used for masonry walls?   13.____

    A. 3   B. 4   C. 7   D. 9

14. Which of the following would NOT be a typical source for a cost-per-square-foot esti-   14.____
mate?

    A. Architect   B. Engineer
    C. Appraiser   D. Building contractor

15. Approximately how many stair treads with risers can a carpenter install in an average   15.____
work day?

    A. 5-8   B. 10-12   C. 15-18   D. 21-25

16. Each of the following materials is commonly used as sheet metal flashing for roof water-   16.____
proofing EXCEPT

    A. lead   B. galvanized steel
    C. copper   D. zinc

17. The MOST commonly used type of metal lath for wall support is   17.____

    A. self-furring   B. flat rib
    C. flat diamond mesh   D. 3/8" rib

18. Approximately how long will it take to install a non-mortised lockset?   18.____

    A. 15 minutes   B. 30 minutes
    C. 1 hour   D. 2 hours

19. What is represented by the architectural symbol shown at   19.____
the right?

    A. Cut stone   B. Concrete block
    C. Rubble stone   D. Brick

20. What type of nails are typically used for installing floor sheathing?   20.____

    A. 4d   B. 8d   C. 12d   D. 16d

21. Each of the following is considered *finish* electrical work EXCEPT   21.___

    A. outlet boxes
    B. light fixtures
    C. connection of fixtures to wiring
    D. switches

22. Which component of cost estimating typically presents the GREATEST difficulty?   22.___

    A. Materials   B. Overhead
    C. Profit   D. Labor

23. Approximately how many hours will it take to install and caulk a typical sliding shower   23.___
door assembly?

    A. 2   B. 4   C. 6   D. 8

24. What is represented by the electrical symbol shown at   24.___
the right?

    A. Single pole switch   B. Lock or key switch
    C. Service weather head   D. Main switch

25. Approximately how many exterior square feet can one painter cover, applying a primer   25.___
coat and two coats of finish paint, in an average work day?

    A. 100   B. 250   C. 350   D. 500

KEY (CORRECT ANSWERS)

1.	D		11.	B
2.	B		12.	D
3.	C		13.	B
4.	B		14.	C
5.	B		15.	C
6.	C		16.	A
7.	A		17.	C
8.	B		18.	B
9.	B		19.	A
10.	B		20.	B

21.	A
22.	D
23.	B
24.	A
25.	D

TEST 3

DIRECTIONS: Each question or incomplete statement is followed by several suggested answers or completions. Select the one that BEST answers the question or completes the statement. *PRINT THE LETTER OF THE CORRECT ANSWER IN THE SPACE AT THE RIGHT.*

1. Irregular shapes and narrow lites typically reduce the rate of glass installation by _____%.

    A. 10-20   B. 25-35   C. 30-50   D. 55-75

    1.____

2. What is represented by the electrical symbol shown at the right?

    A. Exposed wiring   B. Fusible element
    C. Three-way switch   D. Circuit breaker

    2.____

3. Approximately how many square feet of siding can be installed by a crew in a typical work day?

    A. 250   B. 500   C. 750   D. 1,000

    3.____

4. What is the construction term for hinges used on doors?

    A. Gables   B. Butts   C. Hips   D. Plates

    4.____

5. Floor joists are typically spaced about _____ apart.

    A. 16"   B. 2 feet   C. 3 feet   D. 4 feet

    5.____

6. Which of the following paving materials is generally MOST expensive?

    A. Brick on sand bed   B. Random flagstone
    C. Asphalt   D. Concrete

    6.____

7. Approximately how long should it take a 2-person crew to install floor joists for a 100 square-foot area of floor space?

    A. 30 minutes   B. 1 hour
    C. 3 hours   D. 1 work day

    7.____

8. A _____ is represented by the mechanical symbol shown at the right.

    A. pressure-reducing valve   B. motor-operated valve
    C. lock and shield valve   D. globe valve

    8.____

9. On average, labor costs for a job will be about _____% of the total job cost.

    A. 15   B. 35   C. 55   D. 85

    9.____

10. Most exterior paint averages a coverage of about _____ square feet per gallon.

    A. 100   B. 250   C. 400   D. 550

    10.____

11. What type of window includes two sashes which slide vertically? 11.___

    A. Double-hung   B. Screen
    C. Casement   D. Sliding

12. Approximately how many linear feet of drywall tape can be applied during an average work day? 12.___

    A. 250   B. 400   C. 750   D. 1,000

13. What is used to join lengths of copper pipe? 13.___

    A. Molten solder
    B. Threaded ends and sealer
    C. Nipples
    D. Lead-and-oakum seal

14. Typically, one gallon of prepared wallpaper paste will supply adhesive for _____ full rolls of wall covering. 14.___

    A. 8   B. 12   C. 24   D. 36

15. What is represented by the electrical symbol shown at the right? 15.___

    A. Range outlet
    B. Wall bracket light fixture
    C. Split-wired receptacle
    D. Special purpose outlet

16. What size is MOST wire used in residential work? 16.___

    A. 6   B. 8   C. 12   D. 16

17. Most fire codes require fire-resistant floor underneath fireplace units which extends to at least _____ inches beyond the unit. 17.___

    A. 6   B. 12   C. 18   D. 24

18. If a building is constructed without a basement, _____ are typically used as footings. 18.___

    A. joists   B. staked caissons
    C. grade beams   D. mud sills

19. What is the MOST commonly used size range for flashing and gutter sheet metal? 19.___

    A. 8-12   B. 14-18   C. 22-26   D. 24-30

20. Approximately how many square feet of interior wall space can one painter, using a brush, cover in an hour? 20.___

    A. 25-50   B. 100   C. 175-200   D. 250

21. Which of the following downspout materials would be MOST expensive? 21.___

    A. Copper   B. Aluminum
    C. Zinc   D. Stainless steel

22. What is represented by the mechanical symbol shown at the right?   22.____

    A.   Expansion valve   B.   Floor drain
    C.   Shower   D.   Scale trap

23. Approximately how much lead (pounds) is required per joint in one sewer line lead-and-oakum seal?   23.____

    A.   1/4   B.   1/2   C.   1 1/2   D.   3

24. Which of the following caulking materials is MOST expensive?   24.____

    A.   Neoprene   B.   Butyl
    C.   Polyurethane   D.   Latex

25. The assembly inside a tank toilet that controls the water supply is the   25.____

    A.   P trap   B.   bell-and-spigot
    C.   gating   D.   ball cock

KEY (CORRECT ANSWERS)

1.	C	11.	A
2.	B	12.	A
3.	A	13.	A
4.	B	14.	B
5.	A	15.	C
6.	D	16.	C
7.	C	17.	B
8.	D	18.	C
9.	A	19.	C
10.	C	20.	B

21.	A
22.	A
23.	A
24.	B
25.	C

EXAMINATION SECTION
TEST 1

DIRECTIONS: Each question or incomplete statement is followed by several suggested answers or completions. Select the one that BEST answers the question or completes the statement. *PRINT THE LETTER OF THE CORRECT ANSWER IN THE SPACE AT THE RIGHT.*

1. The most common approach used by a prime contractor to hold its subcontractors to their initial bids is the doctrine of promissory estoppel. In order to bind a subcontractor to its bid price, the prime contractor must prove each of the following EXCEPT that the

1.____

    A. prime contractor relied on the subcontractor's offer when making its own bid
    B. subcontractor submitted a clear and definite offer
    C. subcontractor's bid was formally accepted by the prime contractor
    D. subcontractor could have expected the prime contractor to rely on the subcontractor's offer when making its own bid

2. Which type of specification in a construction contract is intended to invite the greatest amount of competition?

2.____

    A. Base bid   B. Closed
    C. Open   D. Bidder's choice

3. Written or graphic instruments issued prior to the execution of a contract, which modify or interpret the bidding documents by additions, deletions, clarifications, or corrections, are generally referred to as

3.____

    A. contract modifications   B. addenda
    C. reference documents   D. supplementary conditions

4. What type of warranty is used to limit the manufacturer's responsibility in a construction contract?

4.____

    A. Service agreement   B. Correction of work
    C. Limited term   D. Material-only

5. Which of the following statements represents the most important difference between drawings and specifications?

5.____

    A. Specifications constitute one of the contract documents.
    B. Specifications segregate information in order to aid in forming subcontracts.
    C. Drawings are used to show which materials are to be used.
    D. Drawings name the quantity of materials to be used.

6. The usual fidelity bond arrangement used in construction contracts is used to protect the contractor against

6.____

    A. loss, damage or excessive wear of rented equipment
    B. catastrophic damage to completed elements of the construction project
    C. dishonest acts of an employee such as theft, forgery or embezzlement
    D. bid stability of subcontractors

7. Each of the following is a common purpose of an agreement in construction contract documents EXCEPT to 7.___

   A. state the work to be done and the price to be paid for it
   B. specifically formalize the construction contract
   C. act as a single instrument that brings together all of the contract segments by reference
   D. list the technical specifications that must be adhered to in the construction project

8. Which of the following is an attribute that might be considered for the ceiling subsystem in a performance specification? 8.___

   A. Maximum claim spread 25
   B. Fire safety
   C. Smoke development shall not exceed 75
   D. ASTM E84

9. Of the following types of hold-harmless clauses, _____ indemnification used in construction contracts indemnifies the owner and/or architect engineer even when the party indemnified is solely responsible for the loss. 9.___

   A. limited-form   B. intermediate-form
   C. broad-form   D. omnibus

10. Unit kitchens are an item that would be described under the _____ Division heading in the CSI Masterformat of specifications. 10.___

   A. Equipment   B. Special Construction
   C. Furnishings   D. Specialties

11. Which of the following information is usually described in contract specifications? 11.___

   A. Test and code requirements
   B. Size of component parts
   C. Overall dimensions
   D. Schedules of finishes, windows, and doors

12. The PRIMARY advantage associated with unit-price construction contracts is 12.___

   A. open competition on projects involving quantities of work that cannot be accurately forecast at the time of bidding or negotiation
   B. fully completed drawings and specifications at the time of bidding or negotiation
   C. greater-than-usual flexibility with regard to special reimbursable costs
   D. flexibility in negotiating a unit price for agreed-upon work items

13. Which of the following information is typically shown by drawings? 13.___

   A. Methods of fabrication, installation, and erection
   B. Alternates and unit prices
   C. Interrelation of materials, equipment, and space
   D. Gages of manufacturer's equipment

14. Which of the following is/are typical purposes of a changed-condition clause in a con-   14.____
struction contract?
    I.   To protect the owner from unforeseen increases in project costs
    II. To reduce the contractor's liability for the unexpected
    III. To alleviate the need for including large contingency sums in the bid
The CORRECT answer is:

    A. I *only*   B. II *only*   C. I, II   D. II, III

15. In construction contracts, a special warranty most frequently applies to the work of a(n)   15.____

    A. architect   B. subcontractor
    C. engineer   D. contractor

16. The MAIN advantage associated with the use of bid bonds as security for submitted pro-   16.____
posals is that they

    A. will hold subcontractors accountable for their subbids
    B. don't require an annual service charge
    C. are estimated according to the minimum bid price
    D. don't immobilize appreciable sums of a contractor's money

17. Under most statutes governing construction contract law, a prime contractor may be   17.____
relieved from its bid at any time after the opening of bids by the *doctrine of mistake.*
Which of the following are conditions that would support an argument for applying the
doctrine of mistake?
The
    I.   mistake relates to a material feature of the contract
    II. mistake is one of judgment, rather than fact
    III. owner is put in a status quo position, to the extent that he suffers no serious
         prejudice except the loss of his bargain
    IV. mistake is of a mechanical or clerical nature
The CORRECT answer is:

    A. I *only*   B. III *only*   C. II, IV   D. I, III, IV

18. Which of the following is NOT typically a disadvantage associated with the use of retain-   18.____
age arrangements in construction contracts?

    A. Reduced bidding competition
    B. Higher construction costs for owners
    C. Tends to sacrifice workmanship for speed of completion
    D. Cash-flow problems for contractors

19. What is the term for a detailed compilation of the quantity of each elementary work item   19.____
that is called for on the project?

    A. Specification   B. Takeoff
    C. Bid invitation   D. Summary sheet

20. Which of the following is NOT one of the general types of specifications used in construc-   20.____
tion contracts?

    A. Proprietary   B. Surety
    C. Descriptive   D. Performance

21. When negotiating a cost-plus contract, the owner and contractor must pay particular attention to each of the following considerations EXCEPT

    A. a list of job costs to be reimbursable to the contractor
    B. a common understanding regarding the accounting methods to be used
    C. the number of work units to be performed in executing the project
    D. a definite and mutually agreeable subcontract-letting procedure

21.__

22. According to construction contract law, what is the term for a promise by a party called the guarantor to make good the mistake, debt, or default of another party?

    A. Guaranty   B. Warranty   C. Guarantee   D. Surety

22.__

23. In a technical section that has been written according to the CSI standard format, which of the following descriptions would be sequenced FIRST?

    A. Warranty   B. Summary
    C. Project/site conditions   D. Maintenance

23.__

24. In a construction contract, addendum changes to _____ are typically sequenced first.

    A. drawings   B. bid form
    C. prior addenda   D. general conditions

24.__

25. Which of the following is typically added to a construction contract as a means of providing financial protection to a contractor?

    I.   Value engineering clause
    II. Escalation clause
    III. Escape clause

The CORRECT answer is:

    A. I *only*   B. I, II   C. I, III   D. II, III

25.__

KEY (CORRECT ANSWERS)

1.	C	11.	A
2.	C	12.	A
3.	B	13.	C
4.	D	14.	D
5.	B	15.	B
6.	C	16.	D
7.	D	17.	D
8.	B	18.	C
9.	C	19.	B
10.	A	20.	B

21.	C
22.	A
23.	B
24.	C
25.	D

TEST 2

DIRECTIONS: Each question or incomplete statement is followed by several suggested answers or completions. Select the one that BEST answers the question or completes the statement. *PRINT THE LETTER OF THE CORRECT ANSWER IN THE SPACE AT THE RIGHT.*

1. Which type of specification is most commonly used for public work?　　　　　1.＿＿＿

   A.　Open　　　　　　　　　　　　　　B.　Closed
   C.　Restricted　　　　　　　　　　　D.　Bidder's choice

2. Changes in the general conditions of a contract are expressed in the form of　　　2.＿＿＿

   A.　contract modifications　　　　　　B.　change orders
   C.　supplementary conditions　　　　D.　addenda

3. The listing of subcontractors is often troublesome for contractors when it comes to bid-　　3.＿＿＿
ding on projects with

   A.　unbalanced bids　　　　　　　　B.　alternates
   C.　contract bonds　　　　　　　　　D.　unit pricing

4. Of the following, it is NOT a typical right assigned to an owner under the terms of a con-　　4.＿＿＿
struction contract to

   A.　inspect the work as it proceeds
   B.　terminate the contract for cause
   C.　intervene in the direction and control of the work
   D.　retain a specified portion of the contractor's periodic payments

5. In most states, oral purchase agreements are NOT enforceable when　　　　5.＿＿＿

   A.　they are carried out without the knowledge or consent of the prime contractor
   B.　the price of goods is $500 or more
   C.　the seller has not been approved by the owner
   D.　the seller is not required under the agreement to deliver the goods to the site

6. Which of the following elements of a project manual is NOT usually included under the　　6.＿＿＿
Sample Forms heading?

   A.　Bid bond
   B.　Supplementary conditions
   C.　Performance and payment bonds
   D.　Agreement

7. As part of a construction contract, a retainage arrangement can substantially serve an　　7.＿＿＿
owner in each of the following ways EXCEPT

   A.　protection against a contractor's failure to remedy defective work
   B.　collection of damages from the contractor for late completion
   C.　protection against breach of contract
   D.　protection against damages to others caused by the contractor's performance

8. In general, the submission of *qualified* bids by a contractor is not permissible in public bidding because it

    A. is considered to be an arbitrary and unfair practice.
    B. will make the bid subject to rejection
    C. avoids fixing a total cost for the project
    D. is an illegal practice

8._

9. Which of the following bonds is given by a self-insured contractor to the state to guarantee payment of statutory benefits to injured employees?

    A. Union wage bond
    B. License bond
    C. Workman's compensation bond
    D. Fidelity bond

9._

10. The Divisions of the CSI Masterformat of specifications are based on four major categories. Which of the following is NOT one of these categories?

    A. Trades
    B. Levels of specialization
    C. Place relationships
    D. Materials

10._

11. In construction contract law, what is the term for the promise that certain facts are true as represented and that they will remain so?

    A. Guaranty   B. Guarantee   C. Surety   D. Warranty

11._

12. An owner may occasionally want a contractor to start construction operations before the formalities associated with the signing of the contract can be completed. In this case, a(n) _____ should be conveyed to authorize the start of work.

    A. letter of intent
    B. escape clause
    C. proviso of estoppel
    D. writ of mediation

12._

13. In performance specifying, the term *criterion* refers to a(n)

    A. set of physical measurements of the materials specified
    B. qualitative statement of the desired performance
    C. evaluative procedure to assure compliance with the standard
    D. quantitative statement of the desired performance

13._

14. A construction contract may be terminated on the grounds of the doctrine of impossibility of performance. Which of the following would be most likely to be interpreted as constituting impossibility of performance?

    A. Prolonged infirmity of prime contractor
    B. Withdrawal of subbids that make the execution of construction too costly to be profitable
    C. Unexpected site conditions found that make the construction impracticable
    D. One party finds it an economic burden to continue

14._

15. Which of the following contracts is NOT typically defined in a contractual liability insurance policy that is included in a construction contract?

    A. Hold-harmless agreements
    B. Lease of premises
    C. Easement agreements
    D. Sidetrack agreements

15._

16. For a contractor, the main disadvantage associated with lump-sum contracts is that   16.____

    A. they increase the likelihood of impossibility of performance
    B. the total amount of payment will be unknown until project completion
    C. they make it more difficult to hold subcontractors to their subbids
    D. adverse changes in the contractor's project costs will not be compensated

17. When a bidder's list of substitutions is used in the specifications of a construction con-   17.____
tract, each of the following is generally true EXCEPT

    A. the bid must include the net difference in cost if the substitutions are accepted
    B. each bidder is free to submit any substitution
    C. it is the best method for achieving pure competition
    D. each of the bidders is unaware of the substitution his competitor may offer

18. In a(n) _____ contract, it is especially important that the work must be of such a nature   18.____
that it can be fairly well-defined and a reasonably good estimate of cost can be approxi-
mated at the time of negotiations.

    A. incentive   B. cost-plus-fixed-fee
    C. progress payment   D. cost-plus-percentage

19. In a typical surety bond arrangement written into a construction contract, the principal is   19.____
the

    A. owner   B. surety company
    C. contractor   D. architect/engineer

20. When several prime contracts are desired in a construction project, the limits of each   20.____
prime contract will usually be established in the

    A. specifications   B. general conditions
    C. agreement   D. bidding requirements

21. Under the terms of a *liquidated damages* bid bond, the surety agrees to pay the _____   21.____
as damages for a contractor's default on a bid.

    A. entire bond amount
    B. difference between the contractor's defaulted low bid and the price the owner must
        pay to the next lowest responsible bidder
    C. agreed-upon percentage, usually 5 to 10 percent, of the minimum bid price
    D. amount of the initial progress payment plus a penalty

22. Which of the following descriptions in a technical section would appear in Part 3, accord-   22.____
ing to the CSI standard fornat?

    A. Manufacturers   B. Installation
    C. Definitions   D. Accessories

23. Before a contract award is made, the bids must be carefully studied and evaluated by the   23.____
owner and architect-engineer, a process which is typically referred to as

    A. prepping   B. polling
    C. canvassing   D. bonding

24. On small projects, office functions are usually carried out in a contractor's main office and particular items of office overhead are difficult to establish. If the contractor is working such a project on a cost-plus basis, it is common practice to   24.__

    A. agree with the owner upon a disinterested third party who will estimate the total office overhead costs of the project, and incorporate this figure into the contract
    B. eliminate office overhead altogether as a reimbursed cost and increase the contractor's fee by a reasonable amount
    C. agree in advance with the owner upon an estimated percentage of total job costs that will be named as office overhead in the accounting of the contract
    D. agree in advance with the owner upon a fixed amount that will be named as office overhead in the accounting of the contract

25. In the absence of any clause in a construction contract that addresses the point of excusable delay by a contractor, the contractor may only expect relief from delays with specified causes. Which of the following is NOT one of these causes?   25.__

    A. The architect-engineer   B. The law
    C. Subcontractors   D. The owner

———

KEY (CORRECT ANSWERS)

1.	A		11.	D
2.	C		12.	A
3.	B		13.	D
4.	C		14.	C
5.	B		15.	A
6.	B		16.	D
7.	C		17.	C
8.	B		18.	B
9.	C		19.	C
10.	B		20.	A

21.	A
22.	B
23.	C
24.	B
25.	C

———

EXAMINATION SECTION
TEST 1

DIRECTIONS: Each question or incomplete statement is followed by several suggested answers or completions. Select the one that BEST answers the question or completes the statement. *PRINT THE LETTER OF THE CORRECT ANSWER IN THE SPACE AT THE RIGHT.*

1. At times there may be a conflict between employees' needs and agency goals. A supervisor's MAIN role in motivating employees in such circumstances is to try to

    A. develop good work habits among the employees whom he supervises
    B. emphasize the importance of material rewards such as merit increases
    C. keep careful records of employees' performance for possible disciplinary action
    D. reconcile employees' objectives with those of the public agency

1.____

2. Organizations cannot function effectively without policies. However, when an organization imposes excessively detailed policy restrictions, it is MOST likely to lead to

    A. conflicts among individual employees
    B. a lack of adequate supervision
    C. a reduction of employee initiative
    D. a reliance on punitive discipline

2.____

3. The PRIMARY responsibility for establishing good employee relations in the public service USUALLY rests with

    A. employees
    B. management
    C. civil service organizations
    D. employee organizations

3.____

4. At times, certain off-the-job conduct of public employees may be of concern to management. This concern stems from the fact that

    A. agency programs could be harmed by adverse publicity if employees' conduct is considered detrimental by the public
    B. fairness to all concerned is usually the major consideration in disciplinary cases
    C. public employees must meet higher standards than employees working in private industry
    D. public employees have high ethical standards and may participate in social action programs

4.____

5. At one time or another, most employees ask for, or expect, special treatment. For a supervisor faced with this problem, the one of the following which is the MOST valid guideline is:

    A. According to the rules, a supervisor must give identical treatment to all his subordinates, regardless of the circumstances.
    B. Although all employees have equal rights, it is sometimes necessary to give an employee special treatment to meet an individual need.
    C. It would damage morale if any employee were to receive special treatment, regardless of circumstances.
    D. Since each employee has different needs, there is little reason to maintain general rules.

5.____

6. Mental health problems exist in many parts of our society and may also be found in the work setting. The BASIC role of the supervisor in relation to the mental health problems of his subordinates is to

    A. restrict himself solely to the taking of disciplinary measures, if warranted, and follow up carefully
    B. avoid involvement in personal matters
    C. identify mental health problems as early as possible
    D. resolve mental health problems through personal counseling

6._

7. Supervisory expectation of high levels of employee performance, where such performance is possible, is MOST likely to lead to employees'

    A. expecting frequent praise and encouragement
    B. gaining a greater sense of satisfaction
    C. needing less detailed instructions then previously
    D. reducing their quantitative output

7._

8. In public agencies, as elsewhere, supervisors sometimes compete with one another to increase their units' productivity. Of the following, the MAJOR disadvantage of such competition, from the general viewpoint of providing good public service, is that

    A. while individual employee effort will increase, unit productivity will decrease
    B. employees will be discouraged from sincere interest in their work
    C. the supervisors' competition may hinder the achievement of agency goals
    D. total payroll costs will increase as the activities of each unit increase

8._

9. If employees are motivated primarily by material compensation, the amount of effort an individual employee will put into performing his work effectively will depend MAINLY upon how he perceives

    A. cooperation to be tied to successful effort
    B. the association between good work and increased compensation
    C. the public status of his particular position
    D. the supervisor's behavior in work situations

9._

10. Cash awards to individual employees are sometimes used to encourage useful suggestions. However, some management experts believe that awards should involve some form of employee recognition other than cash. Which of the following reasons BEST supports opposition to using cash as a reward for worthwhile suggestions?

    A. Cash awards cause employees to expend excessive time in making suggestions.
    B. Taxpayer opposition to cash awards has increased following generous salary increases for public employees in recent years.
    C. Public funds expended on awards lead to a poor image of public employees.
    D. The use of cash awards raises the problem of deciding tne monetary value of suggestions.

10._

11. The BEST general rule for a supervisor to follow in giving praise and criticism is to

    A. criticize and praise publicly
    B. criticize publicly and praise privately
    C. praise and criticize privately
    D. praise publicly and criticize privately

11._

12. An important step in designing an error-control policy is to determine the maximum number of errors that can be considered acceptable for the entire organization. Of the following, the MOST important factor in making such a decision is the

    A. number of clerical staff available to check for errors
    B. frequency of errors by supervisors
    C. human and material costs of errors
    D. number of errors that will become known to the public

12.____

13. When a supervisor tries to correct a situation where errors have been widespread, he should concentrate his efforts, and those of the employees involved, on

    A. avoiding future mistakes   B. fixing appropriate blame
    C. preparing a written report   D. determining fair penalties

13.____

14. When delegating work to a subordinate, a supervisor should ALWAYS tell the subordinate

    A. each step in the procedure for doing the work
    B. how much time to expend
    C. what is to be accomplished
    D. whether reports are necessary

14.____

15. The responsibilities of all employees should be clearly defined and understood. In addition, in order for employees to successfully fulfill their responsibilities, they should also GENERALLY be given

    A. written directives   B. close supervision
    C. corresponding authority   D. daily instructions

15.____

16. The one of the following types of training in which positive transfer of training to the actual work situation is MOST likely to take place is

    A. conference training   B. demonstration training
    C. classroom training   D. on-the-job training

16.____

17. The type of training or instruction in which the subject matter is presented in small units called frames is known as

    A. programmed instruction   B. reinforcement
    C. remediation   D. skills training

17.____

18. In order to bring about maximum learning in a training situation, a supervisor acting as a trainer should attempt to create a setting in which

    A. all trainees experience a large amount of failure as an incentive
    B. all trainees experience a small amount of failure as an incentive
    C. each trainee experiences approximately the same amounts of success and failure
    D. each trainee experiences as much success and as little failure as possible

18.____

19. Assume that, in a training course given by an agency, the instructor conducts a brief quiz, on paper, toward the close of each session. From the point of view of maximizing learning, it would be BEST for the instructor to

    A. wait until the last session to provide the correct answers
    B. give the correct answers aloud immediately after each quiz
    C. permit trainees to take the questions home with them so that they can look up the answers
    D. wait until the next session to provide the correct answers

19._

20. A supervisor, in the course of evaluating employees, should ALWAYS determine whether

    A. employees realize that their work is under scrutiny
    B. the ratings will be included in permanent records
    C. employees meet standards of performance
    D. his statements on the rating form are similar to those made by the previous supervisor

20._

21. All of the following are legitimate objectives of employee performance reporting systems EXCEPT

    A. serving as a check on personnel policies such as job qualification requirements and placement techniques
    B. determining who is the least efficient worker among a large number of employees
    C. improving employee performance by identifying strong and weak points in individual performance
    D. developing standards of satisfactory performance

21._

22. Studies of existing employee performance evaluation schemes have revealed a common tendency to construct guides in order to measure <u>inferred</u> traits. Of the following, the BEST example of an inferred trait is

    A. appearance   B. loyalty   C. accuracy   D. promptness

22._

23. Which of the following is MOST likely to be a positive influence in promoting common agreement at a staff conference?

    A. A mature, tolerant group of participants
    B. A strong chairman with firm opinions
    C. The normal differences of human personalities
    D. The urge to forcefully support one's views

23._

24. Before holding a problem-solving conference, the conference leader sent to each invitee an announcement on which he listed the names of all invitees. His action in listing the names was

    A. *wise,* mainly because all invitees will know who has been invited, and can, if necessary, plan a proper approach
    B. *unwise,* mainly because certain invitees could form factions prior to the conference
    C. *unwise,* mainly because invitees might come to the conference in a belligerent mood if they had had interpersonal conflicts with other invitees
    D. *wise,* mainly because invitees who are antagonistic to each other could decide not to attend

24._

25. Methods analysis is a detailed study of existing or proposed work methods for the pur-   25.____
pose of improving agency operations. Of the following, it is MOST accurate to say that
this type of study

    A.   can sometimes be made informally by the experienced supervisor who can identify
problems and suggest solutions

    B.   is not suitable for studying the operations of a public agency

    C.   will be successfully accomplished only if an outside organization reviews agency
operations

    D.   usually costs more to complete than is justified by the potential economies to be
realized

———

KEY (CORRECT ANSWERS)

1.	D		11.	D
2.	C		12.	C
3.	B		13.	A
4.	A		14.	C
5.	B		15.	C
6.	C		16.	D
7.	B		17.	A
8.	C		18.	D
9.	B		19.	B
10.	D		20.	C

21.	B
22.	B
23.	A
24.	A
25.	A

———

TEST 2

DIRECTIONS: Each question or incomplete statement is followed by several suggested answers or completions. Select the one that BEST answers the question or completes the statement. *PRINT THE LETTER OF THE CORRECT ANSWER IN THE SPACE AT THE RIGHT.*

1. Present-day managerial practices advocate that adequate hierarchical levels of communication be maintained among all levels of management. Of the following, the BEST way to accomplish this is with   1.___

    A. interdepartmental memoranda only
    B. interdepartmental memoranda only
    C. periodic staff meetings, interdepartmental and interdepartmental memoranda
    D. interdepartmental and interdepartmental memoranda

2. It is generally agreed upon that it is important to have effective communications in the unit so that everyone knows exactly what is expected of him. Of the following, the communications system which can assist in fulfilling this objective BEST is one which consists of   2.___

    A. written policies and procedures for administrative functions and verbal policies and procedures for professional functions
    B. written policies and procedures for professional and administrative functions
    C. verbal policies and·procedures for professional and administrative functions
    D. verbal policies and procedures for professional functions

3. If a department manager wishes to build an effective department, he MOST generally must   3.___

    A. be able to hire and fire as he feels necessary
    B. consider the total aspects of his job, his influence and the effects of his decisions
    C. have access to reasonable amounts of personnel and money with which to build his programs
    D. attend as many professional conferences as possible so that he can keep up-to-date with all the latest advances in the field

4. Of the following, the factor which generally contributes MOST effectively to the performance of the unit is that the supervisor   4.___

    A. personally inspect the work of all employees
    B. fill orders at a faster rate than his subordinates
    C. have an exact knowledge of theory
    D. implement a program of professional development for his staff

5. Administrative policies relate MOST closely to   5.___

    A. control of commodities and personnel
    B. general policies emanating from the central office
    C. fiscal management of the department only
    D. handling and dispensing of funds

6. Part of being a good supervisor is to be able to develop an attitude towards employees   6._____
which will motivate them to do their best on the job. The GOOD supervisor, therefore,
should

    A. take an interest in subordinates, but not develop an all-consuming attitude in this
area
    B. remain in an aloof position when dealing with employees
    C. be as close to subordinates as possible on the job
    D. take a complete interest in all the activities of subordinates, both on and off the job

7. The practice of a supervisor assigning an experienced employee to train new employees   7._____
instead of training them himself, is, GENERALLY, considered

    A. *undesirable*; the more experienced employee will resent being taken away from his
regular job
    B. *desirable*; the supervisor can then devote more time to his regular duties
    C. *undesirable*; the more experienced employee is not working at the proper level to
train new employees
    D. *desirable*; the more experienced employee is probably a better trainer than the
supervisor

8. It is generally agreed that on-the-job training is MOST effective when new employees are   8._____

    A. provided with study manuals, standard operating procedures and other written
materials to be studied for at least two weeks before the employees attempt to do
the job
    B. shown how to do the job in detail, and then instructed to do the work under close
supervision
    C. trained by an experienced worker for at least a week to make certain that the
employees can do the job
    D. given work immediately which is checked at the end of each day

9. Employees sometimes form small informal groups, commonly called cliques. With regard   9._____
to the effect of such groups on processing of the workload, the attitude a supervisor
should take towards these cliques is that of

    A. *acceptance*, since they take the employees' minds off their work without wasting
too much time
    B. *rejection*, since those workers inside the clique tend to do less work than the out-
siders
    C. *acceptance*, since the supervisor is usually included in the clique
    D. *rejection*, since they are usually disliked by higher management

10. Of the following, the BEST statement regarding rules and regulations in a unit is that they   10._____

    A. are "necessary evils" to be tolerated by those at and above the first supervisory
level only
    B. are stated in broad, indefinite terms so as to allow maximum amount of leeway in
complying with them
    C. must be understood by all employees in the unit
    D. are primarily for management's needs since insurance regulations mandate them

11. It is sometimes considered desirable for a supervisor to survey the opinions of his employees before taking action on decisions affecting them. Of the following, the greatest DISADVANTAGE of following this approach is that the employees might

    A. use this opportunity to complain rather than to make constructive suggestions
    B. lose respect for their supervisor whom they feel cannot make his own decisions
    C. regard this as an attempt by the supervisor to get ideas for which he can later claim credit
    D. be resentful if their suggestions are not adopted

11.__

12. Of the following, the MOST important reason for keeping statements of duties of employees up-to-date is to

    A. serve as a basis of information for other governmental jurisdictions
    B. enable the department of personnel to develop job-related examinations
    C. differentiate between levels within the occupational groups
    D. enable each employee to know what his duties are

12.__

13. Of the following, the BEST way to evaluate the progress of a new subordinate is to

    A. compare the output of the new employee from week to week as to quantity and quality
    B. obtain the opinions of the new employee's co-workers
    C. test the new employee periodically to see how much he has learned
    D. hold frequent discussions with the employee focusing on his work

13.__

14. Of the following, a supervisor is LEAST likely to contribute to good morale in the unit if he

    A. encourages employees to increase their knowledge and proficiency in their work on their own time
    B. reprimands subordinates uniformly when infractions are committed
    C. refuses to accept explanations for mistakes regardless of who has made them or how serious they are
    D. compliments subordinates for superior work performance in the presence of their peers

14.__

15. The practice of promoting supervisors from within a given unit only, rather than from within the entire agency, may BEST be described as

    A. *desirable*, because the type of work in each unit generally is substantially different from all other units
    B. *undesirable*, since it will severely reduce the number of eligibles from which to select a supervisor
    C. *desirable*, since it enables each employee to know in advance the precise extent of promotion opportunities in his unit
    D. *undesirable*, because it creates numerous administrative and budgetary difficulties

15.__

16. Of the following, the BEST way for a supervisor to make assignments GENERALLY is to

    A. give the easier assignments to employees with greater seniority
    B. give the difficult assignments to the employees with greater seniority
    C. make assignments according to the ability of each employee
    D. rotate the assignments among the employees

16.__

17. Assume that a supervisor makes a proposal through appropriate channels which would delegate final authority and responsibility to a subordinate employee for a major control function within the agency. According to current management theory, this proposal should be   17.____

   A. *adopted,* since this would enable the supervisor to devote more time to non-routine tasks
   B. *rejected,* since final responsibility for this high-level assignment may not properly be delegated to a subordinate employee
   C. *adopted,* since the assignment of increased responsibility to subordinate employees is a vital part of their development and training
   D. *rejected,* since the morale of the subordinate employees not selected for this assignment would be adversely affected

18. If it becomes necessary for a supervisor to improve the performance of a subordinate to assure the achievement of results according to plans, the BEST course of action, of the following, generally, would be to   18.____

   A. emphasize the subordinate's strengths and try to motivate the employee to improve on those factors
   B. emphasize the subordinate's weak areas of performance and try to bring them up to an acceptable standard
   C. issue a memorandum to all employees warning that if performance does not improve, disciplinary measures will be taken
   D. transfer the subordinate to another section engaged in different work

19. A supervisor who specifies each phase of a job in detail, supervises closely and permits very little discretion in performance of tasks, GENERALLY   19.____

   A. provides motivation for his staff to produce more work
   B. finds that his subordinates make fewer mistakes than those with minimal supervision
   C. finds that his subordinates have little or no incentive to work any harder than necessary
   D. provides superior training opportunities for his employees

20. Assume that you supervise two employees who do not get along well with each other. Their relationship has been continuously deteriorating. You decide to take steps to solve this problem by first determining the reason for their inability to get along well with each other. This course of action is   20.____

   A. *desirable,* because their work is probably adversely affected by their differences
   B. *undesirable,* because your inquiries might be is-interpreted by the employees and cause resentment
   C. *desirable,* because you could then learn who is at fault for causing the deteriorating relationship and take appropriate disciplinary measures
   D. *undesirable,* because it is best to let them work their differences out between themselves

21. Routine procedures that have worked well in the past should be reviewed periodically by a supervisor MAINLY because

    A. they may have become outdated or in need of revision
    B. employees may dislike the procedures even though they have proven successful in the past
    C. these reviews are the main part of a supervisor's job
    D. this practice serves to give the supervisor an idea of how productive his subordinates are

21._

22. Assume that an employee tells his supervisor about a grievance he has against a co-worker. The supervisor assures the employee that he will immediately take action to eliminate the grievance. The supervisor's attitude should be considered

    A. *correct*; because a good supervisor is one who can come to a quick decision
    B. *incorrect*; because the supervisor should have told the employee that he will investigate the grievance and then determine a future course of action
    C. *correct*; because the employee's morale will be higher, resulting in greater productivity
    D. *incorrect*; because the supervisor should remain uninvolved and let the employees settle grievances between themselves

22._

23. If an employee's work output is low and of poor quality due to faulty work habits, the MOST constructive of the following ways for a supervisor to correct this situation, GENERALLY, is to

    A. discipline the employee
    B. transfer the employee to another unit
    C. provide additional training
    D. check the employee's work continuously

23._

24. Assume that it becomes necessary for a supervisor to ask his staff to work overtime. Which one of the following techniques is MOST likely to win their willing cooperation to do this?

    A. Point out that this is part of their job specification entitled "performs related work"
    B. Explain the reason it is necessary for the employees to work overtime
    C. Promise the employees special consideration regarding future leave matters
    D. Warn that if the employees do not work overtime, they will face possible disciplinary action

24._

25. If an employee's work performance has recently fallen below established minimum standards for quality and quantity, the threat of demotion or other disciplinary measures as an attempt to improve this employee's performance would probably be the MOST acceptable and effective course of action

    A. *only* after other more constructive measures have failed
    B. *if* applied uniformly to all employees as soon as performance falls below standard
    C. *only* if the employee understands that the threat will not actually be carried out
    D. *if* the employee is promised that, as soon as his work performance improves, he will be reinstated to his previous status

25._

KEY (CORRECT ANSWERS)

1.	C		11.	D
2.	B		12.	D
3.	B		13.	A
4.	D		14.	C
5.	A		15.	B
6.	A		16.	C
7.	B		17.	B
8.	B		18.	B
9.	A		19.	C
10.	C		20.	A

21. A
22. B
23. C
24. B
25. A

————

TEST 3

DIRECTIONS: Each question or incomplete statement is followed by several suggested answers or completions. Select the one that BEST answers the question or completes the statement. *PRINT THE LETTER OF THE CORRECT ANSWER IN THE SPACE AT THE RIGHT.*

1.   If, as a supervisor, it becomes necessary for you to assign an employee to supervise your unit during your vacation, it would generally be BEST to select the employee who

    A.   is the best technician on the staff
    B.   can get the work out smoothly, without friction
    C.   has the most seniority
    D.   is the most popular with the group

1.__

2.   Assume that, as a supervisor, your own work has accumulated to the point where you decide that it is desirable for you to delegate in order to meet your deadlines. The one of the following tasks which would be MOST appropriate to delegate to a subordinate is

    A.   checking the work of the employees for accuracy
    B.   attending a staff conference at which implementation of a new departmental policy will be discussed
    C.   preparing a final report including a recommendation on purchase of expensive new laboratory equipment
    D.   preparing final budget estimates for next year's budget

2.__

3.   Of the following actions, the one LEAST appropriate for you to take during an *initial* interview with a new employee is to

    A.   find out about the experience and education of the new employee
    B.   attempt to determine for what job in your unit the employee would best be suited
    C.   tell the employee about his duties and responsibilities
    D.   ascertain whether the employee will make good promotion material

3.__

4.   If it becomes necessary to reprimand a subordinate employee, the BEST of the following ways to do this is to

    A.   ask the employee to stay after working hours and then reprimand him
    B.   reprimand the employee immediately after the infraction has been committed
    C.   take the employee aside and speak to him privately during regular working hours
    D.   write a short memo to the employee warning that strict adherence to departmental policy and procedures is required of all employees

4.__

5.   If you, as a supervisor, believe that one of your subordinate employees has a serious problem, such as alcoholism or an emotional disturbance, which is adversely affecting his work, the BEST way to handle this situation *initially* would be to

    A.   urge him to seek proper professional help before he is dismissed from his job
    B.   ignore it and let the employee work out the problem himself
    C.   suggest that the employee take an extended leave of absence until he can again function effectively
    D.   frankly tell the employee that unless his work improves, you will take disciplinary measures against him

5.__

6. Of the following, the BEST way to develop a subordinate's potential is to　　　　6._____

    A. give him a fair chance to learn by doing
    B. assign him more than his share of work
    C. criticize only his work
    D. urge him to do his work rapidly

7. During a survey, an employee from another agency asks you to assist him on a job which　　7._____
would require a full day of your time. Of the following, the BEST immediate action for you
to take is to

    A. refuse to assist him
    B. ask for compensation before doing it
    C. assist him promptly
    D. notify his department head

8. Of the following, the BEST way to handle an overly talkative subordinate is to　　　8._____

    A. have your superior talk to him about it
    B. have a subordinate talk to him about it
    C. talk to him about it in a group conference
    D. talk to him about it in private

9. While you are making a survey, a citizen questions you about the work you are doing. Of　　9._____
the following, the BEST thing to do is to

    A. answer the questions tactfully
    B. refuse to answer any questions
    C. advise him to write a letter to the main office
    D. answer the questions in double-talk

10. Respect for a supervisor is MOST likely to increase if he is　　　　　　10._____

    A. morose   B. sporadic   C. vindictive   D. zealous

11. A subordinate who continuously bypasses his immediate supervisor for technical infor-　　11._____
mation should be

    A. reprimanded by his immediate supervisor
    B. ignored by his immediate supervisor
    C. given more difficult work to do
    D. given less difficult work to do

12. Complicated instructions should NOT be written　　　　　　　　12._____

    A. accurately   B. lucidly   C. factually   D. verbosely

13. Of the following, the MOST important reason for checking a report is to　　13._____

    A. check accuracy   B. eliminate unnecessary sections
    C. catch mistakes   D. check for delineation

14. Two subordinates under your supervision dislike each other to the extent that production   14.___
is cut down. Your BEST action as a supervisor is to

    A. ignore the matter and hope for the best
    B. transfer the more aggressive man
    C. cut down on the work load
    D. talk to them together about the matter

15. One of the following characteristics which a supervisor should NOT display while explain-   15.___
ing a job to a subordinate is

    A. enthusiasm   B. confidence
    C. apathy   D. determination

16. Of the following, for BEST production of work, it should be assigned according to a per-   16.___
son's

    A. attitude toward the work   B. ability to do the work
    C. salary   D. seniority

17. You receive an anonymous written complaint from a citizen about a subordinate who   17.___
used abusive language. Of the following, your BEST course of action is to

    A. ignore the letter
    B. report it to your supervisor
    C. discuss the complaint with the subordinate privately
    D. keep the subordinate in the office

18. A supervisor should recognize that the way to get the BEST results from his instructions   18.___
and assignments to the staff is to use

    A. a suggestive approach after he has decided exactly what is to be done and how
    B. the willing and cooperative staff members and avoid the hard-to-handle people
    C. care to select the persons most capable of carrying out the assignments
    D. an authoritative, non-nonsense tone when issuing instructions or giving assign-
       ments

19. As the supervisor of a unit, you find that you are spending too much of your time on rou-   19.___
tine tasks and not enough on coordinating the work of the staff or preparing necessary
reports. Of the following, it would be MOST advisable for you to

    A. discard a great portion of the routine jobs done in the unit
    B. give some of the routine jobs to other members of the staff
    C. postpone the routine jobs and concentrate on coordinating the work of the staff
    D. delegate the job of coordinating the work to the most capable member of the staff

20. At times a supervisor may be called upon to train new employees. Suppose that you are   20.___
giving such training in several sessions to be held on different days. During the first session, a trainee interrupts everal times to ask questions at key points in your discussion.
Of the following, the BEST way to handle this trainee is to

    A. advise him to pay closer attention so he can avoid asking too many questions
    B. tell him to listen without interrupting and he'll hear his questions answered

C. answer his questions to show him that you know your field, but make a mental note that this trainee is a troublemaker
D. answer each question fully and make certain he understands the answers

21. Employee errors can be reduced to a minimum by effective supervision and by training. Which of the following approaches used by a supervisor would usually be MOST effective in handling an employee who has made an avoidable and serious error for the first time?   21.____

A. Tell the worker how other employees avoid making errors
B. Analyze with the employee the situation leading to the error and then take whatever administrative or training steps are needed to avoid such errors
C. Use this error as the basis for a staff meeting at which the employee's error is disclosed and discussed in an effort to improve the performance
D. Urge the employee to modify his behavior in light of his mistake

22. Suppose that a particular staff member, formerly one of your most regular workers, has recently fallen into the habit of arriving a bit late to work several times a week. You feel that such a habit can grow consistently worse and spread to other staff members unless it is checked. Of the following, the BEST action for you to take, as the supervisor in charge of the unit, is to   22.____

A. go immediately to your own supervisor, present the facts, and have this employee disciplined
B. speak privately to this tardy employee, advise him of the need to improve his punctuality, and inform him that he'll be disciplined if late again
C. talk to the co-worker with whom this late employee is most friendly and ask the friend to help him solve his tardiness problem
D. speak privately with this employee, and try to discover and deal with the reasons for the latenesses

23. A supervisor may make an assignment in the form of a request, a command, or a call for volunteers. It is LEAST desirable to make an assignment in the form of a request when   23.____

A. an employee does not like the particular kind of assignment to be given
B. the assignment requires working past the regular closing day
C. an emergency has come up
D. the assignment is not particularly pleasant for anybody

24. When you give a certain task that you normally perform yourself to one of your employees, it is MOST important that you   24.____

A. lead the employee to believe that he has been chosen above others to perform this job
B. describe the job as important even though it is merely a routine task
C. explain the job that needs to be accomplished, but always let the employee decide how to do it
D. tell the employee why you are delegating the job to him and explain exactly what he is to do

25. A supervisor when instructing new trainees in the routine of his unit should include a   25._____
description of the department's overall objectives and programs in order to

    A. insure that individual work assignments will be completed satisfactorily
    B. create a favorable impression of his supervisory capabilities
    C. develop a better understanding of the purposes behind work assignments
    D. produce an immediate feeling of group cooperation

KEY (CORRECT ANSWERS)

1.	B	11.	A
2.	A	12.	D
3.	D	13.	C
4.	C	14.	D
5.	A	15.	C
6.	A	16.	B
7.	A	17.	C
8.	D	18.	C
9.	A	19.	B
10.	D	20.	D

21.	B
22.	D
23.	A
24.	D
25.	C

TEST 4

DIRECTIONS: Each question or incomplete statement is followed by several suggested answers or completions. Select the one that BEST answers the question or completes the statement. *PRINT THE LETTER OF THE CORRECT ANSWER IN THE SPACE AT THE RIGHT.*

1. An integral part of every supervisor's job is getting his ideas or instructions across to his staff. The extent of his success, if he has a reasonably competent staff, is PRIMARILY dependent on the
   1.____

   A. interest of the employee
   B. intelligence of the employee
   C. reasoning behind the ideas or instructions
   D. presentation of the ideas or instructions

2. Generally, what is the FIRST action the supervisor should take when an employee approaches him with a complaint?
   2.____

   A. Review the employee's recent performance with him
   B. Use the complaint as a basis to discuss improvement of procedures
   C. Find out from the employee the details of the complaint
   D. Advise the employee to take his complaint to the head of the department

3. Of the following, which is NOT usually considered one of the purposes of counseling an employee after an evaluation of his performance?
   3.____

   A. Explaining the performance standards used by the supervisor
   B. Discussing necessary disciplinary action to be taken
   C. Emphasizing the employee's strengths and weaknesses
   D. Planning better utilization of the employee's strengths

4. Assume that a supervisor, when reviewing a decision reached by one of his subordinates, finds the decision incorrect. Under these circumstances, it would be MOST desirable for the supervisor to
   4.____

   A. correct the decision and inform the subordinate of this at a staff meeting
   B. correct the decision and suggest a more detailed analysis in the future
   C. help the employee find the reason for the correct decision
   D. refrain from assigning this type of a problem to the employee

5. An IMPORTANT characteristic of a good supervisor is his ability to
   5.____

   A. be a stern disciplinarian
   B. put off the settling of grievances
   C. solve problems   D.   find fault in individuals

6. A new supervisor will BEST obtain the respect of the men assigned to him if he
   6.____

   A. makes decisions rapidly and sticks to them, regardless of whether they are right or wrong
   B. makes decisions rapidly and then changes them just as rapidly if the decisions are wrong
   C. does not make any decisions unless he is absolutely sure that they are right
   D. makes his decisions after considering carefully all available information

7. A newly appointed worker is operating at a level of performance below that of the other   7._
   employees. In this situation, a supervisor should FIRST

   A. lower the acceptable standard for the new man
   B. find out why the new man cannot do as well as the others
   C. advise the new worker he will be dropped from the payroll at the end of the proba-
      tionary period
   D. assign another new worker to assist the first man

8. Assume that you have to instruct a new man on a specific departmental operation. The   8._
   new man seems unsure of what you have said. Of the following, the BEST way for you to
   determine whether the man has understood you is to

   A. have the man explain the operation to you in his own words
   B. repeat your explanation to him slowly
   C. repeat your explanation to him, using simpler wording
   D. emphasize the important parts of the operation to him

9. A supervisor realizes that he has taken an instanteous dislike to a new worker assigned   9._
   to him. The BEST course of action for the supervisor to take in this case is to

   A. be especially observant of the new worker's actions
   B. request that the new worker be reassigned
   C. make a special effort to be fair to the new worker
   D. ask to be transferred himself

10. A supervisor gives detailed instructions to his men as to how a certain type of job is to be   10._
    done. One ADVANTAGE of this practice is that this will

    A. result in a more flexible operation
    B. standardize operations
    C. encourage new men to learn
    D. encourage initiative in the men

11. Of the following, the one that would MOST likely be the result of poor planning is: 11._

    A. Omissions are discovered after the work is completed.
    B. During the course of normal inspection, a meter is found to be inaccessible.
    C. An inspector completes his assignments for that day ahead of schedule.
    D. A problem arises during an inspection and prevents an inspector from completing
       his day's assignments.

12. Of the following, the BEST way for a supervisor to maintain good employee morale is for   12._
    the supervisor to

    A. avoid correcting the employee when he makes mistakes
    B. continually praise the employee's work even when it is of average quality
    C. show that he is willing to assist in solving the employee's problems
    D. accept the employee's excuses for failure even though the excuses are not valid

13. A supervisor takes time to explain to his men why a departmental order has been issued. 13._____
This practice is

    A. *good,* mainly because without this explanation the men will not be able to carry out the order
    B. *bad,* mainly because time will be wasted for no useful purpose
    C. *good,* because understanding the reasons behind an order will lead to more effective carrying out of the order
    D. *bad,* because men will then question every order that they receive

14. Of the following, the MOST important responsibility of a supervisor in charge of a section 14._____
is to

    A. establish close personal relationships with each of his subordinates in the section
    B. insure that each subordinate in the section knows the full range of his duties and responsibilities
    C. maintain friendly relations with his immediate supervisor
    D. protect his subordinates from criticism from any source

15. The BEST way to get a good work output from employees is to 15._____

    A. hold over them the threat of disciplinary action or removal
    B. maintain a steady, unrelenting pressure on them
    C. show them that you can do anything they can do faster and better
    D. win their respect and liking, so they want to work for you

---

KEY (CORRECT ANSWERS)

1.	A	6.	D
2.	C	7.	B
3.	A	8.	A
4.	C	9.	C
5.	C	10.	B

11.	A
12.	C
13.	C
14.	B
15.	D

SUPERVISION, ADMINISTRATION, MANAGEMENT AND ORGANIZATION

EXAMINATION SECTION
TEST 1

DIRECTIONS: Each question or incomplete statement is followed by several suggested answers or completions. Select the one that BEST answers the question or completes the statement. *PRINT THE LETTER OF THE CORRECT ANSWER IN THE SPACE AT THE RIGHT.*

1. A supervisor scheduled an interview with a subordinate in order to discuss his unsatisfactory performance during the previous several weeks. The subordinate's work contained an excessive number of careless errors.
   After the interview, the supervisor, reviewing his own approach for self-examination, listed three techniques he had used in the interview, as follows:
   I. Specifically pointed out to the subordinate where he had failed to meet the standards expected.
   II. Shared the blame for certain management errors that had irritated the subordinate.
   III. Agreed with the subordinate on specific targets to be met during the period ahead.
   Of the following statements the one that is MOST acceptable concerning the above 3 techniques is that

   A. all 3 techniques are correct
   B. techniques I and II are correct; III is not correct
   C. techniques II and III are correct; I is not correct
   D. techniques I and III are correct; II is not correct

1.____

2. Assume that the performance of an employee is not satisfactory. Of the following, the MOST effective way for a supervisor to attempt to improve the performance of the employee is to meet with him *and* to

   A. order him to change his behavior
   B. indicate the actions that are unsatisfactory and the penalties for them
   C. show him alternate ways of behaving and a method for him to evaluate his attempts at change
   D. suggest that he use the behavior of the supervisor as a model of acceptable conduct

2.____

3. Training employees to be productive workers is based on four fundamental principles:
   I. Demonstrate how the job should be done by telling and showing the correct operations step-by-step
   II. Allow the employee to get some of the feel of the job by allowing him to try it a bit
   III. Put him on the job while continuing to check his performance
   IV. Let him know why the job is important and why it must be done right.
   The MOST logical order for these training steps is:

   A. I, III, II, IV   B. I, IV, II, III
   C. II, I, III, IV   D. IV, I, II, III

3.____

4. Sometimes a supervisor is faced with the need to train under-educated new employees. The following five statements relate to training such employees.

    I.   Make the training general rather than specific
    II. Rely upon demonstrations and illustrations whenever possible
    III. Overtrain rather than undertrain by erring on the side of imparting a little more skill than is absolutely necessary
    IV. Provide lots of follow-up on the job
    V. Reassure and recognize frequently in order to increase self-confidence

Which of the following choices lists *all* the above statements that are generally CORRECT?

    A. II, II, and IV
    B. II, III, IV, and V
    C. I, II, and V
    D. I, II, IV, and V

4.__

5. One of the ways in which some supervisors train subordinates is to discuss the subordinate's weaknesses with them. Experts who have explored the actual feelings and reactions of subordinates in such situations have come to the conclusion that such interviews *usually*

    A. are seen by subordinates as a threat to their self-esteem
    B. give subordinates a feeling of importance which leads to better learning
    C. convince subordinates to accept the opinion of the supervisor
    D. result in the development of better supervision

5.__

6. The one of the following which BEST describes the rate at which a trainee learns departmental procedures is that he *probably* will learn

    A. at the same rate throughout if the material to be learned is complex
    B. slowly in the beginning and then learning will accelerate steadily
    C. quickly for a while, than slow down temporarily
    D. at the same rate if the material to be learned is lengthy

6.__

7. Which of the following statements concerning the delegation of work to subordinate employees is *generally* CORRECT?

    A. A supervisor's personal attitude toward delegation has a minimal effect on his skill in delegating.
    B. A willingness to let subordinates make mistakes has a place in work delegation.
    C. The element of trust has little impact on the effectiveness of work delegation.
    D. The establishment of controls does not enhance the process of delegation.

7.__

8. Assume that you are the chairman of a group that has been formed to discuss and solve a particular problem. After a half-hour of discussion, you feel that the group is wandering off the point and is no longer discussing the problem.
In this situation, it would be BEST for you to

    A. wait to see whether the group will get back on the track by itself
    B. ask the group to stop and to try a different approach
    C. ask the group to stop, decide where they are going, and then to decide how to continue
    D. ask the group to stop, decide where they are going, and then to continue in a different direction

8.__

9. One method of group decision-making is the use of committees. Following are four state-   9.____
ments concerning committees.
    I. Considering the value of each individual member's time, committees are costly.
    II. One result of committee decisions is that no one may be held responsible for the decision.
    III. Committees will make decisions more promptly then individuals.
    IV. Committee decisions tend to be balanced and to take different viewpoints into account.

Which of the following choices lists *all* of the above statements that are generally COR-
RECT?

   A. I and II   B. II and III   C. I, II, IV   D. II, III, IV

10. Assume that an employee bypasses his supervisor and comes directly to you, the supe-   10.____
rior officer, to ask for a short leave of absence because of a pressing personal problem.
The employee did not first consult with his immediate supervisor because he believes
that his supervisor is unfavorably biased against him.
Of the following, the MOST desirable way for you to handle this situation is to

   A. instruct the employee that it is not appropriate for him to go over the head of his supervisor regardless of their personal relationship
   B. listen to a brief description of his problem and then tactfully suggest that he take the matter up with his supervisor before coming to you
   C. request that both the employee and his supervisor meet jointly with you in order to discuss the employee's problem and to get at the reasons behind their apparent difficulty
   D. listen carefully to the employee's problem and then, without committing yourself one way or the other, promise to discuss it with his supervisor

11. Which of the following statements concerning the motivation of subordinates is generally   11.____
INCORRECT? The

   A. authoritarian approach as the method of supervision is likely to result in the setting of minimal performance standards for themselves by subordinates
   B. encouragement of competition among subordinates may lead to deterioration of teamwork
   C. granting of benefits by a supervisor to subordinates in order to gain their gratitide will result in maximum output by the subordinates
   D. opportunity to achieve job satisfaction has an important effect on motivating subor-dinates

12. Of the following, the MOST serious disadvantage of having a supervisor evaluate subor-   12.____
dinates on the basis of measurable performance goals that are set jointly by the supervisor and the subordinates is that this results-oriented appraisal method

   A. focuses on past performance rather than plans for the future
   B. fails to provide sufficient feedback to help subordinates learn where they stand
   C. encourages the subordinates to conceal poor performance and set low goals
   D. changes the primary task of the supervisor from helping subordinates improve to criticizing their performance

13. A supervisor can BEST provide on-the-job satisfaction for his subordinates by   13.__

    A. providing rewards for good performance
    B. allowing them to decide when to do the assigned work
    C. motivating them to perform according to accepted procedures
    D. providing challenging work that achieves departmental objectives

14. Which of the following factors *generally* contributes MOST to job satisfaction among   14.__
supervisory employees?

    A. Autonomy and independence on the job
    B. Job security
    C. Pleasant physical working conditions
    D. Adequate economic rewards

15. Large bureaucracies typically exhibit certain characteristics.   15.__
Of the following, it would be CORRECT to state that such bureaucracies *generally*

    A. tend to oversimplify communications
    B. pay undue attention to informal organizations
    C. develop an attitude of "group-think" and conformity
    D. emphasize personal growth among employees

16. When positive methods fail to achieve conformity with accepted standards of conduct or   16.__
performance, a negative type of action, punitive in nature, usually must follow.
The one of the following that is *usually* considered LEAST important for the success of
such punishment or negative discipline is that it be

    A. certain   B. swift   C. severe   D. consistent

17. Assume that you are a supervisor. Philip Smith, who is under your supervision, informs   17.__
you that James Jones, who is also your subordinate, has been creating antagonism and
friction within the unit because of his unnecessarily gruff manner in dealing with his co-
workers. Smith's remarks confirm your own observations of Jones' behavior and its
effects. In handling this situation, the one of the following procedures which will *probably*
be MOST effective is to

    A. ask Smith to act as an informal counselor to Jones and report the results to you
    B. counsel the other employees in your unit on methods of changing attitudes of peo-
ple
    C. interview Jones and help him to understand this problem
    D. order Jones to carry out his responsibilities with greater consideration for the feel-
ings of his co-workers

18. The PRINCIPLE relating to the number of subordinates who can be supervised effec-   18.__
tively by one supervisor is *commonly* known as

    A. span of control   B. delegation of authority
    C. optimum personnel assignment   D. organizational factor

19. Ascertaining and improving the level of morale in a public agency is one of the responsi- 19._____
bilities of a conscientious supervisor.
The one of the following aspects of subordinates' behavior which is NOT an indication
of low morale is

    A. lower-level employees participating in organizational decision-making
    B. careless treatment of equipment
    C. general deterioration of personal appearance
    D. formation of cliques

20. Employees may resist changes in agency operations even though such changes are 20._____
often necessary. If you, as a supervisor, are attempting to introduce a necessary change,
you should *first* fully explain the reasons for it to your staff. Your NEXT step should be to

    A. set specific goals and outline programs for all employees
    B. invite employee participation in effectuating the change by asking for suggestions
       to accomplish it
    C. discuss the need for improved work performance by city employees
    D. point out the penalties for non-cooperation without singling out any employee by
       name

21. A supervisor should *normally* avoid giving orders in an offhand or casual manner 21._____
MAINLY because his subordinates

    A. are like mot people and may resent being treated lightly
    B. may attach little importance to these orders
    C. may work best if given the choice of work methods
    D. are unlikely to need instructions in most matters

22. Assume that, as a supervisor, you have just praised a subordinate. While he expresses 22._____
satisfaction at your praise, he complains that it does not help him get promoted even
though he is on a promotion eligible list, since there is no current vacancy.
In these circumstances, it would be BEST for you to

    A. minimize the importance of advancement and emphasize the satisfaction in the
       work itself
    B. follow up by pointing out some errors he has committed in the past
    C. admit that the situation exists, and express the hope that it will improve
    D. tell him that, until quite recently, advancement was even slower

23. Departmental policies are usually broad rules or guides for action. It is important for a 23._____
supervisor to understand his role with respect to policy implementation.
Of the following, the MOST accurate description of this role is that a supervisor should

    A. be apologetic toward his subordinates when applying unpopular policies to them
    B. act within policy limits, although he can attempt to influence policy change by mak-
       ing his thoughts and observations known to his superior
    C. arrange his activities so that he is able to deal simultaneously with situations that
       involve several policy matters
    D. refrain as much as possible from exercising permissible discretion in applying pol-
       icy to matters under his control

24. A supervisor should be aware that *most* subordinates will ask questions at meetings or   24.__
group discussions *in order to*

    A. stimulate other employees to express their opinions
    B. discover how they may be affected by the subjects under discussion
    C. display their knowledge of the topics under discussion
    D. consume time in order to avoid returning to their normal tasks

25. Don't assign responsibilities with conflicting objectives to the same work group. For   25.__
example, to require a unit to monitor the quality of its own work is a bad practice. This
practice is *most likely* to be bad because

    A. the chain of command will be unnecessarily lengthened
    B. it is difficult to portray mixed duties accurately on an organization chart
    C. employees may act in collusion to cover up poor work
    D. the supervisor may delegate responsibilities which he should retain

---

KEY (CORRECT ANSWERS)

1.	A		11.	C
2.	C		12.	C
3.	D		13.	D
4.	B		14.	A
5.	A		15.	C
6.	C		16.	C
7.	B		17.	C
8.	C		18.	A
9.	C		19.	A
10.	D		20.	B

21.	B
22.	C
23.	B
24.	B
25.	C

TEST 2

DIRECTIONS: Each question or incomplete statement is followed by several suggested answers or completions. Select the one that BEST answers the question or completes the statement. *PRINT THE LETTER OF THE CORRECT ANSWER IN THE SPACE AT THE RIGHT.*

1. Some supervisors use an approach in which each phase of the job is explained in broad terms supervision is general, and employees are allowed broad discretion in performing their job duties.
    Such a supervisory approach *usually* affects employee motivation by

    A. improving morale and providing an incentive to work harder
    B. providing little or no incentive to work harder than the minimum required
    C. creating extra pressure, usually resulting in decreased performance
    D. reducing incentive to work and causing employees to feel neglected, particularly in performing complex tasks

1.____

2. An employee complains to a superior officer that he has been treated unfairly by his supervisor, stating that other employees have been given less work to do and shown other forms of favoritism.
    Of the following, the BEST thing for the superior officer to do FIRST in order to handle this problem is to

    A. try to discover whether the subordinate has a valid complaint or if something else is the real problem
    B. ask other employees whether they feel that their treatment is consistent and fair
    C. ask his supervisor to explain the charges
    D. see that the number of cases assigned to this employee is reduced

2.____

3. Of the following, the MOST important condition needed to help a group of people to work well together and get the job done is

    A. higher salaries and a better working environment
    B. enough free time to relieve the tension
    C. good communication among everyone involved in the job
    D. assurance that everyone likes the work

3.____

4. A supervisor realizes that a subordinate has called in sick for three Mondays out of the past four. These absences have interfered with staff performance and have been part of the cause of the unit's "behind schedule" condition.
    In order to correct this situation, it would be BEST for the supervisor to

    A. order the subordinate to explain his abuse of sick leave
    B. discuss with the subordinate the penalties for abusing sick leave
    C. discuss the matter with his own supervisor
    D. ask the subordinate in private whether he has a problem about coming to work

4.____

5. Of the following, the MOST effective way for a supervisor to minimize undesirable rumors about new policies in the units under his supervision is to

    A. bypass the supervisor and communicate directly with the individual members of the units
    B. supply immediate and accurate information to everyone who is supposed to be informed

5.____

    C.   play down the importance of the rumors
    D.   issue all communications in written form

6. Which of the following is an *indication* that a superior officer is delegating authority   6.__
PROPERLY?

    A.   The superior officer closely checks the work of experienced subordinates at all
          stages in order to maintain standards.
    B.   The superior officer gives overlapping assignments to insure that work is com-
          pleted on time.
    C.   The work of his subordinates can proceed and be completed during the superior
          officer's absence.
    D.   The work of each supervisor is reviewed by him more than once in order to insure
          quality.

7. Of the following supervisory practices, the one which is *MOST LIKELY* to foster   7.__
employee morale is for the supervisor to

    A.   take an active interest in subordinates' personal lives
    B.   ignore mistakes
    C.   give praise when justified
    D.   permit rules to go unenforced occasionally

8. As the supervisor who is responsible for the implementation of a new paperwork proce-   8.__
dure, you note that the workers often do not follow the stipulated procedure.
Before taking action, it would be ADVISABLE to realize that

    A.   unconscious behavior, such as failure to adapt to change, is largely uncontrollable
    B.   new procedures sometimes have to be modified and adapted after being tried out
    C.   threats of disciplinary action will encourage approval of change
    D.   procedures that fail should be abandoned and replaced

9. The one of the following which is *generally* considered to be the MOST significant criti-   9.__
cism of the modern practice of effective human relations in management of large organizations is that human relations

    A.   weakens management authority over employees
    B.   gives employees control of operations
    C.   can be used to manipulate and control employees
    D.   weakens unions

10. Of the following, the MOST important reason why the supervisor should promote *good*   10.__
supervisor-subordinate relations is to encourage his staff to

    A.   feel important   B.   be more receptive to control
    C.   be happy in their work   D.   meet production performance levels

11. A superior officer decides to assign a special report directly to an employee, bypassing   11.__
his supervisor.
In general, this practice is

    A.   *advisable,* chiefly because it broadens the superior officer's span of authority
    B.   *inadvisable,* chiefly because it undermines the authority of the supervisor in the
          eyes of his subordinates

     C.   *advisable,* chiefly because it reduces the number of details the supervisor must know

     D.   *inadvisable,* chiefly because it gives too much work to the employee

12.   Many supervisors make it a practice to solicit suggestions from their subordinates and to   12.____
encourage their participation in decision making.
The success of this type of supervision *usually* depends MOST directly upon the

     A.   quality of leadership provided by the supervisor
     B.   number of the supervisor's immediate subordinates
     C.   availability of opportunities for employee advancement
     D.   degree to which work assignments cause problems

13.   Small informal groups or "cliques" often appear in a work setting.   13.____
The one of the following which is generally an *advantage* of such groups, from an
administrative point of view, is that they

     A.   are not influenced by the administrative set-up of the office
     B.   encourage socializing after working hours
     C.   develop leadership roles among the office staff
     D.   provide a "steam valve" for release of tension and fatigue

14.   Assume that you are a superior officer in charge of several supervisors, who, in turn, are   14.____
in charge of a number of employees. The employees who are supervised by Jones (a
supervisor) come as a group to you and indicate several resons why Jones is
incompetent and "has to go."
Of the following, your *best* course of action to take FIRST is to

     A.   direct the employees to see Jones about the matter
     B.   suggest to the employees that they should attempt to work with Jones until he can
be transferred
     C.   discuss the possibility of terminating Jones with *your* superior
     D.   ask Jones about the comments of the employees after they depart

15.   Of the following, the MAIN effect which the delegation of authority can have on the effi-   15.____
ciency of an organization is to

     A.   reduce the risk of decision-making errors
     B.   produce uniformity of policy and action
     C.   facilitate speedier decisions and actions
     D.   enable closer control of operations

16.   Of the following, the main DISADVANTAGE of temporarily transferring a newly appointed   16.____
worker to another unit because of an unexpected vacancy is that the temporary nature of
his assignment will, *most likely,*

     A.   undermine his incentive to orient himself to his new job
     B.   interfere with his opportunities for future advancement
     C.   result in friction between himself and his new co-workers
     D.   place his new supervisor in a difficult and awkward position

17. Assume that you, as a supervisor, have decided to raise the quality of work produced by   17.___
your subordinates.
The BEST of the following procedures for you to follow is to

   A. develop mathematically precise standards
   B. appoint a committee of subordinates to set firm and exacting guidelines, including
      penalties for deviations
   C. modify standards developed by supervisors in other organizations
   D. provide consistent evaluation of subordinates' work, furnishing training whenever
      advisable

18. Assume that a supervisor under your supervision strongly objects whenever changes are   18.___
proposed which would improve the efficiency of his unit.
Of the following, the MOST desirable way for you to *change* his attitude is to

   A. involve him in the planning and formulation of changes
   B. promise to recommend him for a more challenging assignment if he accepts
      changes
   C. threaten to have him transferred to another unit if he does not accept changes
   D. ask him to go along with the changes on a tentative, trial basis

19. Work goals may be defined in terms of units produced or in terms of standards of perfor-   19.___
mance.
Which of the following statements concerning work goals is CORRECT?

   A. Workers who have a share in establishing goals tend to set a fairly high standard
      for themselves, but fail to work toward it.
   B. Workers tend to produce according to what they believe are the goals actually
      expected of them.
   C. Since workers usually produce less than the established goals, management
      should set goals higher than necessary.
   D. The individual differences of workers can be minimized by using strict goals and
      invariable procedures.

20. Of the following, the type of employee who would respond BEST to verbal instructions   20.___
given in the form of a suggestion or wish is the

   A. experienced worker who is eager to please
   B. sensitive and emotional worker
   C. hostile worker who is somewhat lazy
   D. slow and methodical worker

21. As a supervisor, you note that the output of an experienced staff member has dropped   21.___
dramatically during the last two months. In addition, his error rate is significantly above
that of other staff members. When you ask the employee the reason for his poor performance, he says, "Well, it's rather personal and I would rather not talk about it if you don't
mind."
At this point, which of the following would be the BEST reply?

   A. Tell him that you will give him two weeks to improve or you will discuss the matter
      with your own supervisor
   B. Insist that he tell you the reason for his poor work and assure him that anything
      personal will be kept confidential

    C.   Say that you don't want to interfere, but, at the same time, his work has deterio-
rated, and that you're concerned about it

    D.   Explain in a friendly manner that you are going to place a warning letter in his per-
sonnel folder that states he has one month in which to improve

22.   Research studies have shown that employees who are strongly interested in achievment   22.____
and advancement on the job *usually* want assignments where the chance of success is

    A.   *low,* and desire frequent supervisory evaluation of their performance
    B.   *high,* and desire general supervisory evaluation of their performance
    C.   *high,* and desire infrequent supervisory evaluation of their performance
    D.   *moderate,* and desire specific supervisory evaluation of their performance

23.   Of the following, a function of the supervisor that concerns itself with the process of   23.____
determining a course of action from alternatives is *usually* referred to as

    A.   decentralization   B.   planning
    C.   controlling   D.   input

24.   Favorable working conditions are an important variable in producing an effective work   24.____
unit.
Which of the following would be LEAST conducive in providing a favorable work situation?

    A.   Applying a job enrichment program to a routine clerical position
    B.   Setting practical goals for the work unit which are consistent with the overall objec-
tive of the agency
    C.   Assigning individuals to positions which require a higher level of educational
achievement than that which they possess
    D.   Establishing a communications system which distributes information and provides
feedback to all organizational levels

25.   Every supervisor within an organization should know to whom he reports and who   25.____
reports to him.
Within the organization this will *most likely* insure

    A.   unity of command
    B.   confidentiality of sensitive issues
    C.   excellent morale
    D.   the elimination of the grapevine

KEY (CORRECT ANSWERS)

1.	A		11.	B
2.	A		12.	A
3.	C		13.	D
4.	D		14.	D
5.	B		15.	C
6.	C		16.	A
7.	C		17.	D
8.	B		18.	A
9.	C		19.	B
10.	D		20.	A

21.	C
22.	D
23.	B
24.	C
25.	A

TEST 3

DIRECTIONS: Each question or incomplete statement is followed by several suggested answers or completions. Select the one that BEST answers the question or completes the statement. *PRINT THE LETTER OF THE CORRECT ANSWER IN THE SPACE AT THE RIGHT.*

1. In trying to improve the motivation of his subordinates, a supervisor can achieve the BEST results by taking action based upon the assumption that *most* employees

    A. have an inherent dislike of work
    B. wish to be closely directed
    C. are more interested in security than in assuming responsibility
    D. will exercise self-direction without coercion

1.____

2. Supervisors in public departments have many functions.
Of the following, the function which is LEAST appropriate for a supervisor is to

    A. serve as a deputy for the administrator within his own unit
    B. determine needs within his unit and plan programs to meet these needs
    C. supervise, train, and evaluate all personnel assigned to his unit
    D. initiate and carry out fund-raising projects, such as bazaars and carnivals, to buy needed equipment

2.____

3. When there are conflicts or tensions between top management and lower-level employees in any public department, the supervisor should FIRST attempt to

    A. represent and enforce the mangement point of view
    B. act as the representative of the workers to get their ideas across to management
    C. serve as a two-way spokesman, trying to interpret each side to the other
    D. remain neutral, but keep informed of changes in the situation

3.____

4. A probationary period for new employees is usually provided in public agencies.
The MAJOR purpose of such a period is *usually* to

    A. allow a determination of employee's suitability for the position
    B. obtain evidence as to employee's ability to perform in a higher position
    C. conform to requirements that ethnic hiring goals be met for all positions
    D. train the new employee in the duties of the position

4.____

5. An effective program of orientation for new employees usually includes *all* the following EXCEPT

    A. having the supervisor introduce the new employee to his job, outlining his responsibilities and how to carry them out
    B. permitting the new worker to tour the facility or department, so he can observe all parts of it in action
    C. scheduling meetings for new employees, at which the job requirements are explained to them and they are given personnel manuals
    D. testing the new worker on his skills, and sending him to a centralized in-service workshop

5.____

6. In-service training is an important responsibility of supervisors.
The MAJOR reason for such training is to

6.____

A. avoid future grievance procedures, because employees might say they were not prepared to carry out their jobs
B. maximize the effectiveness of the department by helping each employee perform at his full potential
C. satisfy inspection teams from central headquarters of the department
D. help prevent disagreements with members of the community

7. There are many forms of useful in-service training.
Of the following, the training method which is NOT an appropriate technique for leadership development is to

A. provide special workshops or clinics in activity skills
B. conduct pre-season institutes to familiarize new workers with the program of the department and with their roles
C. schedule team meetings for problem-solving, including both supervisors and leaders
D. have the leader rate himself on an evaluation form periodically

7.__

8. Of the following techniques of evaluating work training programs, the one that is BEST is to

A. pass out a carefully designed questionnaire to the trainees at the completion of the program
B. test the knowledge that trainees have both at the beginning of training and at its completion
C. interview the trainees at the completion of the program
D. evaluate performance before and after training for both a control group and an experimental group

8.__

9. Assume that a new supervisor is having difficulty making his instructions to subordinates clearly understood. The one of the following which is the FIRST step he should take in dealing with this problem is to

A. set up a training workshop in communication skills
B. determine the extent and nature of the communication gap
C. repeat both verbal and written instructions several times
D. simplify his written and spoken vocabulary

9.__

10. Discipline of employees is usually a supervisor's responsibility. There may be several useful forms of disciplinary action in public employment.
Of the following, the form that is LEAST appropriate is the

A. written reprimand or warning
B. involuntary transfer to another work setting
C. demotion or suspension
D. assignment of added hours of work each week

10.__

11. Of the following, the MOST effective means of dealing with employee disciplinary problems is to

A. give personality tests to individuals to identify their psychological problems
B. distribute and discuss a policy manual containing exact rules governing employee behavior

11.__

C.   establish a single, clear penality to be imposed for all wrongdoing irrespective of degree

D.   have supervisors get to know employees well through social mingling

12.   A recently developed technique for appraising work performance is to have the supervisor record on a continual basis all significant incidents in each subordinate's behavior that indicate unsuccessful action and those that indicate poor behavior.
Of the following, a major DISADVANTAGE of this method of performance appraisal is that it

   12.____

   A.   often leads to overly close supervision
   B.   results in competition among those subordinates being evaluated
   C.   tends to result in superficial judgments
   D.   lacks objectivity for evaluating performance

13.   Assume that you are a supervisor and have observed the performance of an employee during a period of time. You have concluded that his performance needs improvement.
In order to improve his performance, it would, therefore, be BEST for you to

   13.____

   A.   note your findings in the employee's personnel folder so that his behavior is a matter of record
   B.   report the findings to the personnel officer so he can take prompt action
   C.   schedule a problem-solving conference with the employee
   D.   recommend his transfer to simpler duties

14.   When an employee's absences or latenesses seem to be nearing excessiveness, the supervisor should speak with him to find out what the problem is.
Of the following, if such a discussion produces no reasonable explanation, the discussion *usually* BEST serves to

   14.____

   A.   affirm clearly the supervisor's adherence to proper policy
   B.   alert other employees that such behavior is unacceptable
   C.   demonstrate that the supervisor truly represents higher management
   D.   notify the employee that his behavior is being observed and evaluated

15.   Assume that an employee willfully and recklessly violates an important agency regulation. The nature of the violation is of such magnitude that it demands immediate action, but the facts of the case are not entirely clear. Further assume that the supervisor is free to make any of the following recommendations.
The MOST appropriate action for the supervisor to take is to recommend that the employee be

   15.____

   A.   discharged   B.   suspended
   C.   forced to resign   D.   transferred

16.   Although employees' titles may be identical, each position in that title may be considerably different.
Of the following, a supervisor should carefully assign each employee to a specific position based PRIMARILY on the employee's

   16.____

   A.   capability   B.   experience   C.   education   D.   seniority

17. The one of the following situations where it is MOST appropriate to transfer an employee to a *similar* assignment is one in which the employee

    A. lacks motivation and interest
    B. experiences a personality conflict with his supervisor
    C. is negligent in the performance of his duties
    D. lacks capacity or ability to perform assigned tasks

18. The one of the following which is LEAST likely to be affected by improvement in the morale of personnel is employee

    A. skill   B. absenteeism   C. turnover   D. job satisfaction

19. The one of the following situations in which it is LEAST appropriate for a supervisor to delegate authority to subordinates is where the supervisor

    A. lacks confidence in his own abilities to perform certain work
    B. is overburdened and cannot handle all his responsibilities
    C. refers all disciplinary problems to his subordinate
    D. has to deal with an emergency or crisis

20. Of the following, the BEST attitude toward the use of volunteers in programs is that volunteers should be

    A. discouraged, since they cannot be depended upon to show up regularly
    B. employed as a last resort when paid personnel are unavailable
    C. seen as an appropriate means of providing leadership, when effectively recruited and supervised
    D. eliminated to raise the professionalism of personnel

21. A supervisor finds that he is spending too much time on routine tasks, and not enough time on coordinating the work of his employees.
It would be MOST advisable for this supervisor to

    A. delegate the task of work coordination to a capable subordinate
    B. eliminate some of the routine tasks that the unit is required to perform
    C. assign some of the routine tasks to his subordinates
    D. postpone the performance of routine tasks until he has achieved proper coordination of his employees' work

22. Of the following, the MOST important reason for having an office manual in looseleaf form rather than in permanent binding is that the looseleaf form

    A. facilitates the addition of new material and the removal of obsolete material
    B. permits several people to use different sections of the manual at the same time
    C. is less expensive to prepare than permanent binding
    D. is more durable than permanent binding

23. In his first discussion with a newly appointed employee, the LEAST important of the following topics for a supervisor of a unit to include is the

    A. duties the subordinate is expected to perform on the job
    B. functions of the unit
    C. methods of determining standards of performance
    D. nature and duration of the training the subordinate will receive on the job

24. A supervisor has just been told by a subordinate, Mr. Jones, that another employee, Mr. Smith, deliberately disobeyed an important rule of the department by taking home some confidential departmental material.
Of the following courses of action, it would be MOST advisable for the supervisor *first* to

    24.____

    A. discuss the matter privately, with both Mr. Jones and Mr. Smith at the same time
    B. call a meeting of the entire staff and discuss the matter generally without mentioning any employee by name
    C. arrange to supervise Mr. Smith's activities more closely
    D. discuss the matter privately with Mr. Smith

25. The one of the following actions which would be MOST effificient and economical for a supervisor to take to minimize the effect of seasonal fluctuations in the work load of his unit is to

    25.____

    A. increase his permanent staff until it is large enough to handle the work of the busy season
    B. request the purchase of time and labor saving equipment to be used primarily during the busy season
    C. lower, temporarily, the standards for quality of work performance during peak loads
    D. schedule for the slow season work that it is not essential to perform during the busy season

---

KEY (CORRECT ANSWERS)

1.	D	11.	B
2.	D	12.	A
3.	C	13.	C
4.	A	14.	D
5.	D	15.	B
6.	B	16.	A
7.	D	17.	B
8.	D	18.	A
9.	B	19.	C
10.	D	20.	C

21.	C
22.	A
23.	C
24.	D
25.	D

TEST 4

DIRECTIONS: Each question or incomplete statement is followed by several suggested answers or completions. Select the one that BEST answers the question or completes the statement. *PRINT THE LETTER OF THE CORRECT ANSWER IN THE SPACE AT THE RIGHT.*

1. Assume that, while instructing a worker on a new procedure, the instructor asks, at frequent intervals, whether there are any questions. His asking for questions is a

    A. *good practice,* because it affords the worker an opportunity to participate actively in the lesson
    B. *good practice,* because it may reveal points that are not understood by the worker
    C. *poor practice,* because workers generally find it embarrassing to ask questions
    D. *poor practice,* because it may result in wasting time on irrelevant matters

1.___

2. Any person thoroughly familiar with the specific steps in a particular type of work is well-qualified to serve as a training course instructor in the work.
This statement is *erroneous* CHIEFLY because

    A. a qualified instructor cannot be expected to have detailed information about many specific fields
    B. a person who knows a field thoroughly may not be good at passing his knowledge along to others
    C. it is practically impossible for any instructor to be acquainted with all the specific steps in a particular type of work
    D. what is true of one type of work is not necessarily true of other types of work

2.___

3. Of the following traits, the one that is LEAST essential for the "ideal" supervisor is that she

    A. be consistent in her interpretation of the rules and policies of the agency for which she works
    B. is able to judge a person's ability at her first meeting with that person
    C. know her own job thoroughly
    D. appreciate and acknowledge honest effort and above-average work

3.___

4. The one of the following which is generally the basic reason for using standard procedures is to

    A. serve as a basis for formulating policies
    B. provide the sequence of steps for handling recurring activities
    C. train new employees in the policies and objectives
    D. facilitate periodic review of standard practices,

4.___

5. An employee, while working at the bookkeeping machine, accidentally kicks off the holdup alarm system. She notifies the supervisor that she can hear the holdup alarm bell ringing, and requests that the holdup alarm system be reset.
After the holdup alarm system has been reset, the supervisor should notify the manager that the alarm

    A. is in proper wdrking order
    B. should be shut off while the employee is working the bookkeeping machine to avoid another such accident

5.___

   C.   kick-plate should be moved away from the worker's reception window so that it cannot be set off accidentally

   D.   should be relocated so that it cannot be heard in the bookkeeping office

6. A supervisor who spends a considerable amount of time correcting subordinates' proce-   6._____
dural errors should consider FIRST the possibility of

   A.   disciplining those who make errors consistently
   B.   instituting refresher training sessions
   C.   redesigning work forms
   D.   requesting that the requirements for entry-level jobs be changed

7. A supervisor has a subordinate who has been late the past four mornings.   7._____
Of the following, the MOST important action for the supervisor to take FIRST is to

   A.   read the rules concerning lateness to the employee in an authoritative manner
   B.   give the subordinate a chance to explain the reason for his lateness
   C.   tell the employee he must come in on time the next day
   D.   ask the friends of the employee whether they can tell him the reason for the employee's lateness

8. During a conversation, a subordinate tells his supervisor about a family problem.   8._____
For the supervisor to give EXPLICIT advice to the subordinate would be

   A.   *desirable,* primarily because a happy employee is more likely to be productive
   B.   *undesirable,* primarily because the supervisor should not allow a subordinate to discuss personal problems
   C.   *desirable,* primarily because their personal relations will show a marked improvement
   D.   *undesirable,* primarily because a supervisor should not take responsibility for handling a subordinate's personal problem

9. As a supervisor, you have received instructions for a drastic change in the procedure for   9._____
processing cases.
Of the following, the approach which is MOST likely to result in acceptance of the
change by your subordinates is for you to

   A.   inform all subordinates of the change by written memo so that they will have guidelines to follow
   B.   ask your superior to inform the unit members about the change at a staff meeting
   C.   recruit the most experienced employee in the unit to give individual instruction to the other unit members
   D.   discuss the change and the reasons for it with the staff so that they understand their role in its implementation

10. Of the following, the principle which should GENERALLY guide: a supervisor in the train-   10._____
ing of employees under his supervision is that

   A.   training of employees should be delegated to more experienced employees in the same title
   B.   primary emphasis should be placed on training for future assignments
   C.   the training process should be a highly individual matter
   D.   training efforts should concentrate on employees who have the greatest potential

KEY (CORRECT ANSWERS)

1. B
2. B
3. B
4. B
5. D

6. B
7. B
8. D
9. D
10. C

EXAMINATION SECTION
TEST 1

DIRECTIONS: Each question or incomplete statement is followed by several suggested answers or completions. Select the one that BEST answers the question or completes the statement. *PRINT THE LETTER OF THE CORRECT ANSWER IN THE SPACE AT THE RIGHT.*

1. The MAJOR responsibility of a director is to

    A. make certain that his line supervisors keep proper control of staff activity
    B. see that training is given to his staff according to individual needs
    C. insure that his total organization is coordinated toward agency goals and objectives
    D. work constructively with groups so that programs will reflect their needs

1.____

2. A good organization chart of a department is an IMPORTANT instrument because it can

    A. make it easier to understand the mission of the department
    B. help new employees become acquainted with department personnel
    C. clarify relationships and responsibilities of the various department components
    D. simplify the task of *going to the top*

2.____

3. Unnecessary and obsolete forms can be eliminated MOST effectively by

    A. appointing a representative committee to review and evaluate all forms in relation to operating procedures
    B. discarding all forms which have not been used during the past year
    C. assembling all forms and destroying those which are duplicates or obsolete
    D. directing office managers to review the forms to determine which should be revised or abolished

3.____

4. The director must adopt methods and techniques to insure that his budgeted allowances are properly spent and that organizational objectives are being reached.
These responsibilities can be fulfilled BEST by

    A. controlling operations with electronic data processing equipment
    B. shifting caseload controls from caseworkers to clerical staff
    C. installing a work simplification program and establishing controls for crucial areas of operation
    D. assigning employees with special skills and training to perform the more important and specialized jobs

4.____

5. The MOST appropriate technique for making the staff thoroughly familiar with departmental policies would be to

    A. maintain an up-to-date loose-leaf binder of written policies in a central point in the office
    B. issue copies of all policy directives to the unit supervisors
    C. distribute copies of policy directives to the entire staff and arrange for follow-up discussion on a unit basis
    D. discuss all major policy directives at an office-wide staff meeting

5.____

6. When a proposed change in a departmental procedure is being evaluated, the factor   6.___
which should be considered MOST important in reaching the decision is the

    A. extent of resistance anticipated from members of the staff
    B. personnel needed to execute the proposed change
    C. time required for training staff in the revised procedure
    D. degree of organizational dislocation compared with gains expected from the change

7. A director anticipates that certain aspects of a new departmental procedure will be dis-   7.___
tasteful to many staff members.
Assuming that the procedure is basically sound in spite of this drawback, the BEST approach for the director to take with his staff is to

    A. advise them to accept the procedure since it has the support of the highest author- ities in the department
    B. point out that other procedures which were resisted initially have come to be accepted in time
    C. challenge staff members to suggest another procedure which will accomplish the same purpose better
    D. ask the staff members to discuss the *pros* and *cons* of the procedure and suggest how it can be improved

8. At a staff meeting at which a basic change in departmental procedure is to be   8.___
announced, a director begins the discussion by asking the participants for criticisms of the existing procedure. He then describes the new procedure to be employed and explains the improvements that are anticipated.
The director's method of introducing the change is

    A. *good,* mainly because the participants would be more receptive to the new proce- dure if they understood the inadequacies of the old one
    B. *good,* mainly because the participants' comments on the old procedure will provide the basis for evaluation of the feasibility of the new one
    C. *bad,* mainly because the participants will realize that the decision for change has been made before the meeting, without consideration of the participants' com- ments
    D. *bad,* mainly because the discussion is focused on the old procedure, rather than on the procedure being introduced

9. Assume that you are conducting a staff conference to discuss the development of a pro-   9.___
cedure implementing a change in state policy. There are twelve participants whose office titles range from unit supervisor to senior supervisor, each of whom has responsibility for some aspect of the program affected by the policy change. After some introductory remarks, the BEST procedure for you to follow is to call upon the participants in the order of their

    A. titles, with the highest titles first because they are likely to have the most experi- ence and knowledge of the subject
    B. titles, with the lower titles first because they are likely to be less inhibited if they are permitted to give their views before the senior participants speak
    C. places around the table, to promote informality and democratic procedure
    D. specialized knowledge of the subject so that those with the most knowledge and competence may lead the discussion

10. A staff member has suggested a way of reducing the time required to prepare a monthly   10.____
report by combining several items of information, separating one item into two parts, and
generally revising definitions of terms.
The CHIEF disadvantage of such a revision is that

    A. comparison of present with past periods will be more difficult
    B. subordinates who prepare the report will require retraining
    C. forms currently in use will have to be discarded
    D. employees using the records will be confused by the changes

11. Assume that a director happens to be present at a regular staff conference conducted by   11.____
a senior supervisor. During the course of the conference, the director frequently takes
over the discussion in order to amplify remarks made by the supervisor, to impart information about departmental policies, and to modify or correct possible misinterpretations
of the supervisor's remarks.
The director's actions in this situation are

    A. *proper,* mainly because the conference members were given the latest and most
       accurate information concerning departmental policies
    B. *proper,* mainly because the director has an obligation to assist and support the
       supervisor
    C. *improper,* mainly because the director did not completely take over the conference
    D. *improper,* mainly because the supervisor was put in a difficult position in the pres-
       ence of his staff

12. A center has a serious staff morale problem because of rumors that it will probably be   12.____
abolished. To handle this situation, the director adopts a policy of promptly corroborating
rumors that he knows to be true and denying false ones.
Although this method of dealing with the situation should have some good results, its
CHIEF weakness is that

    A. it *chases* the rumors instead of forestalling them by giving correct information con-
       cerning the center's future
    B. the director may not have the necessary information at hand
    C. status is given to the rumors as a result of the attention paid to them
    D. the director may inadvertently divulge confidential information

13. Realizing the importance of harmonious staff relationships, one of your supervisors   13.____
makes a practice of unobtrusively intervening in any conflict situation among staff members. Whenever friction seems to be developing, he attempts to soothe ruffled feelings
and remove the source of difficulty by such methods as rescheduling, reassigning personnel, etc. His efforts are always behind the scenes and unknown to the personnel
involved.
This practice may produce some good results, but the CHIEF drawback is that it

    A. permits staff to engage in unacceptable practices without correction
    B. violates the principle of chain of command
    C. involves the supervisor in personal relationships which are not properly his con-
       cern
    D. requires confidential sources of information about personal relationships within the
       center

14. Assume that the department adopts a policy of transferring administrative personnel   14.____
from one center to another after stated periods of service in a center, or in a central office.
Of the following, the MAIN advantage of such a policy is that it helps

    A. prevent the formation of cliques among staff members
    B. key staff members keep abreast of new developments
    C. effect a greater utilization of staff members' special talents
    D. develop a broader outlook and loyalty to the department as a whole, rather than to
        one center

15. A delegation of union members meets with you in your role as director to discuss obtain-   15.____
ing assistance for a group of strikers who live in the neighborhood covered by the center.
In the course of discussion, you learn that the strike has been called by the local union
against the explicit directive of the national union's leadership.
The MOST appropriate course of action for you to take in this instance is to advise the
union committee

    A. of your sympathy and assure them that individual applications from the strikers for
        assistance will receive priority
    B. that if the strikers are in need, they will be able to receive assistance as long as
        they are on strike
    C. that since the strike is illegal, none of the workers will be eligible for assistance
    D. that there is no bar to any of the strikers receiving assistance provided they are in
        need and are ready and willing to accept other employment if offered

16. The quality control system is a management tool used to test the validity of the eligibility   16.____
caseload.
This system can be helpful to a director in the following ways, with the EXCEPTION of

    A. obtaining objective data to use in evaluating the performance of specific staff mem-
        bers
    B. identifying the need for policy changes
    C. sorting out the source of errors in determining eligibility
    D. setting up training objectives for his staff

17. As director, you observe that there has been a sharp rise in the number of fair hearings,   17.____
The increase seems to coincide with the intensified activities of the local recipients' orga-
nization.
The MOST appropriate action under the circumstances is to

    A. determine whether the fair hearing requests result from weaknesses in the center's
        operation, and remedy the causes, if feasible
    B. disregard the matter for the time being because complaints have been stirred up by
        an organized client group
    C. emphasize to your staff the importance of meeting client needs promptly in order to
        avoid fair hearing requests
    D. resolve the grievances with the leaders of the recipients' organization

18. As director, you receive notice of a fair hearing decision from the State Commissioner 18.____
ordering you to restore assistance to a family. You are appalled by the order because the
facts cited by the hearing officer are at complete variance with what actually occurred,
according to your personal knowledge of the case.
Of the following, the MOST appropriate course of action for you to take first is to

    A. point out to central office that the decision should be reconsidered and appropri-
ately modified
    B. comply with the decision under protest because it is patently wrong
    C. recommend to central office that it consider court action through an Article 78 pro-
ceeding to correct the erroneous decision
    D. comply with the decision, although an order of the State Commissioner has no
force and effect of law

19. In your capacity as director, you have received a copy of the monthly statistical report 19.____
issued by the department. In reviewing the report, you note that your center is showing a
rise in caseload which is substantially higher than the average rise throughout the city.
Which of the alternatives listed below would be MOST appropriate in order to deal with
this situation?

    A. Make plans to discuss the situation with central office so that appropriate corrective
action can be taken on the basis of your consultation
    B. Collect necessary information and data about the operations of your center and the
area it serves to determine the cause of the trend, and plan appropriate action on
the basis of your findings
    C. Call a meeting of your unit supervisors in order to impress upon them the impor-
tance of more diligent efforts to assist clients
    D. Assume that the rise in caseload is an inevitable result of the substantial increase
in unemployment, and take no immediate action

20. Of the following phases of a training program for administrative personnel, the one which 20.____
is usually the MOST difficult to formulate is the

    A. selection of training methods for the program
    B. obtaining of frank opinions of the participants as to the usefulness of the program
    C. chief executive officer's judgment as to the need for such a program
    D. evaluation of the effectiveness of the program

21. Assume that you are conducting a conference dealing with problems of the center of 21.____
which you are the director. The problem being discussed is one with which you have had
no experience. However, two of the participants, who have had considerable experience
with it, carry on an extended discussion, showing that they understand the problem thoroughly. The others are very much interested in the discussion and are taking notes on
the material presented. To permit the two staff members to continue for the length of time
allowed for discussion of the problem is

    A. *desirable,* chiefly because introduction of the material by the two participants them-
selves may encourage others to contribute their work experience
    B. *desirable,* chiefly because their discussion may be more meaningful to the others
than a discussion which is not based on work experience
    C. *undesirable,* chiefly because they are discussing material only in light of their own
experience rather than in general terms
    D. *undesirable,* chiefly because it would reveal your own lack of experience with the
problem and undermine your authority with the staff

22. In dealing with staff members, it is a commonly accepted principle that individual differ-   22.___
ences exist, suggesting that employees should be treated in an unlike manner in order to
achieve maximum results from their work assignments.
This statement means MOST NEARLY that

    A. supervisors should be aware of the personal problems of their subordinates and
make allowances for poor performance because of such problems
    B. standardized work rules are ineffective because of the different capabilities of
employees to maintain such work rules
    C. employees' individual needs should be considered by their supervisors to the
greatest extent possible, within the practical limitations of the work situation
    D. knowledge of general principles of human behavior is generally of little use to a
supervisor in assisting him to supervise his subordinates effectively

23. A supervisor under your jurisdiction reports to you that one of his subordinates has been   23.___
taking unusually long lunch hours, has been absent from work frequently, and has been
doing poorer work than previously.
The BEST procedure for you to follow FIRST is to advise the supervisor to

    A. prefer charges against the employee
    B. arrange for a psychological consultation for the employee
    C. ascertain whether the employee is ill and, if so, arrange a medical examination for
him
    D. have a private conversation with the employee to obtain more information about
the reasons for his behavior

24. If the term *executive development* is defined as the continuous, on-going, on-the-job pro-   24.___
cess of constructing plans to improve individuals in specific positions, both for the purpose of present improvement as well as for any future advancement which is envisaged
for the employee, it follows that the emphasis in an executive development program
should

    A. provide learning experiences through formal or informal classes, seminars, or con-
ferences,for which the focus is on the function of the position
    B. be oriented to the individual participant and may include a host of planned activi-
ties, such as appraisal, coaching, counseling, and job rotation
    C. attempt to create needs, to awaken, enlarge, and stimulate the individual so as to
broaden his outlook and potentialities as a human being
    D. insure that the individual is able to plan, organize, direct, and control operations in
the bureau, division, or agency

25. Most psychologists agree that employees have a need for recognition for the work they   25.___
perform. Therefore, it can be concluded that

    A. employees should be praised every time they complete a job satisfactorily
    B. praise is a more effective incentive to good performance than is punishment
    C. administrative personnel should be aware that subordinates do not have needs
similar to their own
    D. a formalized system of rewards and punishment is better than no system at all, as
long as there is a built-in consistency in its administration

---

KEY (CORRECT ANSWERS)

1.	C		11.	D
2.	C		12.	A
3.	A		13.	A
4.	C		14.	D
5.	C		15.	D
6.	D		16.	A
7.	D		17.	A
8.	C		18.	A
9.	D		19.	B
10.	A		20.	D

21.	B
22.	C
23.	D
24.	B
25.	B

———

TEST 2

DIRECTIONS: Each question or incomplete statement is followed by several suggested answers or completions. Select the one that BEST answers the question or completes the statement. *PRINT THE LETTER OF THE CORRECT ANSWER IN THE SPACE AT THE RIGHT.*

1. Studies have shown that the MOST effective kind of safety training program is one in which the

    A. training is conducted by consultants who are expert in the nature of the work performed
    B. lectures are given by the top executives in an agency
    C. employees participate in all phases of the program
    D. supervisors are responsible for the safety training

1.___

2. Of the following, the MOST effective method of selecting potential top executives would be

    A. situational testing which simulates actual conditions
    B. a written test which covers the knowledge required to perform the job
    C. an oral test which requires candidate to discuss significant aspects of the job
    D. a confidential interview with his former employee

2.___

3. With regard to staff morale, MOST evidence shows that

    A. employees with positive job attitudes always outproduce those with negative job attitudes
    B. morale always relates to the employee's attitude toward his working conditions and his job
    C. low morale always results in poor job performance
    D. high morale has a direct relationship to effective union leadership

3.___

4. Of the following groups of factors, the group which has been shown to be related to the incidence of job accidents is

    A. personality characteristics, intelligence, defective vision
    B. experience, fatigue, motor and perceptual speed
    C. coordination, fatigue, intelligence
    D. defective vision, motor and perceptual speed, intelligence

4.___

5. Executives who have difficulty making decisions when faced with a number of choices USUALLY

    A. have domestic problems which interfere with the decision-making process
    B. can be trained to improve their ability to make decisions
    C. are production-oriented rather than employee-centered
    D. do not know their jobs well enough to act decisively

5.___

6. Studies of disciplinary dismissals of workers reveal that

    A. the majority of employees were dismissed because of lack of technical competence
    B. the supervisors were unusually demanding of employee competence
    C. most employees were dismissed because of inability to work with their co-workers
    D. the chief executive set unrealistic standards of performance

6.___

7. One philosophy of assigning workers to a specific job is that the worker and his job are   7.____
   an integral unit.
   This means, MOST NEARLY, that the

   A. employee and the job may both require adjustment
   B. employee must meet all the specifications of the job as a prerequisite for employ-
      ment
   C. employee's morale will be affected by his salary
   D. employee's job satisfaction has a direct effect on his emotional health

8. The statement that the supervisor and the administrator are the *primary personnel men*   8.____
   means, MOST NEARLY, that

   A. supervisors and administrators are more skilled in personnel techniques than are
      professional personnel technicians
   B. they are in the best position to implement personnel policies and procedures
   C. employees have more confidence in their supervisors and administrators than in
      the professional personnel administrator
   D. personnel administration is most effective when it combines both centralized and
      decentralized approaches

9. Administrators frequently have to interview people in order to obtain information.   9.____
   Although the interview is a legitimate fact-gathering technique, it has limitations which
   should not be overlooked.
   The one of the following which is an IMPORTANT limitation is that

   A. individuals generally hesitate to give information orally which they would usually
      answer in writing
   B. the material derived from the interview can usually be obtained at lower cost from
      existing records
   C. the emotional attitudes of individuals during an interview often affect the accuracy
      of the information given
   D. the interview is a poor technique for discovering how well clients understand
      departmental policies

10. Leadership styles have frequently been categorized as authoritarian, laissez-faire, and   10.____
    democratic.
    In general, management's reliance on leadership to produce desired results would be
    MOST effectively implemented through

    A. the laissez-faire approach when group results are desired
    B. the authoritarian approach in a benevolent manner when quick decisions are
       required
    C. the democratic approach, when quick decisions are unimportant
    D. all three approaches, depending upon circumstances

11. As director, you are responsible for enforcing a recently established regulation which has   11.___
aroused antagonism among many clients.
You should deal with this situation by

    A. explaining to the clients that you are not responsible for making regulations
    B. enforcing the regulation but reporting to your superior the number and kind of com-
plaints against it
    C. carrying out your duty of enforcing the regulation as well as you can without com-
ment
    D. suggesting to your clients that you may overlook violations of the regulation

12. One of the observations made in a recent psychological study of leadership is that the   12.___
behavior of a new employee in a leadership position can be predicted more accurately on
the basis of the behavior of the previous incumbent in the post than on the behavior of
the new employee in his previous job.
The BEST explanation for this observation is that there is a tendency

    A. for a newly appointed executive to avoid making basic changes in operational pro-
cedures
    B. to choose similar types of personalities to fill the same type of position
    C. for a given organizational structure and set of duties and responsibilities to produce
similar patterns of behavior
    D. for executives to develop more mature patterns of behavior as a result of increased
responsibility

13. A director finds that reports submitted to him by his subordinates tend to emphasize the   13.___
favorable and minimize the unfavorable aspects of situations.
The MOST valid reason for this is that

    A. subordinates usually hesitate to give their supervisors an honest picture of a situa-
tion
    B. the director may not have been sufficiently critical of previous reports submitted by
his subordinates
    C. subordinates have a normal tendency to represent themselves and their actions in
the best possible light
    D. many subordinates in the field have developed a tendency to understatement in
the depiction of unfavorable situations

14. Effective delegation of authority and responsibility to subordinates is essential for the   14.___
proper administration of a center. However, the director should retain some activities
under his direct control.
Of the following activities, the one for which there is LEAST justification for delegation
by the director to a subordinate is one involving

    A. relationships with client groups
    B. physical danger to clients
    C. policies which are unpopular with staff
    D. matters for which there are no established policies

15. According to the principle of *span of control,* there should be a limited number of subordi-   15.___
nates reporting to one supervisor.
Of the following, the CHIEF disadvantage which may result from the application of this
principle is a reduction in the

A.   contact between lower ranking staff members and higher ranking administrative personnel
B.   freedom of action of subordinates
C.   authority and responsibility of subordinates
D.   number of organizational levels through which a matter must pass before action is taken

16.   The CHIEF objection to a practice of decentralizing the preparation and distribution of memoranda by bureaus, rather than controlling distribution through central office, is that it is LIKELY to result in

A.   overloading bureaus with a multiplicity of communications
B.   limited and specialized rather than broad and general viewpoints in the memoranda
C.   violation of the principle of unity of command
D.   unimportant information being communicated to all bureaus

17.   A report has been completed by members of your staff. As director, you have reviewed the report and feel that the information revealed could be damaging to the department. You find yourself in conflict in your multiple role as director, as a professional, and as a citizen.
The one of the following actions which would be MOST desirable for you to take FIRST would be to

A.   send a copy of the report to your supervisor and request an immediate conference with him
B.   instruct staff to re-check the report and defer issuance of the report until the findings are confirmed
C.   immediately share the report with your supervisors and your advisory committee
D.   file the report until your advisory committee makes a request for it

18.   In order for employees to function effectively, they should have a feeling of being treated fairly by management. Which of the following general policies is MOST likely to give employees such a feeling?

A.   An employee publication should be mailed directly to the home of each employee.
B.   Employee attitude surveys should be conducted at regular intervals.
C.   Employees should be consulted and kept informed on all matters that affect them.
D.   Employees should be informed when the press publishes statements of policy.

19.   In order to give employees greater job satisfaction, some management experts advocate a policy of job enrichment. The one of the following which would be the BEST example of job enrichment is to

A.   allow an aide to decide which portion of his normal duties and responsibilities he prefers
B.   increase the fringe benefits currently available to paraprofessional employees
C.   add variety to the duties of an employee
D.   permit more flexible working schedules for professional employees

16.____
17.____
18.____
19.____

20. Management of large organizations has often emphasized high salaries and fringe bene-   20.____
fits as the most important means of motivating employees.
The one of the following which is NOT an argument used to support this approach is

    A. most people endure work mainly in order to collect the rewards and to have the opportunity to enjoy them
    B. material incentives have proved to be the best means of stimulating creative capacity and the will to work
    C. the majority of employees place little emphasis on work-centered motivation to perform
    D. numerous research studies have shown that pay ranks first on a scale of factors motivating employees in government and industry in the United States

21. Some organizations provide psychologists or other professionally trained persons with   21.____
whom employees can consult on a confidential basis regarding personal problems. Of
the following, which is MOST likely to be a benefit management can derive from such a
practice?

    A. Increase in the authority of management
    B. Disclosure of the corrupt practices of those handling money
    C. Receipt of new ideas and approaches to organizational problems
    D. Obtaining tighter control on employees' private behavior

22. Authorities agree that it is generally most desirable for an employee experiencing mental   22.____
health problems to seek competent professional help without being required or forced to
do so by another person.
They view self-referral as a most desirable action PRIMARILY because

    A. it shows that the employee probably is more aware of the problem and more highly motivated to solve his problems
    B. the employee's right to privacy in his personal affairs is maintained
    C. another person cannot be blamed in the event the outcome of the referral is not successful
    D. the employee knows best his problems and will do what is necessary to serve his own best interests

Questions 23-25.

DIRECTIONS: Questions 23 through 25 consist of three excerpts each. Consider an excerpt
correct if all the statements in the excerpt are correct. Mark your answer as follows:

    A. if only excerpts 1 and 2 are correct
    B. if only excerpts 2 and 3 are correct
    C. if only excerpt 1 is correct
    D. if only excerpt 2 is correct

23.   1. Many executive decisions are based on assumptions.   23.____

They may be assumptions supported by sketchy data about future needs for services; assumptions about the attitudes and future behavior of employees, perhaps based on reports of staff members or hearsay evidence; or assumptions about agency values that are as much a reflection of personal desires as of agency goals.

2. A good pattern of well-conceived plans is only a first step in administration. The administrator must also create an organization to formulate and carry out such plans. Resources must be assembled; supervision of actual operations is necessary; and before the executive's task is completed, he must exercise control.

3. When a problem is well defined, good alternatives identified, and the likely consequences of each alternative forecast as best we can, one can assume that the final choice of action to be taken would be easy, if not obvious.

24.   1. Principles of motivation are not difficult to establish because human behavior is not   24.____
complex and is easily understood; individual differences in human beings are substantial; and people are continuously learning and changing.

2. What gives employees satisfaction or dissatisfaction indicates the nature of the motivation problem and provides positive guidance to the administrator who faces the problem of trying to get people to carry out a set of plans.

3. The administrator's job of motivation can be described as that of creating a situation in which actions that provide net satisfaction to individual members of the enterprise are at the same time actions that make appropriate contributions toward the objectives of the enterprise.

25.   1. Administrative organization is primarily concerned with legal, technical, or ultimate   25.____
authority; the operational authority relationships that may be created by organization are of major significance.

2. Accountability is not removed by delegation. Appraisal of results should be tempered by the extent to which an administrator must rely on subordinates.

3. In delegations to operating subordinates, authority to plan exceeds authority to do, inasmuch as the executive typically reserves some of the planning for himself.

KEY (CORRECT ANSWERS)

1.	C	11.	B
2.	A	12.	C
3.	B	13.	C
4.	B	14.	D
5.	B	15.	A
6.	C	16.	A
7.	A	17.	B
8.	B	18.	C
9.	C	19.	C
10.	D	20.	D

21.	C
22.	A
23.	A
24.	B
25.	D

PREPARING WRITTEN MATERIAL

PARAGRAPH REARRANGEMENT
COMMENTARY

The sentences which follow are in scrambled order. You are to rearrange them in proper order and indicate the letter choice containing the correct answer at the space at the right.

Each group of sentences in this section is actually a paragraph presented in scrambled order. Each sentence in the group has a place in that paragraph; no sentence is to be left out. You are to read each group of sentences and decide upon the best order in which to put the sentences so as to form as well-organized paragraph.

The questions in this section measure the ability to solve a problem when all the facts relevant to its solution are not given.

More specifically, certain positions of responsibility and authority require the employee to discover connections between events sometimes, apparently, unrelated. In order to do this, the employee will find it necessary to correctly infer that unspecified events have probably occurred or are likely to occur. This ability becomes especially important when action must be taken on incomplete information.

Accordingly, these questions require competitors to choose among several suggested alternatives, each of which presents a different sequential arrangement of the events. Competitors must choose the MOST logical of the suggested sequences.

In order to do so, they may be required to draw on general knowledge to infer missing concepts or events that are essential to sequencing the given events. Competitors should be careful to infer only what is essential to the sequence. The plausibility of the wrong alternatives will always require the inclusion of unlikely events or of additional chains of events which are NOT essential to sequencing the given events.

It's very important to remember that you are looking for the best of the four possible choices, and that the best choice of all may not even be one of the answers you're given to choose from.

There is no one right way to solve these problems. Many people have found it helpful to first write out the order of the sentences, as they would have arranged them, on their scrap paper before looking at the possible answers. If their optimum answer is there, this can save them some time. If it isn't, this method can still give insight into solving the problem. Others find it most helpful to just go through each of the possible choices, contrasting each as they go along. You should use whatever method feels comfortable, and works, for you.

While most of these types of questions are not that difficult, we've added a higher percentage of the difficult type, just to give you more practice. Usually there are only one or two questions on this section that contain such subtle distinctions that you're unable to answer confidently, and you then may find yourself stuck deciding between two possible choices, neither of which you're sure about.

Preparing Written Material

EXAMINATION SECTION
TEST 1

DIRECTIONS: The following groups of sentences need to be arranged in an order that makes sense. Select the letter preceding the sequence that represents the best sentence order. *PRINT THE LETTER OF THE CORRECT ANSWER IN THE SPACE AT THE RIGHT.*

Question 1   1.____

1. The ostrich egg shell's legendary toughness makes it an excellent substitute for certain types of dishes or dinnerware, and in parts of Africa ostrich shells are cut and decorated for use as containers for water.
2. Since prehistoric times, people have used the enormous egg of the ostrich as a part of their diet, a practice which has required much patience and hard work-to hard-boil an ostrich egg takes about four hours.
3. Opening the egg's shell, which is rock hard and nearly an inch thick, requires heavy tools, such as a saw or chisel; from inside, a baby ostrich must use a hornlike projection on its beak as a miniature pick-axe to escape from the egg.
4. The offspring of all higher-order animals originate from single egg cells that are carried by mothers, and most of these eggs are relatively small, often microscopic.
5. The egg of the African ostrich, however, weighs a massive thirty pounds, making it the largest single cell on earth, and a common object of human curiosity and wonder.

The best order is

A. 5 4 1 2 3
B. 1 4 5 3 2
C. 4 2 3 5 1
D. 4 5 2 3 1

Question 2   2.____

1. Typically only a few feet high on the open sea, individual tsunami have been known to circle the entire globe two or three times if their progress is not interrupted, but are not usually dangerous until they approach the shallow water that surrounds land masses.
2. Some of the most terrifying and damaging hazards caused by earthquakes are tsunami, which were once called "tidal waves"— a poorly chosen name, since these waves have nothing to do with tides.
3. Then a wave, slowed by the sudden drag on the lower part of its moving water column, will pile upon itself, sometimes reaching a height of over 100 feet.
4. Tsunami (Japanese for "great harbor wave") are seismic waves that are caused by earthquakes near oceanic trenches, and once triggered, can travel up to 600 miles an hour on the open ocean.
5. A land-shoaling tsunami is capable of extraordinary destruction; some tsunami have deposited large boats miles inland, washed out two-foot-thick seawalls, and scattered locomotive trains over long distances.

The best order is

A. 4 1 3 2 5
B. 1 3 4 2 5
C. 5 1 3 2 4
D. 2 4 1 3 5

Question 3   3._

1. Soon, by the 1940's, jazz was the most popular type of music among American intellectuals and college students.
2. In the early days of jazz, it was considered "lowdown" music, or music that was played only in rough, disreputable bars and taverns.
3. However, jazz didn't take long to develop from early ragtime melodies into more complex, sophisticated forms, such as Charlie Parker's "bebop" style of jazz.
4. After charismatic band leaders such as Duke Ellington and Count Basic brought jazz to a larger audience, and jazz continued to evolve into more complicated forms, white audiences began to accept and even to enjoy the new American art form.
5. Many white Americans, who then dictated the tastes of society, were wary of music that was played almost exclusively in black clubs in the poorer sections of cities and towns.

The best order is

A. 5 4 3 2 1
B. 2 5 3 4 1
C. 4 5 3 1 2
D. 1 2 4 3 5

Question 4   4._

1. Then, hanging in a windless place, the magnetized end of the needle would always point to the south.
2. The needle could then be balanced on the rim of a cup, or the edge of a fingernail, but this balancing act was hard to maintain, and the needle often fell off.
3. Other needles would point to the north, and it was important for any traveler finding his way with a compass to remember which kind of magnetized needle he was carrying.
4. To make some of the earliest compasses in recorded history, ancient Chinese "magicians" would rub a needle with a piece of magnetized iron called a lodestone.
5. A more effective method of keeping the needle free to swing with its magnetic pull was to attach a strand of silk to the center of the needle with a tiny piece of wax.

The best order is

A. 4 2 5 1 3
B. 4 3 5 2 1
C. 4 5 2 1 3
D. 4 1 3 5 2

Question 5

5.____

1. The now-famous first mate of the *HMS Bounty,* Fletcher Christian, founded one of the world's most peculiar civilizations in 1790.
2. The men knew they had just committed a crime for which they could be hanged, so they set sail for Pitcairn, a remote, abandoned island in the far eastern region of the Polynesian archipelago, accompanied by twelve Polynesian women and six men.
3. In a mutiny that has become legendary, Christian and the others forced Captain Bligh into a lifeboat and set him adrift off the coast of Tonga in April of 1789.
4. In early 1790, the *Bounty* landed at Pitcairn Island, where the men lived out the rest of their lives and founded an isolated community which to this day includes direct descendants of Christian and the other crewmen.
5. The *Bounty,* commanded by Captain William Bligh, was in the middle of a global voyage, and Christian and his shipmates had come to the conclusion that Bligh was a reckless madman who would lead them to their deaths unless they took the ship from him.

The best order is

A. 4 5 3 2 1
B. 1 3 5 2 4
C. 1 5 3 2 4
D. 3 1 5 4 2

Question 6

6.____

1. But once the vines had been led to make orchids, the flowers had to be carefully hand-pollinated, because unpollinated orchids usually lasted less than a day, wilting and dropping off the vine before it had even become dark.
2. The Totonac farmers discovered that looping a vine back around once it reached a five-foot height on its host tree would cause the vine to flower.
3. Though they knew how to process the fruit pods and extract vanilla's flavoring agent, the Totonacs also knew that a wild vanilla vine did not produce abundant flowers or fruit.
4. Wild vines climbed along the trunks and canopies of trees, and this constant upward growth diverted most of the vine's energy to making leaves instead of the orchid flowers that, once pollinated, would produce the flavorful pods.
5. Hundreds of years before vanilla became a prized food flavoring in Europe and the Western World, the Totonac Indians of the Mexican Gulf Coast were skilled cultivators of the vanilla vine, whose fruit they literally worshipped as a goddess.

The best order is

A. 2 3 4 1 5
B. 2 4 3 1 5
C. 5 3 4 2 1
D. 3 4 1 2 5

Question 7   7.___

1. Once airborne, the spider is at the mercy of the air currents—usually the spider takes a brief journey, traveling close to the ground, but some have been found in air samples collected as high as 10,000 feet, or been reported landing on ships far out at sea.

2. Once a young spider has hatched, it must leave the environment into which it was born as quickly as possible, in order to avoid competing with its hundreds of brothers and sisters for food.

3. The silk rises into warm air currents, and as soon as the pull feels adequate the spider lets go and drifts up into the air, suspended from the silk strand in the same way that a person might parasail.

4. To help young spiders do this, many species have adapted a practice known as "aerial dispersal," or, in common speech, "ballooning."

5. A spider that wants to leave its surroundings quickly will climb to the top of a grass stem or twig, face into the wind, and aim its back end into the air, releasing a long stream of silk from the glands near the tip of its abdomen.

The best order is

   A. 5 4 2 3 1
   B. 5 2 4 1 3
   C. 2 5 4 3 1
   D. 2 4 5 3 1

Question 8   8.___

1. For about a year, Tycho worked at a castle in Prague with a scientist named Johannes Kepler, but their association was cut short by another argument that drove Kepler out of the castle, to later develop, on his own, the theory of planetary orbits.

2. Tycho found life without a nose embarrassing, so he made a new nose for himself out of silver, which reportedly remained glued to his face for the rest of his life.

3. Tycho Brahe, the 17th-century Danish astronomer, is today more famous for his odd and arrogant personality than for any contribution he has made to our knowledge of the stars and planets.

4. Early in his career, as a student at Rostock University, Tycho got into an argument with the another student about who was the better mathematician, and the two became so angry that the argument turned into a sword fight, during which Tycho's nose was sliced off.

5. Later in his life, Tycho's arrogance may have kept him from playing a part in one of the greatest astronomical discoveries in history: the elliptical orbits of the solar system's planets.

The best order is

   A. 1 4 2 3 5
   B. 4 2 3 5 1
   C. 4 2 1 3 5
   D. 3 4 2 5 1

Question 9

1. The processionaries are so used to this routine that if a person picks up the end of a silk line and brings it back to the origin—creating a closed circle—the caterpillars may travel around and around for days, sometimes starving ar freezing, without changing course.
2. Rather than relying on sight or sound, the other caterpillars, who are lined up end-to-end behind the leader, travel to and from their nests by walking on this silk line, and each will reinforce it by laying down its own marking line as it passes over.
3. In order to insure the safety of individuals, the processionary caterpillar nests in a tree with dozens of other caterpillars, and at night, when it is safest, they all leave together in search of food.
4. The processionary caterpillar of the European continent is a perfect illustration of how much some insect species rely on instinct in their daily routines.
5. As they leave their nests, the processionaries form a single-file line behind a leader who spins and lays out a silk line to mark the chosen path.

The best order is

A. 4 3 5 2 1
B. 3 5 4 2 1
C. 3 5 2 1 4
D. 4 5 3 1 2

Question 10

1. Often, the child is also given a handcrafted walker or push cart, to provide support for its first upright explorations.
2. In traditional Indian families, a child's first steps are celebrated as a ceremonial event, rooted in ancient myth.
3. These carts are often intricately designed to resemble the chariot of Krishna, an important figure in Indian mythology.
4. The sound of these anklet bells is intended to mimic the footsteps of the legendary child Rama, who is celebrated in devotional songs throughout India.
5. When the child's parents see that the child is ready to begin walking, they will fit it with specially designed ankle bracelets, adorned with gently ringing bells.

The best order is

A. 2 3 4 1 5
B. 2 5 3 1 4
C. 5 4 1 3 2
D. 5 3 2 1 4

Question 11   11.

   1.   The settlers planted Osage orange all across Middle America, and today long lines and rectangles of Osage orange trees can still be seen on the prairies, running along the former boundaries of farms that no longer exist.

   2.   After trying sod walls and water-filled ditches with no success, American farmers began to look for a plant that was adaptable to prairie weather, and that could be trimmed into a hedge that was "pig-tight, horse-high, and bull-strong."

   3.   The tree, so named because it bore a large (but inedible) fruit the size of an orange, was among the sturdiest and hardiest of American trees, and was prized among Native Americans for the strength and flexibility of bows which were made from its wood.

   4.   The first people to practice agriculture on the American flatlands were faced with an important problem: what would they use to fence their land in a place that was almost entirely without trees or rocks?

   5.   Finally, an Illinois farmer brought the settlers a tree that was native to the land between the Red and Arkansas rivers, a tree called the Osage orange.

The best order is

   A.   2 1 5 3 4
   B.   1 2 3 4 5
   C.   4 2 5 3 1
   D.   4 2 1 3 5

Question 12   12.

   1.   After about ten minutes of such spirited and complicated activity, the head dancer is free to make up his or her own movements while maintaining the interest of the New Year's crowd.

   2.   The dancer will then perform a series of leg kicks, while at the same time operating the lion's mouth with his own hand and moving the ears and eyes by means of a string which is attached to the dancer's own mouth.

   3.   The most difficult role of this dance belongs to the one who controls the lion's head; this person must lead all the other "parts" of the lion through the choreographed segments of the dance.

   4.   The head dancer begins with a complex series of steps, alternately stepping forward with the head raised, and then retreating a few steps while lowering the head, a movement that is intended to create the impression that the lion is keeping a watchful eye for anything evil.

   5.   When performing a traditional Chinese New Year's lion dance, several performers must fit themselves inside a large lion costume and work together to enact different parts of the dance.

The best order is

   A.   5 3 4 2 1
   B.   3 4 2 5 1
   C.   3 1 5 4 2
   D.   4 2 3 5 1

Question 13

1. For many years the shell of the chambered nautilus was treasured in Europe for its beauty and intricacy, but collectors were unaware that they were in possession of the structure that marked a "missing link" in the evolution of marine mollusks.

2. The nautilus, however, evolved a series of enclosed chambers in its shell, and invented a new use for the structure: the shell began to serve as a buoyancy device.

3. Equipped with this new flotation device, the nautilus did not need the single, muscular foot of its predecessors, but instead developed flaps, tentacles, and a gentle form of jet propulsion that transformed it into the first mollusk able to take command of its own destiny and explore a three-dimensional world.

4. By pumping and adjusting air pressure into the chambers, the nautilus could spend the day resting on the bottom, and then rise toward the surface at night in search of food.

5. The nautilus shell looks like a large snail shell, similar to those of its ancestors, who used their shells as protective coverings while they were anchored to the sea floor.

The best order is

A. 5 2 4 1 3
B. 5 1 2 3 4
C. 1 2 5 3 4
D. 1 5 2 4 3

Question 14

1. While France and England battled for control of the region, the Acadiens prospered on the fertile farmland, which was finally secured by England in 1713.

2. Early in the 17th century, settlers from western France founded a colony called Acadie in what is now the Canadian province of Nova Scotia.

3. At this time, English officials feared the presence of spies among the Acadiens who might be loyal to their French homeland, and the Acadiens were deported to spots along the Atlantic and Caribbean shores of America.

4. The French settlers remained on this land, under English rule, for around forty years, until the beginning of the French and Indian War, another conflict between France and England.

5. As the Acadien refugees drifted toward a final home in southern Louisiana, neighbors shortened their name to "Cadien," and finally "Cajun," the name which the descendants of early Acadiens still call themselves.

The best order is

A. 1 4 2 3 5
B. 2 1 3 5 4
C. 2 1 4 3 5
D. 5 2 3 4 1

Question 15

15.___

1. Traditional households in the Eastern and Western regions of Africa serve two meals a day-one at around noon, and the other in the evening.
2. The starch is then used in the way that Americans might use a spoon, to scoop up a portion of the main dish on the person's plate.
3. The reason for the starch's inclusion in every meal has to do with taste as well as nutrition; African food can be very spicy, and the starch is known to cool the burning effect of the main dish.
4. When serving these meals, the main dish is usually served on individual plates, and the starch is served on a communal plate, from which diners break off a piece of bread or scoop rice or fufu in their fingers.
5. The typical meals usually consist of a thick stew or soup as the main course, and an accompanying starch—either bread, rice, *or fufu, a* starchy grain paste similar in consistency to mashed potatoes.

The best order is

A. 5 2 3 4 1
B. 5 1 4 3 2
C. 1 4 5 3 2
D. 1 5 4 2 3

Question 16

16.___

1. In the early days of the American Midwest, Indiana settlers sometimes came together to hold an event called an apple peeling, where neighboring settlers gathered at the home-stead of a host family to help prepare the hosts' apple crop for cooking, canning, and making apple butter.
2. At the beginning of the event, each peeler sat down in front of a ten- or twenty-gallon stone jar and was given a crock of apples and a paring knife.
3. Once a peeler had finished with a crock, another was placed next to him; if the peeler was an unmarried man, he kept a strict count of the number of apples he had peeled, because the winner was allowed to kiss the girl of his choice.
4. The peeling usually ended by 9:30 in the evening, when the neighbors gathered in the host family's parlor for a dance social.
5. The apples were peeled, cored, and quartered, and then placed into the jar.

The best order is

A. 1 5 3 4 2
B. 2 5 3 4 1
C. 1 2 5 3 4
D. 2 1 5 4 3

Question 17   17._____

1. If your pet turtle is a land turtle and is native to temperate climates, it will stop eating some time in October, which should be your cue to prepare the turtle for hibernation.
2. The box should then be covered with a wire screen, which will protect the turtle from any rodents or predators that might want to take advantage of a motionless and helpless animal.
3. When your turtle hasn't eaten for a while and appears ready to hibernate, it should be moved to its winter quarters, most likely a cellar or garage, where the temperature should range between 40° and 45° F.
4. Instead of feeding the turtle, you should bathe it every day in warm water, to encourage the turtle to empty its intestines in preparation for its long winter sleep.
5. Here the turtle should be placed in a well-ventilated box whose bottom is covered with a moisture-absorbing layer of clay beads, and then filled three-fourths full with almost dry peat moss or wood chips, into which the turtle will burrow and sleep for several months.

The best order is

A. 1 4 3 5 2
B. 3 4 2 5 1
C. 3 2 4 1 5
D. 4 5 2 3 1

Question 18   18._____

1. Once he has reached the nest, the hunter uses two sturdy bamboo poles like huge chopsticks to pull the nest away from the mountainside, into a large basket that will be lowered to people waiting below.
2. The world's largest honeybees colonize the Nepalese mountainsides, building honeycombs as large as a person on sheer rock faces that are often hundreds of feet high.
3. In the remote mountain country of Nepal, a small band of "honey hunters" carry out a tradition so ancient that 10,000 year-old drawings of the practice have been found in the caves of Nepal.
4. To harvest the honey and beeswax from these combs, a honey hunter climbs above the nests, lowers a long bamboo-fiber ladder over the cliff, and then climbs down.
5. Throughout this dangerous practice, the hunter is stung repeatedly, and only the veterans, with skin that has been toughened over the years, are able to return from a hunt without the painful swelling caused by stings.

The best order is

A. 2 4 3 5 1
B. 2 4 1 5 3
C. 5 3 2 4 1
D. 3 2 4 1 5

Question 19

19.__

1. After the Romans left Britain, there were relentless attacks on the islands from the barbarian tribes of northern Germany—the Angles, Saxons, and Jutes.
2. As the empire weakened, Roman soldiers withdrew from Britain, leaving behind a country that continued to practice the Christian religion that had been introduced by the Romans.
3. Early Latin writings tell of a Christian warrior named Arturius (Arthur, in English) who led the British citizens to defeat these barbarian invaders, and brought an extended period of peace to the lands of Britain.
4. Long ago, the British Isles were part of the far-flung Roman Empire that extended across most of Europe and into Africa and Asia.
5. The romantic legend of King Arthur and his knights of the Round Table, one of the most popular and widespread stories of all time, appears to have some foundation in history.

The best order is

A. 5 4 3 2 1
B. 5 4 2 1 3
C. 4 5 2 3 1
D. 4 3 2 1 5

Question 20

20.__

1. The cylinder was allowed to cool until it sould stand on its own, and then it was cut from the tube and split down the side with a single straight cut.
2. Nineteenth-century glassmakers, who had not yet discovered the glazier's modern techniques for making panes of glass, had to create a method for converting their blown glass into flat sheets.
3. The bubble was then pierced at the end to make a hole that opened up while the glassmaker gently spun it, creating a cylinder of glass.
4. Turned on its side and laid on a conveyor belt, the cylinder was strengthened, or tempered, by being heated again and cooled very slowly, eventually flattening out into a single rectangular piece of glass.
5. To do this, the glassmaker dipped the end of a long tube into melted glass and blew into the other end of the tube, creating an expanding bubble of glass.

The best order is

A. 2 5 3 4 1
B. 2 4 5 3 1
C. 3 5 2 4 1
D. 3 1 4 5 2

Question 21

21.____

1. The splints are almost always hidden, but horses are occasionally born whose splinted toes project from the leg on either side, just above the hoof.
2. The second and fourth toes remained, but shrank to thin splints of bone that fused invisibly to the horse's leg bone.
3. Horses are unique among mammals, having evolved feet that each end in what is essentially a single toe, capped by a large, sturdy hoof.
4. Julius Caesar, an emperor of ancient Rome, was said to have owned one of these three-toed horses, and considered it so special that he would not permit anyone else to ride it.
5. Though the horse's earlier ancestors possessed the traditional mammalian set of five toes on each foot, the horse has retained only its third toe; its first and fifth toes disappeared completely as the horse evolved.

The best order is

A. 3 5 2 1 4
B. 5 3 2 4 1
C. 3 2 5 1 4
D. 5 2 3 1 4

Question 22

22.____

1. The new building materials—some of which are twenty feet long, and weigh nearly six tons—were transported to Pohnpei on rafts, and were brought into their present position by using hibiscus fiber ropes and leverage to move the stone columns upward along the inclined trunks of coconut palm trees.
2. The ancestors built great fires to heat the stone, and then poured cool seawater on the columns, which caused the stone to contract and split along natural fracture lines.
3. The now-abandoned enclave of Nan Madol, a group of 92 man-made islands off the shore of the Micronesian island of Pohnpei, is estimated to have been built around the year 500 A.D.
4. The islanders say their ancestors quarried stone columns from a nearby island, where large basalt columns were formed by the cooling of molten lava.
5. The structures of Nan Madol are remarkable for the sheer size of some of the stone "logs" or columns that were used to create the walls of the offshore community, and today anthropologists can only rely on the information of existing local people for clues about how Nan Madol was built.

The best order is

A. 5 4 3 2 1
B. 5 3 1 4 2
C. 3 5 4 2 1
D. 3 1 4 2 5

Question 23   23.__

   1.   One of the most easily manipulated substances on earth, glass can be made into ceramic tiles that are composed of over 90% air.

   2.   NASA's space shuttles are the first spacecraft ever designed to leave and re-enter the earth's atmosphere while remaining intact.

   3.   These ceramic tiles are such effective insulators that when a tile emerges from the oven in which it was fired, it can be held safely in a person's hand by the edges while its interior still glows at a temperature well over 2000° F.

   4.   Eventually, the engineers were led to a material that is as old as our most ancient civilizationsglass.

   5.   Because the temperature during atmospheric re-entry is so incredibly hot, it took NASA's engineers some time to find a substance capable of protecting the shuttles.

The best order is

    A.   5 2 1 3 4
    B.   2 5 4 1 3
    C.   2 3 1 2 5
    D.   5 4 3 1 2

Question 24   24.__

   1.   The secret to teaching any parakeet to talk is patience, and the understanding that when a bird "talks," it is simply imitating what it hears, rather than putting ideas into words.

   2.   You should stay just out of sight of the bird and repeat the phrase you want it to learn, for at least fifteen minutes every morning and evening.

   3.   It is important to leave the bird without any words of encouragement or farewell; otherwise it might combine stray remarks or phrases, such as "Good night," with the phrase you are trying to teach it.

   4.   For this reason, to train your bird to imitate your words you should keep it free of any distractions, especially other noises, while you are giving it "lessons."

   5.   After your repetition, you should quietly leave the bird alone for a while, to think over what it has just heard.

The best order is

    A.   1 4 2 5 3
    B.   1 2 4 3 5
    C.   3 2 1 5 4
    D.   3 1 5 4 2

Question 25   25.____

1. As a school approaches, fishermen from neighboring communities join their fishing boats together as a fleet, and string their gill nets together to make a huge fence that is held up by cork floats.
2. At a signal from the party leaders, or *nakura,* the family members pound the sides of the boats or beat the water with long poles, creating a sudden and deafening noise.
3. The fishermen work together to drag the trap into a half-circle that may reach 300 yards in diameter, and then the families move their boats to form the other half of the circle around the school of fish.
4. The school of fish flee from the commotion into the awaiting trap, where a final wall of net is thrown over the open end of the half-circle, securing the day's haul.
5. Indonesian people from the area around the Sulu islands live on the sea, in floating villages made of lashed-together or stilted homes, and make much of their living by fishing their home waters for migrating schools of snapper, scad, and other fish.

The best order is

A. 1 5 3 4 2
B. 1 2 4 3 5
C. 5 1 2 3 4
D. 5 1 3 2 4

———

KEY (CORRECT ANSWERS)

1. D		11. C	
2. D		12. A	
3. B		13. D	
4. A		14. C	
5. C		15. D	
6. C		16. C	
7. D		17. A	
8. D		18. D	
9. A		19. B	
10. B		20. A	

21. A
22. C
23. B
24. A
25. D

———

PREPARING WRITTEN MATERIALS

EXAMINATION SECTION

TEST 1

DIRECTIONS: Each question consists of a sentence which may be classified appropriately under one of the following four categories:
    A. Incorrect because of faulty grammar or sentence structure.
    B. Incorrect because of faulty punctuation.
    C. Incorrect because of faulty spelling or capitalization.
    D. Correct

Examine each sentence carefully. Then, in the space at the right, print the capital letter preceding the option which is the BEST of the four suggested above. All incorrect sentences contain only one type of error. Consider a sentence correct if it contains none of the types of errors mentioned, although there may be other correct ways of expressing the same thought.

1. The fire apparently started in the storeroom, which is usually locked.   1._____

2. On approaching the victim two bruises were noticed by this officer.   2._____

3. The officer, who was there examined the report with great care.   3._____

4. Each employee in the office had a separate desk.   4._____

5. The suggested procedure is similar to the one now in use.   5._____

6. No one was more pleased with the new procedure than the chauffeur.   6._____

7. He tried to pursuade her to change the procedure.   7._____

8. The total of the expenses charged to petty cash were high.   8._____

9. An understanding between him and I was finally reached.   9._____

10. It was at the supervisor's request that the clerk agreed to postpone his vacation.   10._____

11. We do not believe that it is necessary for both he and the clerk to attend the conference.   11._____

12. All employees, who display perseverance, will be given adequate recognition.   12._____

13. He regrets that some of us employees are dissatisfied with our new assignments.   13._____

14. "Do you think that the raise was merited," asked the supervisor?   14._____

15. The new manual of procedure is a valuable supplament to our rules and   15._____
    regulation.

16. The typist admitted that she had attempted to pursuade the other employees 16._____
    to assist her in her work.

17. The supervisor asked that all amendments to the regulations be handled by   17._____
    you and I.

18. They told both he and I that the prisoner had escaped.   18._____

19. Any superior officer, who, disregards the just complaints of his subordinates, 19._____
    is remiss in the performance of his duty.

20. Only those members of the national organization who resided in the Middle   20._____
    west attended the conference in Chicago.

21. We told him to give the investigation assignment to whoever was available. 21._____

22. Please do not disappoint and embarass us by not appearing in court.   22._____

23. Despite the efforts of the Supervising mechanic, the elevator could not be 23._____
    started.

24. The U.S. Weather Bureau, weather record for the accident date was checked. 24._____

KEY (CORRECT ANSWERS)

1.	D		11.	A
2.	A		12.	B
3.	B		13.	D
4.	D		14.	B
5.	D		15.	C
6.	D		16.	C
7.	C		17.	A
8.	A		18.	A
9.	A		19.	B
10.	D		20.	C

21.	D
22.	C
23.	C
24.	B

———

TEST 2

DIRECTIONS: Each question consists of a sentence. Some of the sentences contain errors in English grammar or usage, punctuation, spelling, or capitalization. A sentence does not contain an error simply because it could be written in a different manner. Choose answer:
- A. If the sentence contains an error in English grammar or usage.
- B. if the sentence contains an error in punctuation.
- C. If the sentence contains an error in spelling or capitalization
- D. If the sentence does not contain any errors.

1. The severity of the sentence prescribed by contemporary statutes—including both the former and the revised New York Penal Laws—do not depend on what crime was intended by the offender.

1.____

2. It is generally recognized that two defects in the early law of attempt played a part in the birth of burglary: (1) immunity from prosecution for conduct short of the last act before completion of the crime, and (2) the relatively minor penalty imposed for an attempt (it being a common law misdemeanor) vis-à-vis the completed offense.

2.____

3. The first sentence of the statute is applicable to employees who enter their place of employment, invited guests, and all other persons who have an express or implied license or privilege to enter the premises.

3.____

4. Contemporary criminal codes in the United States generally divide burglary into various degrees, differentiating the categories according to place, time and other attendent circumstances.

4.____

5. The assignment was completed in record time but the payroll for it has not yet been prepaid.

5.____

6. The operator, on the other hand, is willing to learn me how to use the mimeograph.

6.____

7. She is the prettiest of the three sisters.

7.____

8. She doesn't know; if the mail has arrived.

8.____

9. The doorknob of the office door is broke.

9.____

10. Although the department's supply of scratch pads and stationery have diminished considerably, the allotment for our division has not been reduced.

10.____

11. You have not told us whom you wish to designate as your secretary.

11.____

12. Upon reading the minutes of the last meeting, the new proposal was taken up for consideration.

12.____

13. Before beginning the discussion, we locked the door as a precautionery measure.

13.____

14. The supervisor remarked, "Only those clerks, who perform routine work, are permitted to take a rest period."

14.____

15. Not only will this duplicating machine make accurate copies, but it will also produce a quantity of work equal to fifteen transcribing typists.

15.____

16. "Mr. Jones," said the supervisor, "we regret our inability to grant you an extention of your leave of absence."

16.____

17. Although the employees find the work monotonous and fatigueing, they rarely complain.

17.____

18. We completed the tabulation of the receipts on time despite the fact that Miss Smith our fastest operator was absent for over a week.

18.____

19. The reaction of the employees who attended the meeting, as well as the reaction of those who did not attend, indicates clearly that the schedule is satisfactory to everyone concerned.

19.____

20. Of the two employees, the one in our office is the most efficient.

20.____

21. No one can apply or even understand, the new rules and regulations.

21.____

22. A large amount of supplies were stored in the empty office.

22.____

23. If an employee is occassionally asked to work overtime, he should do so willingly.

23.____

24. It is true that the new procedures are difficult to use but, we are certain that you will learn them quickly.

24.____

25. The office manager said that he did not know who would be given a large allotment under the new plan.

25.____

KEY (CORRECT ANSWERS)

1.	A		11.	D
2.	D		12.	A
3.	D		13.	C
4.	C		14.	B
5.	C		15.	A
6.	A		16.	C
7.	D		17.	C
8.	B		18.	B
9.	A		19.	D
10.	A		20.	A

21.	B
22.	A
23.	C
24.	B
25.	D

TEST 3

DIRECTIONS: Each of the following sentences may be classified MOST appropriately under one of the following categories:
   A. Faulty because of incorrect grammar
   B. Faulty because of incorrect punctuation
   C. Faulty because of incorrect capitalization
   D. Correct

Examine each sentence carefully. Then, in the space at the right, print the capital letter preceding the option which is the BEST of the four suggested above. All incorrect sentence contain but one type of error. Consider a sentence correct if it contains none of the types of errors mentioned, even though there may be other correct ways of expressing the same thought.

1. The desk, as well as the chairs, were moved out of the office.   1._____

2. The clerk whose production was greatest for the month won a day's vacation as first prize.   2._____

3. Upon entering the room, the employees were found hard at work at their desks.   3._____

4. John Smith our new employee always arrives at work on time.   4._____

5. Punish whoever is guilty of stealing the money.   5._____

6. Intelligent and persistent effort lead to success no matter what the job may be.   6._____

7. The secretary asked, "can you call again at three o'clock?"   7._____

8. He told us, that if the report was not accepted at the next meeting, it would have to be rewritten.   8._____

9. He would not have sent the letter if he had known that it would cause so much excitement.   9._____

10. We all looked forward to him coming to visit us.   10._____

11. If you find that you are unable to complete the assignment please notify me as soon as possible.   11._____

12. Every girl in the office went home on time but me; there was still some work for me to finish.   12._____

13. He wanted to know who the letter was addressed to, Mr. Brown or Mr. Smith.   13._____

14. "Mr. Jones, he said, please answer this letter as soon as possible."   14._____

15. The new clerk had an unusual accent inasmuch as he was born and educated in the south.   15._____

16. Although he is younger than her, he earns a higher salary.   16._____

17. Neither of the two administrators are going to attend the conference being held in Washington, D.C.   17._____

18. Since Miss Smith and Miss Jones have more experience than us, they have been given more responsible duties.   18._____

19. Mr. Shaw the supervisor of the stock room maintains an inventory of stationery and office supplies.   19._____

20. Inasmuch as this matter affects both you and I, we should take joint action.   20._____

21. Who do you think will be able to perform this highly technical work?   21._____

22. Of the two employees, John is considered the most competent.   22._____

23. He is not coming home on tuesday; we expect him next week.   23._____

24. Stenographers, as well as typists must be able to type rapidly and accurately.   24._____

25. Having been placed in the safe we were sure that the money would not be stolen.   25._____

_____

KEY (CORRECT ANSWERS)

1.	A		11.	B
2.	D		12.	D
3.	A		13.	A
4.	B		14.	B
5.	D		15.	C
6.	A		16.	A
7.	C		17.	A
8.	B		18.	A
9.	D		19.	B
10.	A		20.	A

21.	D
22.	A
23.	C
24.	B
25.	A

TEST 4

DIRECTIONS: Each of the following sentences consist of four sentences lettered A, B, C, and D. One of the sentences in each group contains an error in grammar or punctuation. Indicate the INCORRECT sentence in each group. *PRINT THE LETTER OF THE CORRECT ANSWER IN THE SPACE AT THE RIGHT.*

1. A. Give the message to whoever is on duty.
   B. The teacher who's pupil won first prize presented the award.
   C. Between you and me, I don't expect the program to succeed.
   D. His running to catch the bus caused the accident.

   1.____

2. A. The process, which was patented only last year is already obsolete.
   B. His interest in science (which continues to the present) led him to convert his basement into a laboratory.
   C. He described the book as "verbose, repetitious, and bombastic".
   D. Our new director will need to possess three qualities: vision, patience, and fortitude.

   2.____

3. A. The length of ladder trucks varies considerably.
   B. The probationary fireman reported to the officer to who he was assigned.
   C. The lecturer emphasized the need for we firemen to be punctual.
   D. Neither the officers nor the members of the company knew about the new procedure.

   3.____

4. A. Ham and eggs is the specialty of the house.
   B. He is one of the students who are on probation.
   C. Do you think that either one of us have a chance to be nominated for president of the class?
   D. I assume that either he was to be in charge or you were.

   4.____

5. A. Its a long road that has no turn.
   B. To run is more tiring than to walk.
   C. We have been assigned three new reports: namely, the statistical summary, the narrative summary, and the budgetary summary.
   D. Had the first payment been made in January, the second would be due in April.

   5.____

6. A. Each employer has his own responsibilities.
   B. If a person speaks correctly, they make a good impression.
   C. Every one of the operators has had her vacation.
   D. Has anybody filed his report?

   6.____

7. A. The manager, with all his salesmen, was obliged to go.
   B. Who besides them is to sign the agreement?
   C. One report without the others is incomplete.
   D. Several clerks, as well as the proprietor, was injured.

   7.____

8.   A.   A suspension of these activities is expected.   8.____
      B.   The machine is economical because first cost and upkeep are low.
      C.   A knowledge of stenography and filing are required for this position.
      D.   The condition in which the goods were received shows that the packing was not done properly.

9.   A.   There seems to be a great many reasons for disagreement.   9.____
      B.   It does not seem possible that they could have failed.
      C.   Have there always been too few applicants for these positions?
      D.   There is no excuse for these errors.

10. A.   We shall be pleased to answer your question.   10.____
      B.   Shall we plan the meeting for Saturday?
      C.   I will call you promptly at seven.
      D.   Can I borrow your book after you have read it?

11. A.   You are as capable as I.   11.____
      B.   Everyone is willing to sign but him and me.
      C.   As for he and his assistant, I cannot praise them too highly.
      D.   Between you and me, I think he will be dismissed.

12. A.   Our competitors bid above us last week.   12.____
      B.   The survey which was began last year has not yet been completed.
      C.   The operators had shown that they understood their instructions.
      D.   We have never ridden over worse roads.

13. A.   Who did they say was responsible?   13.____
      B.   Whom did you suspect?
      C.   Who do you suppose it was?
      D.   Whom do you mean?

14. A.   Of the two propositions, this is the worse.   14.____
      B.   Which report do you consider the best—the one in January or the one in July?
      C.   I believe this is the most practicable of the many plans submitted.
      D.   He is the youngest employee in the organization.

15. A.   The firm had but three orders last week.   15.____
      B.   That doesn't really seem possible.
      C.   After twenty years scarcely none of the old business remains.
      D.   Has he done nothing about it?

KEY (CORRECT ANSWERS)

1.	B	6.	B	11.	C
2.	A	7.	D	12.	B
3.	C	8.	C	13.	A
4.	C	9.	A	14.	B
5.	A	10.	D	15.	C

———

English Expression
CHOICE OF EXPRESSION
COMMENTARY

One special form of the English Expression multiple-choice question in current use requires the candidate to select from among five (5) versions of a particular part of a sentence (or of an entire sentence), the one version that expresses the idea of the sentence most clearly, effectively, and accurately. Thus, the candidate is required not only to recognize errors, but also to choose the best way of phrasing a particular part of the sentence.

This is a test of choice of expression, which assays the candidate's ability to express himself correctly and effectively, including his sensitivity to the subleties and nuances of the language.

SAMPLE QUESTIONS

DIRECTIONS: In each of the following sentences some part of the sentence or the entire sentence is underlined. The underlined part presents a problem in the appropriate use of language. Beneath each sentence you will find five ways of writing the underlined part. The first of these indicates no change (that is, it repeats the original), but the other four are all different. If you think the original sentence is better than any of the suggested changes, you should choose answer A; otherwise you should mark one of the other choices. Select the best answer and blacken the corresponding space on the answer sheet.

This is a test of correctness and effectiveness of expression. In choosing answers, follow the requirements of standard written English; that is, pay attention to acceptable usage in grammar, diction (choice of words), sentence construction, and punctuation. Choose the answer that produces the most effective sentence - clear and exact, without awkwardness or ambiguity. Do not make a choice that changes the meaning of the original sentence.

SAMPLE QUESTION 1
Although these states now trade actively with the West, and although they are willing to exchange technological information, their arts and thoughts and social structure <u>remains substantially similar to what it has always been</u>.
    A.   remains substantially similar to what it has always been
    B.   remain substantially unchanged
    C.   remains substantially unchanged
    D.   remain substantially similar to what they have always been
    E.   remain substantially without being changed

The purpose of questions of this type is to determine the candidate's ability to select the clearest and most effective means of expressing what the statement attempts to say. In this example, the phrasing in the statement, which is repeated in A, presents a problem of agreement between a subject and its verb <u>(their arts and thought and social structure</u> and <u>remains)</u>, a problem of agreement between a pronoun and its antecedent <u>(their arts and thought and social structure</u> and <u>it)</u>, and a problem of precise and concise phrasing <u>(remains substantially similar to what it has always been</u> for <u>remains substantially unchanged)</u>. Each of the four remaining choices in some way corrects one or more of the faults in the sentence, but only one deals with all three problems satisfactorily. Although C presents a more careful and concise wording of the phrasing of the statement and, in the process, eliminates the problem of agreement between pronoun and antecedent, it fails to correct the problem of agreement between the subject and its verb. In D, the subject agrees with its verb and the pronoun agrees with its antecedent, but the phrasing is not so accurate as it should be. The same difficulty persists in E. Only in B are all the problems presented corrected satisfactorily. The question is not difficult.

SAMPLE QUESTION 2

Her latest novel is the largest in scope, the most accomplished in technique, and <u>it is more significant in theme than anything</u> she has written.

   A.   it is more significant in theme than anything
   B.   it is most significant in theme of anything
   C.   more significant in theme than anything
   D.   the most significant in theme than anything
   E.   the most significant in theme of anything

This question is of greater difficulty than the preceding one.

The problem posed in the sentence and repeated in A, is essentially one of parallelism: Does the underlined portion of the sentence follow the pattern established by the first two elements of the series (the largest ... the most accomplished)? It does not, for it introduces a pronoun and verb (it is) that the second term of the series indicates should be omitted and a degree of comparison (more significant) that is not in keeping with the superlatives used earlier in the sentence. B uses the superlative degree of <u>significant</u> but retains the unnecessary <u>it is</u>; C removes the <u>it is.</u> but retains the faulty comparative form of the adjective. D corrects both errors in parallelism, but introduces an error in idiom (the most ...than). Only E corrects all the problems without introducing another fault.

SAMPLE QUESTION 3

Desiring to insure the continuity of their knowledge, <u>magical lore is transmitted by the chiefs</u> to their descendants.

   A.   magical lore is transmitted by the chiefs
   B.   transmission of magical lore is made by the chiefs
   C.   the chiefs' magical lore is transmitted
   D.   the chiefs transmit magical lore
   E.   the chiefs make transmission of magical lore
The CORRECT answer is D.

SAMPLE QUESTION 4

<u>As Malcolm walks quickly and confident</u> into the purser's office, the rest of the crew wondered whether he would be charged with the theft.

   A.   As Malcolm walks quickly and confident
   B.   As Malcolm was walking quick and confident
   C.   As Malcolm walked quickly and confident
   D.   As Malcolm walked quickly and confidently
   E.   As Malcolm walks quickly and confidently
The CORRECT answer is D.

SAMPLE QUESTION 5

The chairman, <u>granted the power to assign any duties to whoever he </u>wished,was still unable to prevent bickering.

    A.   granted the power to assign any duties to whoever he wished
    B.   granting the power to assign any duties to whoever he wished
    C.   being granted the power to assign any duties to whoever he wished
    D.   having been granted the power to assign any duties to whosoever he wished
    E.   granted the power to assign any duties to whomever he wished

The CORRECT answer is E.

SAMPLE QUESTION 6

Certainly, well-seasoned products are more expensive, <u>but those kinds prove cheaper</u> in the end.

    A.   but those kinds prove cheaper
    B.   but these kinds prove cheaper
    C.   but that kind proves cheaper
    D.   but those kind prove cheaper
    E.   but this kind proves cheaper

The CORRECT answer is A.

SAMPLE QUESTION 7

"We shall not," he shouted, "whatever the <u>difficulties." "lose faith in the success of our </u>plan!"

    A.   difficulties," "lose faith in the success of our plan!"
    B.   difficulties, "lose faith in the success of our plan"!
    C.   "difficulties, lose faith in the success of our plan!"
    D.   difficulties, lose faith in the success of our plan"!
    E.   difficulties, lose faith in the success of our plan!"

The CORRECT answer is E.

SAMPLE QUESTION 8

<u>Climbing up the tree,</u> the lush foliage obscured the chattering monkeys.

    A.   Climbing up the tree
    B.   Having climbed up the tree
    C.   Clambering up the tree
    D.   After we had climbed up the tree
    E.   As we climbed up the tree

The CORRECT answer is E.

EXAMINATION SECTION
TEST 1

DIRECTIONS: See DIRECTIONS for Sample Questions on page 1. *PRINT THE LETTER OF THE CORRECT ANSWER IN THE SPACE AT THE RIGHT.*

1.   At the opening of the story, Charles Gilbert <u>has just come</u> to make his home with his two unmarried aunts.   1.___

    A.   No change   B.   hadn't hardly come   C.   has just came
    D.   had just come   E.   has hardly came

2.   The sisters, who are no longer young, <u>are use to living</u> quiet lives.   2.___

    A.   No change   B.   are used to live
    C.   are use'd to living   D.   are used to living
    E.   are use to live

3.   They <u>willingly except</u> the child.   3.___

    A.   No change   B.   willingly eccepted
    C.   willingly accepted   D.   willingly acepted
    E.   willingly accept

4.   As the months pass, Charles' presence <u>affects many changes</u> in their household.   4.___

    A.   No change   B.   affect many changes
    C.   effects many changes   D.   effect many changes
    E.   affected many changes

5.   These changes <u>is not all together</u> to their liking.   5.___

    A.   No change   B.   is not altogether
    C.   are not all together   D.   are not altogether
    E.   is not alltogether

6.   In fact, they have some difficulty in adapting <u>theirselves</u> to these changes.   6.___

    A.   No change   B.   in adopting theirselves
    C.   in adopting themselves   D.   in adapting theirselves
    E.   in adapting themselves

7.   That is the man <u>whom I believe</u> was the driver of the car.   7.___

    A.   No change   B.   who I believed   C.   whom I believed
    D.   who to believe   E.   who I believe

8.   John's climb to fame was more rapid <u>than his brother's</u>.   8.___

    A.   No change   B.   than his brother
    C.   than that of his brother's   D.   than for his brother
    E.   than the brother

9.   We knew that he <u>had formerly swam</u> on an Olympic team.   9.___

    A.   No change   B.   has formerly swum
    C.   did formerly swum   D.   had formerly swum
    E.   has formerly swam

10. Not one of us loyal supporters <u>ever get a pass</u> to a game   10.____

   A. No change   B. ever did got a pass
   C. ever has get a pass   D. ever had get a pass
   E. ever gets a pass

11. He <u>was complemented</u> on having done a fine job.   11.____

   A. No change   B. was compliminted
   C. was compleminted   D. was complimented
   E. did get complimented

12. This play is different from the one we <u>had seen</u> last night.   12.____

   A. No change   B. have seen   C. had saw
   D. have saw   E. saw

13. A row of trees <u>was planted</u> in front of the house.   13.____

   A. No change   B. was to be planted   C. were planted
   D. were to be planted   E. are planted

14. The house <u>looked its age</u> in spite of our attempts to beautify it.   14.____

   A. No change   B. looks its age   C. looked its' age
   D. looked it's age E. looked it age

15. I do not know <u>what to council</u> in this case.   15.____

   A. No change   B. where to council
   C. when to councel   D. what to counsel
   E. what to counsil

16. She is more capable <u>than any other girl</u> in the office.   16.____

   A. No change   B. than any girl
   C. than any other girls   D. than other girl
   E. than other girls

17. At the picnic the young children <u>behaved very good</u>.   17.____

   A. No change   B. behave very good
   C. behaved better   D. behave very well
   E. behaved very well

18. I resolved <u>to go irregardless of</u> the consequences.   18.____

   A. No change   B. to depart irregardless of
   C. to go regarding of   D. to go regardingly of
   E. to go regardless of

19. The new movie has a number of actors <u>which have been famous</u> on Broadway.   19.____

   A. No change   B. which had been famous
   C. who had been famous   D. that are famous
   E. who have been famous

175

20. I am certain that these books <u>are not our's</u>.   20.___

   A. No change   B. have not been ours'
   C. have not been our's   D. are not ours
   E. are not ours'

21. <u>Each of your papers is filed</u> for future reference.   21.___

   A. No change
   B. Each of your papers are filed
   C. Each of your papers have been filed
   D. Each of your papers are to be filed
   E. Each of your paper is filed

22. I wish that <u>he would take his work more serious</u>.   22.___

   A. No change
   B. he took his work more serious
   C. he will take his work more serious
   D. he shall take his work more seriously
   E. he would take his work more seriously

23. <u>After the treasurer report had been read</u>, the chairman called for the reports of the com-   23.___
    mittees.

   A. No change
   B. After the treasure's report had been read
   C. After the treasurers' report had been read
   D. After the treasurer's report had been read
   E. After the treasurer's report had been read

24. Last night the stranger <u>lead us down the mountain</u>.   24.___

   A. No change
   B. leaded us down the mountain
   C. let us down the mountain
   D. led us down the mountain
   E. had led us down the mountain

25. It would not be safe <u>for either you or I</u> to travel in Viet Nam.   25.___

   A. No change   B. for either you or me
   C. for either I or you   D. for either of you or I
   E. for either of I or you

KEY (CORRECT ANSWERS)

1.	A	11.	D
2.	D	12.	E
3.	E	13.	A
4.	C	14.	A
5.	D	15.	D
6.	E	16.	A
7.	E	17.	E
8.	A	18.	E
9.	D	19.	E
10.	E	20.	D

21.	A
22.	E
23.	E
24.	D
25.	B

———

TEST 2

DIRECTIONS: See DIRECTIONS for Sample Questions on page 1. *PRINT THE LETTER OF THE CORRECT ANSWER IN THE SPACE AT THE RIGHT.*

1. Both the body and the mind <u>needs exercise</u>.   1.___

    A. No change   B. have needs of exercise
    C. is needful of exercise   D. needed exercise
    E. need exercise

2. <u>It's paw injured</u>, the animal limped down the road.   2.___

    A. No change   B. It's paw injured
    C. Its paw injured   D. Its' paw injured
    E. Its paw injure

3. The butter <u>tastes rancidly</u>.   3.___

    A. No change   B. tastes rancid
    C. tasted rancidly   D. taste rancidly
    E. taste rancid

4. <u>Who do you think</u> has sent me a letter?   4.___

    A. No change   B. Whom do you think
    C. Whome do you think   D. Who did you think
    E. Whom can you think

5. If more nations <u>would have fought</u> against tyranny, the course of history would have been   5.___
different.

    A. No change   B. would fight
    C. could have fought   D. fought
    E. had fought

6. Radio and television programs, along with other media of communication, <u>helps us to</u>   6.___
<u>appreciate the arts and to keep informed</u>.

    A. No change
    B. helps us to appreciate the arts and to be informed
    C. helps us to be appreciative of the arts and to keep informed
    D. helps us to be appreciative of the arts and to be informed
    E. help us to appreciate the arts and to keep informed

7. Music, <u>for example most always</u> has listening and viewing audiences numbering in the   7.___
hundreds of thousands.

    A. No change   B. for example, most always
    C. for example, almost always   D. for example nearly always
    E. for example, near always

8. When operas are performed on radio or television, <u>they effect the listener</u>.   8.___

    A. No change   B. they inflict the listener
    C. these effect the listeners   D. they affects the listeners
    E. they affect the listener

9. <u>After hearing then the listener wants</u> to buy recordings of the music.   9._____

    A.   No change
    B.   After hearing them, the listener wants
    C.   After hearing them, the listener want
    D.   By hearing them the listener wants
    E.   By hearing them, the listener wants

10. <u>To we Americans</u> the daily news program has become important.   10._____

    A.   No change   B.   To we the Americans
    C.   To us Americans   D.   To us the Americans
    E.   To we and us Americans

11. This has resulted from <u>it's coverage of a days' events</u>.   11._____

    A.   No change
    B.   from its coverage of a days' events
    C.   from it's coverage of a day's events
    D.   from its' coverage of a day's events
    E.   from its coverage of a day's events

12. In schools, <u>teachers advice their students</u> to listen to or to view certain programs.   12._____

    A.   No change
    B.   teachers advise there students
    C.   teachers advise their students
    D.   the teacher advises their students
    E.   teachers advise his students

13. In these ways <u>we are preceding toward the goal</u> of an educated and an informed public.   13._____

    A.   No change
    B.   we are preeceding toward the goal
    C.   we are proceeding toward the goal
    D.   we are preceding toward the goal
    E.   we are proceeding toward the goal

14. The cost of living <u>is raising again</u>.   14._____

    A.   No change   B.   are raising again
    C.   is rising again   D.   are rising again
    E.   is risen again

15. We did not realize that the boys' father <u>had forbidden them to keep there puppy</u>.   15._____

    A.   No change
    B.   had forbade them to keep there puppy
    C.   had forbade them to keep their puppy
    D.   has forbidden them to keep their puppy
    E.   had forbidden them to keep their puppy

16. <u>Her willingness to help others</u>' was her outstanding characteristic.   16._____

    A.   No change
    B.   Her willingness to help other's,

C. Her willingness to help others's
D. Her willingness to help others
E. Her willingness to help each other

17. Because he did not have an invitation, the girls objected to him going,   17.___

    A. No change
    B. the girls object to him going
    C. the girls objected to him's going
    D. the girls objected to his going
    E. the girls object to his going

18. Weekly dances have become a popular accepted feature of the summer schedule.   18.___

    A. No change
    B. have become a popular accepted feature
    C. have become a popular excepted feature
    D. have become a popularly excepted feature
    E. have become a popularly accepted feature

19. I couldn't hardly believe that he would desert our party.   19.___

    A. No change   B. would hardly believe
    C. didn't hardly believe   D. should hardly believe
    E. could hardly believe

20. I found the place in the book more readily than she.   20.___

    A. No change   B. more readily than her
    C. more ready than she   D. more quickly than her
    E. more ready than her

21. A good example of American outdoor activities are sports.   21.___

    A. No change   B. is sports   C. are sport
    D. are sports events   E. are to be found in sports

22. My point of view is much different from your's.   22.___

    A. No change
    B. much different than your's
    C. much different than yours
    D. much different from yours
    E. much different than yours'

23. The cook was suppose to use two spoonfuls of dressing for each serving.   23.___

    A. No change
    B. was supposed to use two spoonsful
    C. was suppose to use two spoonsful
    D. was supposed to use two spoonsfuls
    E. was supposed to use two spoonfuls

24. If anyone has any doubt about the values of the tour, refer him to me.   24.___

    A. No change   B. refer him to I   C. refer me to he
    D. refer them to me   E. refer he to I

25. We expect that the affects of <u>the trip will be beneficial</u>.   25.____

   A. No change
   B. the effects of the trip will be beneficial
   C. the effects of the trip should be beneficial
   D. the affects of the trip would be beneficial
   E. the effects of the trip will be benificial

KEY (CORRECT ANSWERS)

1.	E		11.	E
2.	C		12.	C
3.	B		13.	E
4.	A		14.	C
5.	E		15.	E
6.	E		16.	D
7.	C		17.	D
8.	E		18.	E
9.	B		19.	E
10.	C		20.	A

21.	B
22.	D
23.	E
24.	A
25.	B

TEST 3

DIRECTIONS: See DIRECTIONS for Sample Questions on page 1. *PRINT THE LETTER OF THE CORRECT ANSWER IN THE SPACE AT THE RIGHT.*

1. <u>That, my friend</u> is not the proper attitude.

   A. No change
   B. That my friend
   C. That my friend,
   D. That -- my friend
   E. That, my friend,

   1.___

2. The girl refused <u>to admit that the not was her's</u>.

   A. No change
   B. that the note were her's
   C. that the note was hers'
   D. that the note was hers
   E. that the note might be hers

   2.___

3. There <u>were fewer candidates that we had been lead</u> to expect.

   A. No change
   B. was fewer candidates than we had been lead
   C. were fewer candidates than we had been lead
   D. was fewer candidates than we had been led
   E. were fewer candidates than we had been led

   3.___

4. When I first saw the car, <u>its steering wheel was broke</u>.

   A. No change
   B. its' steering wheel was broken
   C. it's steering wheel had been broken
   D. its steering wheel were broken
   E. its steering wheel was broken

   4.___

5. I find that the essential spirit for <u>we beginners is missing</u>.

   A. No change
   B. we who begin are missing
   C. us beginners are missing
   D. us beginners is missing
   E. we beginners are missing

   5.___

6. I believe that <u>you had ought</u> to study harder.

   A. No change
   B. you should have ought
   C. you had better
   D. you ought to have
   E. you ought

   6.___

7. This is <u>Tom, whom I am sure</u>, will be glad to help you.

   A. No change
   B. Tom whom, I am sure,
   C. Tom, whom I am sure,
   D. Tom who I am sure,
   E. Tom, who, I am sure,

   7.___

8. His father or his mother <u>has read to him</u> every night since he was very small.

   A. No change
   B. did read to him
   C. have been reading to him
   D. had read to him
   E. have read to him

   8.___

9. He <u>become</u> an authority on the theater and its great personalities.   9.____

    A. No change
    C. become the authority
    E. becamed an authority
    B. becomed an authority
    D. became an authority

10. I know of no other person in the club <u>who is more kind-hearted than her</u>.   10.____

    A. No change
    B. who are more kind-hearted than they
    C. who are more kind-hearted than them
    D. whom are more kind-hearted than she
    E. who is more kind-hearted than she

11. After Bill <u>had ran the mile</u>, he was breathless.   11.____

    A. No change
    C. has ran the mile
    E. had run the mile
    B. had runned the mile
    D. had ranned the mile

12. Wilson <u>has scarcely no equal</u> as a pitcher.   12.____

    A. No change
    C. has hardly no equal
    E. has scarcely any equals
    B. has scarcely an equal
    D. had scarcely no equal

13. It <u>was the worse storm</u> that the inhabitants of the island could remember.   13.____

    A. No change
    C. was the worst storm
    E. was the most worse storm
    B. were the worse storm
    D. was the worsest storm

14. If only <u>we had began</u> before it was too late'.   14.____

    A. No change
    C. we would have begun
    E. we had beginned
    B. we had began
    D. we had begun

15. <u>Lets evaluate</u> our year's work.   15.____

    A. No change
    C. Lets' evaluate
    E. Let's evaluate
    B. Let us' evaluate
    D. Lets' us evaluate

16. This is an organization <u>with which I wouldn't want to be associated with</u>.   16.____

    A. No change
    B. with whom I wouldn't want to be associated with
    C. that I wouldn't want to be associated
    D. with which I would want not to be associated with
    E. with which I wouldn't want to be associated

17. The enemy fled in many directions, <u>leaving there weapons</u> on the field.   17.____

    A. No change
    C. letting their weapons
    E. leaving their weapons
    B. leaving its weapons
    D. leaving alone there weapons

18. I hoped that John could effect a compromise between the approved forces.   18.___

    A. No change
    B. could accept a compromise between
    C. could except a compromise between
    D. would have effected a compromise among
    E. could effect a compromise among

19. I was surprised to learn that he has not always spoke English fluently.   19.___

    A. No change
    B. that he had not always spoke English
    C. that he did not always speak English
    D. that he has not always spoken English
    E. that he could not always speak English

20. The lawyer promised to notify my father and I of his plans for a new trial.   20.___

    A. No change
    B. to notify I and my father
    C. to notify me and our father
    D. to notify my father and me
    E. to notify mine father and me

21. The most important feature of the series of tennis lessons were the large amount of   21.___
strokes taught.

    A. No change
    B. were the large number
    C. was the large amount
    D. was the largeness of the amount
    E. was the large number

22. That the prize proved to be beyond her reach did not surprise him.   22.___

    A. No change
    B. has not surprised him
    C. had not ought to have surprised him
    D. should not surprise him
    E. would not have surprised him

23. I am not all together in agreement with the author's point of view.   23.___

    A. No change   B. all together of agreement
    C. all together for agreement   D. altogether with agreement
    E. altogether in agreement

24. Windstorms have recently established a record which meteorologists hope will not be   24.___
equal for many years to come.

    A. No change   B. will be equal
    C. will not be equalized   D. will be equaled
    E. will not be equaled

25. A large number of Shakespeare's soliloquies must be considered <u>as representing thought</u>, not speech.

    A. No change
    B. as representative of speech, not thought
    C. as represented by thought, not speech
    D. as indicating thought, not speech
    E. as representative of thought, more than speech

25.____

KEY (CORRECT ANSWERS)

1.	E		11.	E
2.	D		12.	B
3.	E		13.	C
4.	E		14.	D
5.	D		15.	E
6.	E		16.	E
7.	E		17.	E
8.	A		18.	A
9.	D		19.	D
10.	E		20.	D

21.	E
22.	A
23.	E
24.	E
25.	A

TEST 4

DIRECTIONS: See DIRECTIONS for Sample Questions on page 1. *PRINT THE LETTER OF THE CORRECT ANSWER IN THE SPACE AT THE RIGHT.*

1.   A sight to inspire fear <u>are wild animals on the lose</u>.   1.___

    A.   No change
    B.   are wild animals on the loose
    C.   is wild animals on the loose
    D.   is wild animals on the lose
    E.   are wild animals loose

2.   For many years, the settlers <u>had been seeking to workship as they please</u>.   2.___

    A.   No change
    B.   had seeked to workship as they pleased
    C.   sought to workship as they please
    D.   sought to have worshiped as they pleased
    E.   had been seeking to worship as they pleased

3.   The girls stated that the dresses were <u>their's</u>.   3.___

    A.   No change   B.   there's   C.   theirs   D.   theirs'   E.   there own

4.   <u>Please fellows</u> don't drop the ball.   4.___

    A.   No change   B.   Please, fellows   C.   Please fellows;
    D.   Please, fellows,   E.   Please! fellows

5.   Your sweater <u>has laid</u> on the floor for a week.   5.___

    A.   No change   B.   has been laying
    C.   has been lying   D.   laid
    E.   has been lain

6.   I wonder whether <u>you're sure that scheme of yours</u>' will work.   6.___

    A.   No change
    B.   your sure that scheme of your's
    C.   you're sure that scheme of yours
    D.   your sure that scheme of yours
    E.   you're sure that your scheme's

7.   Please let <u>her and me</u> do it.   7.___

    A.   No change   B.   she and I   C.   she and me
    D.   her and I   E.   her and him

8.   I expected him to be angry <u>and to scold</u> her.   8.___

    A.   No change   B.   and that he would scold
    C.   and that he might scold   D.   and that he should scold
    E.   , scolding

9.   Knowing little about algebra, <u>it was difficult to solve the equation</u>.   9.___

A. No change
B. the equation was difficult to solve
C. the solution to the equation was difficult to find
D. I found it difficult to solve the equation
E. it being difficult to solve the equation

10. He <u>worked more diligent</u> now that he had become vice president of the company.　　10._____

   A. No change　　　　　　　　　　B. works more diligent
   C. works more diligently　　　　　D. began to work more diligent
   E. worked more diligently

11. <u>Flinging himself at the barricade</u> he pounded on it furiously.　　11._____

   A. No change
   B. Flinging himself at the barricade: he
   C. Flinging himself at the barricade - he
   D. Flinging himself at the barricade; he
   E. Flinging himself at the barricade, he

12. When he <u>begun to give us advise</u>, we stopped listening.　　12._____

   A. No change　　　　　　　　　　B. began to give us advise
   C. begun to give us advice　　　　D. began to give us advice
   E. begin to give us advice

13. John was only one of the boys whom as you know was not eligible.　　13._____

   A. No change　　　　　　　　　　B. who as you know were
   C. whom as you know were　　　　D. who as you know was
   E. who as you know is

14. Why was Jane and he permitted to go?　　14._____

   A. No change　　　　　　　　　　B. was Jane and him
   C. were Jane and he　　　　　　　D. were Jane and him
   E. weren't Jane and he

15. <u>Take courage Tom: we</u> all make mistakes.　　15._____

   A. No change　　　　　　　　　　B. Take courage Tom - we
   C. Take courage, Tom; we　　　　D. Take courage, Tom we
   E. Take courage! Tom: we

16. Henderson, the president of the class and <u>who is also captain of the team</u>, will lead the　　16._____
    rally.

   A. No change
   B. since he is captain of the team
   C. captain of the team
   D. also being captain of the team
   E. who be also captain of the team

17. Our car has always <u>run good</u> on that kind of gasoline.　　17._____

   A. No change　　　B. run well　　　C. ran good
   D. ran well　　　　E. done good

18. There was a serious difference of opinion <u>among her and I</u>. 18.___

    A. No change
    B. among she and I
    C. between her and I
    D. between her and me
    E. among her and me

19. "This is most unusual," said <u>Helen, "the</u> mailman has never been this late before." 19.___

    A. No change
    B. Helen, "The
    C. Helen - "The
    D. Helen; "The
    E. Helen." The

20. The three main characters in the story are Johnny Hobart a <u>teenager, his mother a widow, and</u> the local druggist. 20.___

    A. No change
    B. teenager; his mother, a widow; and
    C. teenager; his mother a widow; and
    D. teenager, his mother, a widow and
    E. teenager, his mother, a widow; and

21. How much <u>has food costs raised</u> during the past year? 21.___

    A. No change
    B. have food costs rose
    C. have food costs risen
    D. has food costs risen
    E. have food costs been raised

22. "Will you come <u>too" she pleaded</u>? 22.___

    A. No change
    B. too,?"she pleaded.
    C. too?" she pleaded.
    D. too," she pleaded?
    E. too, she pleaded?"

23. If he <u>would have drank</u> more milk, his health would have been better. 23.___

    A. No change
    B. would drink
    C. had drank
    D. had he drunk
    E. had drunk

24. Jack had <u>no sooner laid down and fallen asleep when</u> the alarm sounded. 24.___

    A. No change
    B. no sooner lain down and fallen asleep than
    C. no sooner lay down and fell asleep when
    D. no sooner laid down and fell asleep than
    E. no sooner lain down than he fell asleep when

25. Jackson is <u>one of the few Sophomores, who has</u> ever made the varsity team. 25.___

    A. No change
    B. one of the few Sophomores, who have
    C. one of the few sophomores, who has
    D. one of the few sophomores who have
    E. one of the few sophomores who has

KEY (CORRECT ANSWERS)

1.	C	11.	E
2.	E	12.	D
3.	C	13.	B
4.	D	14.	C
5.	C	15.	C
6.	C	16.	C
7.	A	17.	B
8.	A	18.	D
9.	D	19.	E
10.	E	20.	B

21.	C
22.	C
23.	E
24.	B
25.	D

———

TEST 5

DIRECTIONS: See DIRECTIONS for Sample Questions on page 1. *PRINT THE LETTER OF THE CORRECT ANSWER IN THE SPACE AT THE RIGHT.*

1. The lieutenant had ridden almost a kilometer when the scattering shells <u>begin landing</u>   1.___
    uncomfortably close.

    A. No change   B. beginning to land   C. began to land
    D. having begun to land   E. begin to land

2. <u>Having studied eight weeks,</u> he now feels sufficiently prepared for the examination.   2.___

    A. No change
    B. For eight weeks he studies so
    C. Due to eight weeks of study
    D. After eight weeks of studying
    E. Since he's been spending the last eight weeks in study

3. <u>Coming from the Greek, and the word "democracy" means government by the people.</u>   3.___

    A. No change
    B. "Democracy," the word which comes from the Greek, means government by the people.
    C. Meaning government by the people, the word "democracy" comes from the Greek.
    D. Its meaning being government by the people in Greek, the word is "democracy."
    E. The word "democracy" comes from the Greek and means government by the people.

4. Moslem universities were one of the chief agencies <u>in the development</u> and spreading   4.___
    Arabic civilization.

    A. No change   B. in the development of
    C. to develop   D. in developing
    E. for the developing of

5. The water of Bering Strait <u>were closing</u> to navigation by ice early in the fall.   5.___

    A. No change   B. has closed   C. have closed
    D. had been closed   E. closed

6. The man, <u>since he grew up</u> on the block, felt sentimental when returning to it.   6.___

    A. No change   B. having grown up
    C. growing up   D. since he had grown up
    E. whose growth had been

7. <u>Jack and Jill watched the canoe to take their parents out of sight round the bend of the</u>   7.___
    <u>creek.</u>

    A. No change
    B. The canoe, taking their parents out of sight, rounds the bend as Jack and Jill watch.
    C. Jack and Jill watched the canoe round the bend of the creek, taking their parents out of sight.

D. The canoe rounded the bend of the creek as it took their parents out of sight, Jack and Jill watching.

E. Jack and Jill watching,the canoe is rounding the bend of the creek to take their parents out of sight.

8. Chaucer's best-known work is THE CANTERBURY TALES, a collection of stories <u>which he tells</u> with a group of pilgrims as they travel to the town of Canterbury.　　　8.____

   A. No change   B. which he tells through   C. who tell
   D. told by   E. told through

9. The Estates-General, the old feudal assembly of France, <u>had not met</u> for one hundred and sevety-five years when it convened in 1789.　　　9.____

   A. No change   B. has not met   C. has not been meeting
   D. had no meeting   E. has no meeting

10. Just forty years ago, <u>there had been</u> fewer than one hundred symphony orchestras in the United States.　　　10.____

   A. No change   B. there had   C. there were
   D. there was   E. there existed

11. Mrs. Smith complained that her son's temper tantrums <u>aggragravated her</u> and caused her to have a headache.　　　11.____

   A. No change   B. gave her aggravation
   C. were aggravating to her   D. aggravated her condition
   E. instigated

12. A girl <u>like I</u> would never be seen in a place like that.　　　12.____

   A. No change B. as I   C. as me   D. like I am   E. like me

13. <u>Between you and me</u>. my opinion is that this room is certainly nicer than the first one we saw.　　　13.____

   A. No change   B. between you and I   C. among you and me
   D. betwixt you and I   E. between we

14. It is important to know for <u>what kind of a person you are working</u>.　　　14.____

   A. No change
   B. what kind of a person for whom you are working
   C. what kind of person you are working
   D. what kind of person you are working for
   E. what kind of a person you are working for

15. I had <u>all ready</u> finished the book before you came in.　　　15.____

   A. No change B. already   C. previously D. allready   E. all

16. <u>Ask not for who the bell tolls, it tolls for thee</u>.　　　16.____

   A. No change
   B. Ask not for whom the bell tolls, it tolls for thee.
   C. Ask not whom the bell tolls for; it tolls for thee.

D. Ask not for whom the bell tolls; it tolls for thee.
E. Ask not who the bell tolls for: It tolls for thee.

17. It is a far better thing I do, than <u>ever I did</u> before.   17.___

   A. No change   B. never I did   C. I have ever did
   D. I have ever been done   E. ever have I done

18. <u>Ending a sentence with a preposition is something up with which I will not put.</u>   18.___

   A. No change
   B. Ending a sentence with a preposition is something with which I will not put up.
   C. To end a sentence with a preposition is that which I will not put up with.
   D. Ending a sentence with a preposition is something of which I will not put up.
   E. Something I will not put up with is ending a sentence with a preposition.

19. Everyone <u>took off their hats and stand up</u> to sing the national anthem.   19.___

   A. No change
   B. took off their hats and stood up
   C. take off their hats and stand up
   D. took off his hat and stood up
   E. have taken off their hats and standing up

20. <u>She promised me that if she had the opportunity she would have came irregardless of</u>   20.___
    <u>the weather.</u>

   A. No change
   B. She promised me that if she had the opportunity she would have come regardless
       of the weather.
   C. She assured me that had she had the opportunity she would have come regard-
       less of the weather.
   D. She assured me that if she would have had the opportunity she would have come
       regardless of the weather.
   E. She promised me that if she had had the opportunity she would have came irre-
       gardless of the weather.

21. The man decided it would be advisable to marry a girl <u>somewhat younger than him.</u>   21.___

   A. No change   B. somehow younger than him
   C. some younger than him   D. somewhat younger from him
   E. somewhat younger than he

22. Sitting near the campfire, the old man told <u>John and I about many exciting adventures he</u>   22.___
    <u>had had</u>.

   A. No change
   B. John and me about many exciting adventures he had.
   C. John and I about much exciting adventure which he'd had.
   D. John and me about many exciting adventures he had had.
   E. John and me about many exciting adventures he has had.

23. If you had stood at home and done your homework, you would not have failed the course.   23.____

    A. No change
    B. If you had stood at home and done you're homework,
    C. If you had staid at home and done your homework,
    D. Had you stayed at home and done your homework,
    E. Had you stood at home and done your homework,

24. The children didn't, as a rule, do anything beyond what they were told to do.   24.____

    A. No change   B. do hardly anything beyond
    C. do anything except   D. do hardly anything except for
    E. do nothing beyond

25. Either the girls or him is right.   25.____

    A. No change
    B. Either the girls or he is
    C. Either the girls or him are
    D. Either the girls or he are
    E. Either the girls nor he is

KEY (CORRECT ANSWERS)

1. C	11. D
2. A	12. E
3. E	13. A
4. D	14. C
5. D	15. B
6. B	16. D
7. C	17. E
8. D	18. E
9. A	19. D
10. C	20. C

21. E
22. D
23. D
24. A
25. B

PHILOSOPHY, PRINCIPLES, PRACTICES AND TECHNICS
OF
SUPERVISION, ADMINISTRATION, MANAGEMENT AND ORGANIZATION

TABLE OF CONTENTS

PHILOSOPHY, PRINCIPLES, PRACTICES, AND TECHNICS
OF
SUPERVISION, ADMINISTRATION, MANAGEMENT AND ORGANIZATION

I. MEANING OF SUPERVISION

The extension of the democratic philosophy has been accompanied by an extension in the scope of supervision. Modern leaders and supervisors no longer think of supervision in the narrow sense of being confined chiefly to visiting employees, supplying materials, or rating the staff. They regard supervision as being intimately related to all the concerned agencies of society, they speak of the supervisor's function in terms of "growth", rather than the "improvement," of employees.

This modern concept of supervision may be defined as follows:

Supervision is leadership and the development of leadership within groups which are cooperatively engaged in inspection, research, training, guidance and evaluation.

II. THE OLD AND THE NEW SUPERVISION

TRADITIONAL
1. Inspection
2. Focused on the employee
3. Visitation
4. Random and haphazard
5. Imposed and authoritarian
6. One person usually

MODERN
1. Study and analysis
2. Focused on aims, materials, methods, supervisors, employees, environment
3. Demonstrations, intervisitation, workshops, directed reading, bulletins, etc.
4. Definitely organized and planned (scientific)
5. Cooperative and democratic
6. Many persons involved (creative)

III THE EIGHT (8) BASIC PRINCIPLES OF THE NEW SUPERVISION

1. PRINCIPLE OF RESPONSIBILITY
Authority to act and responsibility for acting must be joined.
   a. If you give responsibility, give authority.
   b. Define employee duties clearly.
   c. Protect employees from criticism by others.
   d. Recognize the rights as well as obligations of employees.
   e. Achieve the aims of a democratic society insofar as it is possible within the area of your work.
   f. Establish a situation favorable to training and learning.
   g. Accept ultimate responsibility for everything done in your section, unit, office, division, department.
   h. Good administration and good supervision are inseparable.

2. PRINCIPLE OF AUTHORITY
The success of the supervisor is measured by the extent to which the power of authority is no used.
   a. Exercise simplicity and informality in supervision.
   b. Use the simplest machinery of supervision.
   c. If it is good for the organization as a whole, it is probably justified.
   d. Seldom be arbitrary or authoritative.
   e. Do not base your work on the power of position or of personality.
   f. Permit and encourage the free expression of opinions.

3. PRINCIPLE OF SELF-GROWTH
The success of the supervisor is measured by the extent to which, and the speed with which, he is no longer needed.
   a. Base criticism on principles, not on specifics.
   b. Point out higher activities to employees.
   c. Train for self-thinking by employees, to meet new situations.
   d. Stimulate initiative, self-reliance and individual responsibility.
   e. Concentrate on stimulating the growth of employees rather than on removing defects.

4. PRINCIPLE OF INDIVIDUAL WORTH
Respect for the individual is a paramount consideration in supervision.
   a. Be human and sympathetic in dealing with employees.
   b. Don't nag about things to be done.
   c. Recognize the individual differences among employees and seek opportunities to permit best expression of each personality.

5. PRINCIPLE OF CREATIVE LEADERSHIP
The best supervision is that which is not apparent to the employee.
   a. Stimulate, don't drive employees to creative action.
   b. Emphasize doing good things.
   c. Encourage employees to do what they do best.
   d. Do not be too greatly concerned with details of subject or method.
   e. Do not be concerned exclusively with immediate problems and activities.
   f. Reveal higher activities and make them both desired and maximally possible.
   g. Determine procedures in the light of each situation but see that these are derived from a sound basic philosophy.
   h. Aid, inspire and lead so as to liberate the creative spirit latent in all good employees.

6. PRINCIPLE OF SUCCESS AND FAILURE
There are no unsuccessful employees, only unsuccessful supervisors who have failed to give proper leadership.
   a. Adapt suggestions to the capacities, attitudes, and prejudices of employees.
   b. Be gradual, be progressive, be persistent.
   c. Help the employee find the general principle; have the employee apply his own problem to the general principle.
   d. Give adequate appreciation for good work and honest effort.
   e. Anticipate employee difficulties and help to prevent them.
   f. Encourage employees to do the desirable things they will do anyway.
   g. Judge your supervision by the results it secures.

7. *PRINCIPLE OF SCIENCE*
Successful supervision is scientific, objective, and experimental. It is based on facts, not on prejudices.
    a. Be cumulative in results.
    b. Never divorce your suggestions from the goals of training.
    c. Don't be impatient of results.
    d. Keep all matters on a professional, not a personal level.
    e. Do not be concerned exclusively with immediate problems and activities.
    f. Use objective means of determining achievement and rating where possible.

8. *PRINCIPLE OF COOPERATION*
Supervision is a cooperative enterprise between supervisor and employee.
    a. Begin with conditions as they are.
    b. Ask opinions of all involved when formulating policies.
    c. Organization is as good as its weakest link.
    d. Let employees help to determine policies and department programs.
    e. Be approachable and accessible - physically and mentally.
    f. Develop pleasant social relationships.

IV. WHAT IS ADMINISTRATION?

Administration is concerned with providing the environment, the material facilities, and the operational procedures that will promote the maximum growth and development of supervisors and employees. (Organization is an aspect, and a concomitant, of administration.)

There is no sharp line of demarcation between supervision and administration; these functions are intimately interrelated and, often, overlapping. They are complementary activities.

1. *PRACTICES COMMONLY CLASSED AS "SUPERVISORY"*
    a. Conducting employees conferences
    b. Visiting sections, units, offices, divisions, departments
    c. Arranging for demonstrations
    d. Examining plans
    e. Suggesting professional reading
    f. Interpreting bulletins
    g. Recommending in-service training courses
    h. Encouraging experimentation
    i. Appraising employee morale
    j. Providing for intervisitation

2. *PRACTICES COMMONLY CLASSIFIED AS "ADMINISTRATIVE"*
    a. Management of the office
    b. Arrangement of schedules for extra duties
    c. Assignment of rooms or areas
    d. Distribution of supplies
    e. Keeping records and reports
    f. Care of audio-visual materials
    g. Keeping inventory records
    h. Checking record cards and books
    i. Programming special activities
    j. Checking on the attendance and punctuality of employees

3. *PRACTICES COMMONLY CLASSIFIED AS BOTH "SUPERVISORY" AND "ADMINISTRATIVE"*
   a. Program construction
   b. Testing or evaluating outcomes
   c. Personnel accounting
   d. Ordering instructional materials

V. RESPONSIBILITIES OF THE SUPERVISOR

A person employed in a supervisory capacity must constantly be able to improve his own efficiency and ability. He represents the employer to the employees and only continuous self-examination can make him a capable supervisor.

Leadership and training are the supervisor's responsibility. An efficient working unit is one in which the employees work with the supervisor. It is his job to bring out the best in his employees. He must always be relaxed, courteous and calm in his association with his employees. Their feelings are important, and a harsh attitude does not develop the most efficient employees.

VI. COMPETENCIES OF THE SUPERVISOR

1. Complete knowledge of the duties and responsibilities of his position.
2. To be able to organize a job, plan ahead and carry through.
3. To have self-confidence and initiative.
4. To be able to handle the unexpected situation and make quick decisions.
5. To be able to properly train subordinates in the positions they are best suited for.
6. To be able to keep good human relations among his subordinates.
7. To be able to keep good human relations between his subordinates and himself and to earn their respect and trust.

VII. THE PROFESSIONAL SUPERVISOR-EMPLOYEE RELATIONSHIP

There are two kinds of efficiency: one kind is only apparent and is produced in organizations through the exercise of mere discipline; this is but a simulation of the second, or true, efficiency which springs from spontaneous cooperation. If you are a manager, no matter how great or small your responsibility, it is your job, in the final analysis, to create and develop this involuntary cooperation among the people whom you supervise. For, no matter how powerful a combination of money, machines, and materials a company may have, this is a dead and sterile thing without a team of willing, thinking and articulate people to guide it.

The following 21 points are presented as indicative of the exemplary basic relationship that should exist between supervisor and employee:

1. Each person wants to be liked and respected by his fellow employee and wants to be treated with consideration and respect by his superior.
2. The most competent employee will make an error. However, in a unit where good relations exist between the supervisor and his employees, tenseness and fear do not exist. Thus, errors are not hidden or covered up and the efficiency of a unit is not impaired.
3. Subordinates resent rules, regulations, or orders that are unreasonable or unexplained.
4. Subordinates are quick to resent unfairness, harshness, injustices and favoritism.
5. An employee will accept responsibility if he knows that he will be complimented for a job well done, and not too harshly chastised for failure; that his supervisor will check the cause of the failure, and, if it was the supervisor's fault, he will assume the blame therefore. If it was the employee's fault, his supervisor will explain the correct method or means of handling the responsibility.

6. An employee wants to receive credit for a suggestion he has made, that is used. If a suggestion cannot be used, the employee is entitled to an explanation. The supervisor should not say "no" and close the subject.
7. Fear and worry slow up a worker's ability. Poor working environment can impair his physical and mental health. A good supervisor avoids forceful methods, threats and arguments to get a job done.
8. A forceful supervisor is able to train his employees individually and as a team, and is able to motivate them in the proper channels.
9. A mature supervisor is able to properly evaluate his subordinates and to keep them happy and satisfied.
10. A sensitive supervisor will never patronize his subordinates.
11. A worthy supervisor will respect his employees' confidences.
12. Definite and clear-cut responsibilities should be assigned to each executive.
13. Responsibility should always be coupled with corresponding authority.
14. No change should be made in the scope or responsibilities of a position without a definite understanding to that effect on the part of all persons concerned.
15. No executive or employee, occupying a single position in the organization, should be subject to definite orders from more than one source.
16. Orders should never be given to subordinates over the head of a responsible executive. Rather than do this, the officer in question should be supplanted.
17. Criticisms of subordinates should, whoever possible, be made privately, and in no case should a subordinate be criticized in the presence of executives or employees of equal or lower rank.
18. No dispute or difference between executives or employees as to authority or responsibilities should be considered too trivial for prompt and careful adjudication.
19. Promotions, wage changes, and disciplinary action should always be approved by the executive immediately superior to the one directly responsible.
20. No executive or employee should ever be required, or expected, to be at the same time an assistant to, and critic of, another.
21. Any executive whose work is subject to regular inspection should, whever practicable, be given the assistance and facilities necessary to enable him to maintain an independent check of the quality of his work.

VIII. MINI-TEXT IN SUPERVISION, ADMINISTRATION, MANAGEMENT, AND ORGANIZATION

A. BRIEF HIGHLIGHTS

Listed concisely and sequentially are major headings and important data in the field for quick recall and review.

1. *LEVELS OF MANAGEMENT*

Any organization of some size has several levels of management. In terms of a ladder the levels are:

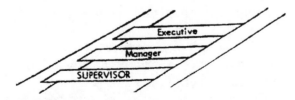

The first level is very important because it is the beginning point of management leadership.

2. WHAT THE SUPERVISOR MUST LEARN

A supervisor must learn to:
- (1) Deal with people and their differences
- (2) Get the job done through people
- (3) Recognize the problems when they exist
- (4) Overcome obstacles to good performance
- (5) Evaluate the performance of people
- (6) Check his own performance in terms of accomplishment

3. A DEFINITION OF SUPERVISOR

The term supervisor means any individual having authority, in the interests of the employer, to hire, transfer, suspend, lay-off, recall, promote, discharge, assign, reward, or discipline other employees or responsibility to direct them, or to adjust their grievances, or effectively to recommend such action, if, in connection with the foregoing, exercise of such authority is not of a merely routine or clerical nature but requires the use of independent judgment.

4. ELEMENTS OF THE TEAM CONCEPT

What is involved in teamwork? The component parts are:

(1) Members	(3) Goals	(5) Cooperation
(2) A leader	(4) Plans	(6) Spirit

5. PRINCIPLES OF ORGANIZATION

- (1) A team member must know what his job is.
- (2) Be sure that the nature and scope of a job are understood.
- (3) Authority and responsibility should be carefully spelled out.
- (4) A supervisor should be permitted to make the maximum number of decisions affecting his employees.
- (5) Employees should report to only one supervisor.
- (6) A supervisor should direct only as many employees as he can handle effectively.
- (7) An organization plan should be flexible.
- (8) Inspection and performance of work should be separate.
- (9) Organizational problems should receive immediate attention.
- (10) Assign work in line with ability and experience.

6. THE FOUR IMPORTANT PARTS OF EVERY JOB

- (1) Inherent in every job is the *accountability* for results.
- (2) A second set of factors in every job is *responsibilities*.
- (3) Along with duties and responsibilities one must have the *authority* to act within certain limits without obtaining permission to proceed.
- (4) No job exists in a vacuum. The supervisor is surrounded by key *relationships*.

7. PRINCIPLES OF DELEGATION

Where work is delegated for the first time, the supervisor should think in terms of these questions:
- (1) Who is best qualified to do this?
- (2) Can an employee improve his abilities by doing this?
- (3) How long should an employee spend on this?
- (4) Are there any special problems for which he will need guidance?
- (5) How broad a delegation can I make?

8. PRINCIPLES OF EFFECTIVE COMMUNICATIONS
  (1) Determine the media
  (2) To whom directed?
  (3) Identification and source authority
  (4) Is communication understood?

9. PRINCIPLES OF WORK IMPROVEMENT
  (1) Most people usually do only the work which is assigned to them
  (2) Workers are likely to fit assigned work into the time available to perform it
  (3) A good workload usually stimulates output
  (4) People usually do their best work when they know that results will be reviewed or inspected
  (5) Employees usually feel that someone else is responsible for conditions of work, workplace layout, job methods, type of tools/equipment, and other such factors
  (6) Employees are usually defensive about their job security
  (7) Employees have natural resistance to change
  (8) Employees can support or destroy a supervisor
  (9) A supervisor usually earns the respect of his people through his personal example of diligence and efficiency

10. AREAS OF JOB IMPROVEMENT
The areas of job improvement are quite numerous, but the most common ones which a supervisor can identify and utilize are:

(1) Departmental layout	(5) Work methods
(2) Flow of work	(6) Materials handling
(3) Workplace layout	(7) Utilization
(4) Utilization of manpower	(8) Motion economy

11. SEVEN KEY POINTS IN MAKING IMPROVEMENTS
  (1) Select the job to be improved
  (2) Study how it is being done now
  (3) Question the present method
  (4) Determine actions to be taken
  (5) Chart proposed method
  (6) Get approval and apply
  (7) Solicit worker participation

12. CORRECTIVE TECHNIQUES OF JOB IMPROVEMENT

Specific Problems	General Improvement	Corrective Techniques
(1) Size of workload	(1) Departmental layout	(1) Study with scale model
(2) Inability to meet schedules	(2) Flow of work	(2) Flow chart study
(3) Strain and fatigue	(3) Work plan layout	(3) Motion analysis
(4) Improper use of men and skills	(4) Utilization of manpower	(4) Comparison of units produced to standard allowance
(5) Waste, poor quality, unsafe conditions	(5) Work methods	(5) Methods analysis
(6) Bottleneck conditions that hinder output	(6) Materials handling	(6) Flow chart & equipment study
(7) Poor utilization of equipment and machine	(7) Utilization of equipment	(7) Down time vs. running time
(8) Efficiency and productivity of labor	(8) Motion economy	(8) Motion analysis

13. A *PLANNING CHECKLIST*

(1) Objectives	(6) Resources	(11) Safety
(2) Controls	(7) Manpower	(12) Money
(3) Delegations	(8) Equipment	(13) Work
(4) Communications	(9) Supplies and materials	(14) Timing of improvements
(5) Resources	(10) Utilization of time	

14. *FIVE CHARACTERISTICS OF GOOD DIRECTIONS*

In order to get results, directions must be:

(1) Possible of accomplishment   (3) Related to mission   (5) Unmistakably clear

(2) Agreeable with worker interests   (4) Planned and complete

15. *TYPES OF DIRECTIONS*

(1) Demands or direct orders   (3) Suggestion or implication

(2) Requests   (4) Volunteering

16. *CONTROLS*

A typical listing of the overall areas in which the supervisor should establish controls might be:

(1) Manpower	(3) Quality of work	(5) Time	(7) Money
(2) Materials	(4) Quantity of work	(6) Space	(8) Methods

17. *ORIENTING THE NEW EMPLOYEE*

(1) Prepare for him   (3) Orientation for the job

(2) Welcome the new employee   (4) Follow-up

18. *CHECKLIST FOR ORIENTING NEW EMPLOYEES*

                                                                         Yes   No

(1) Do your appreciate the feelings of new employees when they first report for work?

(2) Are you aware of the fact that the new employee must make a big adjustment to his job?

(3) Have you given him good reasons for liking the job and the organization?

(4) Have you prepared for his first day on the job?

(5) Did you welcome him cordially and make him feel needed?

(6) Did you establish rapport with him so that he feels free to talk and discuss matters with you?

(7) Did you explain his job to him and his relationship to you?

(8) Does he know that his work will be evaluated periodically on a basis that is fair and objective?

(9) Did you introduce him to his fellow workers in such a way that they are likely to accept him?

(10) Does he know what employee benefits he will receive?

(11) Does he understand the importance of being on the job and what to do if he must leave his duty station?

(12) Has he been impressed with the importance of accident prevention and safe practice?

(13) Does he generally know his way around the department?

(14) Is he under the guidance of a sponsor who will teach the right ways of doing things?

(15) Do you plan to follow-up so that he will continue to adjust successfully to his job?

19. *PRINCIPLES OF LEARNING*
      (1) Motivation   (2) Demonstration or explanation   (3) Practice

20. *CAUSES OF POOR PERFORMANCE*
      (1) Improper training for job
      (2) Wrong tools
      (3) Inadequate directions
      (4) Lack of supervisory follow-up
      (5) Poor communications
      (6) Lack of standards of performance
      (7) Wrong work habits
      (8) Low morale
      (9) Other

21. *FOUR MAJOR STEPS IN ON-THE-JOB INSTRUCTION*
      (1) Prepare the worker
      (2) Present the operation
      (3) Tryout performance
      (4) Follow-up

22. *EMPLOYEES WANT FIVE THINGS*
      (1) Security (2) Opportunity (3) Recognition (4) Inclusion (5) Expression

23. *SOME DON'TS IN REGARD TO PRAISE*
      (1) Don't praise a person for something he hasn't done
      (2) Don't praise a person unless you can be sincere
      (3) Don't be sparing in praise just because your superior withholds it from you
      (4) Don't let too much time elapse between good performance and recognition of it

24. *HOW TO GAIN YOUR WORKERS' CONFIDENCE*
    Methods of developing confidence include such things as:
      (1) Knowing the interests, habits, hobbies of employees
      (2) Admitting your own inadequacies
      (3) Sharing and telling of confidence in others
      (4) Supporting people when they are in trouble
      (5) Delegating matters that can be well handled
      (6) Being frank and straightforward about problems and working conditions
      (7) Encouraging others to bring their problems to you
      (8) Taking action on problems which impede worker progress

25. *SOURCES OF EMPLOYEE PROBLEMS*
    On-the-job causes might be such things as:
      (1) A feeling that favoritism is exercised in assignments
      (2) Assignment of overtime
      (3) An undue amount of supervision
      (4) Changing methods or systems
      (5) Stealing of ideas or trade secrets
      (6) Lack of interest in job
      (7) Threat of reduction in force
      (8) Ignorance or lack of communications
      (9) Poor equipment
    (10) Lack of knowing how supervisor feels toward employee
    (11) Shift assignments

    Off-the-job problems might have to do with:
      (1) Health   (2) Finances   (3) Housing   (4) Family

26. *THE SUPERVISOR'S KEY TO DISCIPLINE*
There are several key points about discipline which the supervisor should keep in mind:
   (1) Job discipline is one of the disciplines of life and is directed by the supervisor.
   (2) It is more important to correct an employee fault than to fix blame for it.
   (3) Employee performance is affected by problems both on the job and off.
   (4) Sudden or abrupt changes in behavior can be indications of important employee problems.
   (5) Problems should be dealt with as soon as possible after they are identified.
   (6) The attitude of the supervisor may have more to do with solving problems than the techniques of problem solving.
   (7) Correction of employee behavior should be resorted to only after the supervisor is sure that training or counseling will not be helpful.
   (8) Be sure to document your disciplinary actions.
   (9) Make sure that you are disciplining on the basis of facts rather than personal feelings.
   (10) Take each disciplinary step in order, being careful not to make snap judgments, or decisions based on impatience.

27. *FIVE IMPORTANT PROCESSES OF MANAGEMENT*
   (1) Planning   (2) Organizing   (3) Scheduling
   (4) Controlling   (5) Motivating

28. *WHEN THE SUPERVISOR FAILS TO PLAN*
   (1) Supervisor creates impression of not knowing his job
   (2) May lead to excessive overtime
   (3) Job runs itself -- supervisor lacks control
   (4) Deadlines and appointments missed
   (5) Parts of the work go undone
   (6) Work interrupted by emergencies
   (7) Sets a bad example
   (8) Uneven workload creates peaks and valleys
   (9) Too much time on minor details at expense of more important tasks

29. *FOURTEEN GENERAL PRINCIPLES OF MANAGEMENT*
   (1) Division of work
   (2) Authority and responsibility
   (3) Discipline
   (4) Unity of command
   (5) Unity of direction
   (6) Subordination of individual interest to general interest
   (7) Remuneration of personnel
   (8) Centralization
   (9) Scalar chain
   (10) Order
   (11) Equity
   (12) Stability of tenure of personnel
   (13) Initiative
   (14) Esprit de corps

30. *CHANGE*
Bringing about change is perhaps attempted more often, and yet less well understood, than anything else the supervisor does. How do people generally react to change? (People tend to resist change that is imposed upon them by other individuals or circumstances.

Change is characteristic of every situation. It is a part of every real endeavor where the efforts of people are concerned.

A. Why do people resist change?
　　People **may** resist change because of:
　　　　(1) Fear of the unknown
　　　　(2) Implied criticism
　　　　(3) Unpleasant experiences in the past
　　　　(4) Fear of loss of status
　　　　(5) Threat to the ego
　　　　(6) Fear of loss of economic stability

B. How can we best overcome the resistance to change?
　　In initiating change, take these steps:
　　　　(1) Get ready to sell
　　　　(2) Identify sources of help
　　　　(3) Anticipate objections
　　　　(4) Sell benefits
　　　　(5) Listen in depth
　　　　(6) Follow up

B. BRIEF TOPICAL SUMMARIES

I. WHO/WHAT IS THE SUPERVISOR?

1. The supervisor is often called the "highest level employee and the lowest level manager."
2. A supervisor is a member of both management and the work group. He acts as a bridge between the two.
3. Most problems in supervision are in the area of human relations, or people problems.
4. Employees expect: Respect, opportunity to learn and to advance, and a sense of belonging, and so forth.
5. Supervisors are responsible for directing people and organizing work. Planning is of paramount importance.
6. A position description is a set of duties and responsibilities inherent to a given position.
7. It is important to keep the position description up-to-date and to provide each employee with his own copy.

II. THE SOCIOLOGY OF WORK

1. People are alike in many ways; however, each individual is unique.
2. The supervisor is challenged in getting to know employee differences. Acquiring skills in evaluating individuals is an asset.
3. Maintaining meaningful working relationships in the organization is of great importance.
4. The supervisor has an obligation to help individuals to develop to their fullest potential.
5. Job rotation on a planned basis helps to build versatility and to maintain interest and enthusiasm in work groups.
6. Cross training (job rotation) provides backup skills.
7. The supervisor can help reduce tension by maintaining a sense of humor, providing guidance to employees, and by making reasonable and timely decisions. Employees respond favorably to working under reasonably predictable circumstances.
8. Change is characteristic of all managerial behavior. The supervisor must adjust to changes in procedures, new methods, technological changes, and to a number of new and sometimes challenging situations.
9. To overcome the natural tendency for people to resist change, the supervisor should become more skillful in initiating change.

III. PRINCIPLES AND PRACTICES OF SUPERVISION

1. Employees should be required to answer to only one superior.
2. A supervisor can effectively direct only a limited number of employees, depending upon the complexity, variety, and proximity of the jobs involved.
3. The organizational chart presents the organization in graphic form. It reflects lines of authority and responsibility as well as interrelationships of units within the organization.
4. Distribution of work can be improved through an analysis using the "Work Distribution Chart."
5. The "Work Distribution Chart" reflects the division of work within a unit in understandable form.
6. When related tasks are given to an employee, he has a better chance of increasing his skills through training.
7. The individual who is given the responsibility for tasks must also be given the appropriate authority to insure adequate results.
8. The supervisor should delegate repetitive, routine work. Preparation of recurring reports, maintaining leave and attendance records are some examples.
9. Good discipline is essential to good task performance. Discipline is reflected in the actions of employees on the job in the absence of supervision.
10. Disciplinary action may have to be taken when the positive aspects of discipline have failed. Reprimand, warning, and suspension are examples of disciplinary action.
11. If a situation calls for a reprimand, be sure it is deserved and remember it is to be done in private.

IV. DYNAMIC LEADERSHIP

1. A style is a personal method or manner of exerting influence.
2. Authoritarian leaders often see themselves as the source of power and authority.
3. The democratic leader often perceives the group as the source of authority and power.
4. Supervisors tend to do better when using the pattern of leadership that is most natural for them.
5. Social scientists suggest that the effective supervisor use the leadership style that best fits the problem or circumstances involved.
6. All four styles -- telling, selling, consulting, joining -- have their place. Using one does not preclude using the other at another time.
7. The theory X point of view assumes that the average person dislikes work, will avoid it whenever possible, and must be coerced to achieve organizational objectives.
8. The theory Y point of view assumes that the average person considers work to be as natural as play, and, when the individual is committed, he requires little supervision or direction to accomplish desired objectives.
9. The leader's basic assumptions concerning human behavior and human nature affect his actions, decisions, and other managerial practices.
10. Dissatisfaction among employees is often present, but difficult to isolate. The supervisor should seek to weaken dissatisfaction by keeping promises, being sincere and considerate, keeping employees informed, and so forth.
11. Constructive suggestions should be encouraged during the natural progress of the work.

V. PROCESSES FOR SOLVING PROBLEMS

1. People find their daily tasks more meaningful and satisfying when they can improve them.
2. The causes of problems, or the key factors, are often hidden in the background. Ability to solve problems often involves the ability to isolate them from their backgrounds. There is some substance to the cliché that some persons "can't see the forest for the trees."
3. New procedures are often developed from old ones. Problems should be broken down into manageable parts. New ideas can be adapted from old ones.

4. People think differently in problem-solving situations. Using a logical, patterned approach is often useful. One approach found to be useful includes these steps:

   (a) Define the problem   (d) Weigh and decide

   (b) Establish objectives   (e) Take action

   (c) Get the facts   (f) Evaluate action

VI. TRAINING FOR RESULTS

1. Participants respond best when they feel training is important to them.
2. The supervisor has responsibility for the training and development of those who report to him.
3. When training is delegated to others, great care must be exercised to insure the trainer has knowledge, aptitude, and interest for his work as a trainer.
4. Training (learning) of some type goes on continually. The most successful supervisor makes certain the learning contributes in a productive manner to operational goals.
5. New employees are particularly susceptible to training. Older employees facing new job situations require specific training, as well as having need for development and growth opportunities.
6. Training needs require continuous monitoring.
7. The training officer of an agency is a professional with a responsibility to assist supervisors in solving training problems.
8. Many of the self-development steps important to the supervisor's own growth are equally important to the development of peers and subordinates. Knowledge of these is important when the supervisor consults with others on development and growth opportunities.

VII. HEALTH, SAFETY, AND ACCIDENT PREVENTION

1. Management-minded supervisors take appropriate measures to assist employees in maintaining health and in assuring safe practices in the work environment.
2. Effective safety training and practices help to avoid injury and accidents.
3. Safety should be a management goal. All infractions of safety which are observed should be corrected without exception.
4. Employees' safety attitude, training and instruction, provision of safe tools and equipment, supervision, and leadership are considered highly important factors which contribute to safety and which can be influenced directly by supervisors.
5. When accidents do occur they should be investigated promptly for very important reasons, including the fact that information which is gained can be used to prevent accidents in the future.

VIII. EQUAL EMPLOYMENT OPPORTUNITY

1. The supervisor should endeavor to treat all employees fairly, without regard to religion, race, sex, or national origin.
2. Groups tend to reflect the attitude of the leader. Prejudice can be detected even in very subtle form. Supervisors must strive to create a feeling of mutual respect and confidence in every employee.
3. Complete utilization of all human resources is a national goal. Equitable consideration should be accorded women in the work force, minority-group members, the physically and mentally handicapped, and the older employee. The important question is: "Who can do the job?"
4. Training opportunities, recognition for performance, overtime assignments, promotional opportunities, and all other personnel actions are to be handled on an equitable basis.

IX. IMPROVING COMMUNICATIONS

1. Communications is achieving understanding between the sender and the receiver of a message. It also means sharing information -- the creation of understanding.
2. Communication is basic to all human activity. Words are means of conveying meanings; however, real meanings are in people.
3. There are very practical differences in the effectiveness of one-way, impersonal, and two-way communications. Words spoken face-to-face are better understood. Telephone conversations are effective, but lack the rapport of person-to-person exchanges. The whole person communicates.
4. Cooperation and communication in an organization go hand in hand. When there is a mutual respect between people, spelling out rules and procedures for communicating is unnecessary.
5. There are several barriers to effective communications. These include failure to listen with respect and understanding, lack of skill in feedback, and misinterpreting the meanings of words used by the speaker. It is also common practice to listen to what we want to hear, and tune out things we do not want to hear.
6. Communication is management's chief problem. The supervisor should accept the challenge to communicate more effectively and to improve interagency and intra-agency communications.
7. The supervisor may often plan for and conduct meetings. The planning phase is critical and may determine the success or the failure of a meeting.
8. Speaking before groups usually requires extra effort. Stage fright may never disappear completely, but it can be controlled.

X. SELF-DEVELOPMENT

1. Every employee is responsible for his own self-development.
2. Toastmaster and toastmistress clubs offer opportunities to improve skills in oral communications.
3. Planning for one's own self-development is of vital importance. Supervisors know their own strengths and limitations better than anyone else.
4. Many opportunities are open to aid the supervisor in his developmental efforts, including job assignments; training opportunities, both governmental and non-governmental -- to include universities and professional conferences and seminars.
5. Programmed instruction offers a means of studying at one's own rate.
6. Where difficulties may arise from a supervisor's being away from his work for training, he may participate in televised home study or correspondence courses to meet his self-develop- ment needs.

XI. TEACHING AND TRAINING

A. The Teaching Process

Teaching is encouraging and guiding the learning activities of students toward established goals. In most cases this process consists in five steps: preparation, presentation, summarization, evaluation, and application.

1. Preparation
   Preparation is twofold in nature; that of the supervisor and the employee.
   Preparation by the supervisor is absolutely essential to success. He must know what, when, where, how, and whom he will teach. Some of the factors that should be considered are:

(1) The objectives	(5) Employee interest
(2) The materials needed	(6) Training aids
(3) The methods to be used	(7) Evaluation
(4) Employee participation	(8) Summarization

Employee preparation consists in preparing the employee to receive the material. Probably the most important single factor in the preparation of the employee is arousing and maintaining his interest. He must know the objectives of the training, why he is there, how the material can be used, and its importance to him.

2. Presentation

In presentation, have a carefully designed plan and follow it.
The plan should be accurate and complete, yet flexible enough to meet situations as they arise. The method of presentation will be determined by the particular situation and objectives.

3. Summary

A summary should be made at the end of every training unit and program. In addition, there may be internal summaries depending on the nature of the material being taught. The important thing is that the trainee must always be able to understand how each part of the new material relates to the whole.

4. Application

The supervisor must arrange work so the employee will be given a chance to apply new knowledge or skills while the material is still clear in his mind and interest is high. The trainee does not really know whether he has learned the material until he has been given a chance to apply it. If the material is not applied, it loses most of its value.

5. Evaluation

The purpose of all training is to promote learning. To determine whether the training has been a success or failure, the supervisor must evaluate this learning.

In the broadest sense evaluation includes all the devices, methods, skills, and techniques used by the supervisor to keep him self and the employees informed as to their progress toward the objectives they are pursuing. The extent to which the employee has mastered the knowledge, skills, and abilities, or changed his attitudes, as determined by the program objectives, is the extent to which instruction has succeeded or failed.

Evaluation should not be confined to the end of the lesson, day, or program but should be used continuously. We shall note later the way this relates to the rest of the teaching process.

B. Teaching Methods

A teaching method is a pattern of identifiable student and instructor activity used in presenting training material.

All supervisors are faced with the problem of deciding which method should be used at a given time.

As with all methods, there are certain advantages and disadvantages to each method.

1. Lecture

The lecture is direct oral presentation of material by the supervisor. The present trend is to place less emphasis on the trainer's activity and more on that of the trainee.

2. Discussion

Teaching by discussion or conference involves using questions and other techniques to arouse interest and focus attention upon certain areas, and by doing so creating a learning situation. This can be one of the most valuable methods because it gives the employees 'an opportunity to express their ideas and pool their knowledge.

3. Demonstration

The demonstration is used to teach how something works or how to do something. It can be used to show a principle or what the results of a series of actions will be. A well-staged demonstration is particularly effective because it shows proper methods of performance in a realistic manner.

4. Performance

Performance is one of the most fundamental of all learning techniques or teaching methods. The trainee may be able to tell how a specific operation should be performed but he cannot be sure he knows how to perform the operation until he has done so.

5. Which Method to Use

Moreover, there are other methods and techniques of teaching. It is difficult to use any method without other methods entering into it. In any learning situation a combination of methods is usually more effective than anyone method alone.

Finally, evaluation must be integrated into the other aspects of the teaching-learning process.

It must be used in the motivation of the trainees; it must be used to assist in developing understanding during the training; and it must be related to employee application of the results of training.

This is distinctly the role of the supervisor.

———